Cicero

On the Commonwealth and *On the Laws*

Cicero's *On the Commonwealth* and *On the Laws* were his first and most substantial attempt to adapt Greek theories of political life to the circumstances of the Roman Republic. They represent Cicero's vision of an ideal society and remain his most important works of political philosophy. *On the Commonwealth* survives only in part, and *On the Laws* was never completed. The present volume offers a new scholarly reconstruction of the fragments of *On the Commonwealth* and a masterly translation of both dialogues. The texts are supported by a helpful, concise introduction, notes, synopsis, biographical notes, and bibliography; students in politics, philosophy, ancient history, law, and classics will gain new understanding of one of the great philosophers and political figures of antiquity thanks to this volume.

JAMES E. G. ZETZEL is Professor of Classics and James R. Barker Professor of Contemporary Civilization at Columbia University in the City of New York. He has lectured and published widely on Latin literature and the transmission of texts, including a commentary on the Latin text of *On the Commonwealth* (Cambridge, 1995) and an essay, "Rome and Its Traditions," in *The Cambridge Companion to Virgil* (1997).

CAMBRIDGE TEXTS IN THE HISTORY OF POLITICAL THOUGHT

Cambridge Texts in the History of Political Thought is now firmly established as the major student textbook series in political theory. It aims to make available to students all the most important texts in the history of western political thought, from ancient Greece to the early twentieth century. All the familiar classic texts will be included, but the series seeks at the same time to enlarge the conventional canon by incorporating an extensive range of less well-known works, many of them never before available in a modern English edition. Wherever possible, texts are published in complete and unabridged form, and translations are specially commissioned for the series. Each volume contains a critical introduction together with chronologies, biographical sketches, a guide to further reading and any necessary glossaries and textual apparatus. When completed, the series will aim to offer an outline of the entire evolution of western political thought.

For a list of titles published in the series, please see end of book.

CICERO

On the Commonwealth and On the Laws

EDITED BY

JAMES E. G. ZETZEL

Columbia University in the City of New York

CAMBRIDGE UNIVERSITY PRESS
Cambridge, New York, Melbourne, Madrid, Cape Town, Singapore, São Paulo,
Delhi, Dubai, Tokyo, Mexico City

Cambridge University Press
The Edinburgh Building, Cambridge CB2 8RU, UK

Published in the United States of America by Cambridge University Press, New York

www.cambridge.org
Information on this title: www.cambridge.org/9780521453448

First published 1999
10th printing 2010

Printed in the United Kingdom at the University Press, Cambridge

A catalogue record for this book is available from the British Library

Library of Congress cataloguing in publication data

Cicero, Marcus Tullius.
[De republica. English]
On the commonwealth; and, On the laws/Cicero; edited by James E. G. Zetzel.
p. cm. – (Cambridge texts in the history of political thought)
Includes bibliographical references and index.
ISBN 0 521 45344 5 (hardback). – ISBN 0 521 45959 1 (paperback)
1. Political science – Early works to 1800. 2. State, The – Early works to 1800. 3. Rome – Politics and government – 265–30 B.C.
I. Zetzel, James E. G. II. Cicero, Marcus Tullius. De legibus. English. III. Title. IV. Title: On the commonwealth; and, On the laws. V. Title: On the laws. VI. Series.
JC81.C613 1999
320.1 – dc21 98-49660 CIP

ISBN 978-0-521-45344-8 hardback
ISBN 978-0-521-45959-4 paperback

Contents

Editor's note

Raymond Geuss originally encouraged me to undertake this translation; I owe him and Quentin Skinner thanks for publishing it in this series, and I am also grateful to Richard Fisher, Elizabeth Howard, Caroline Drake, and Jane Van Tassel of Cambridge University Press for their expert advice and assistance.

A preliminary draft of the translation of Book 1 of *On the Laws* was used by students in Contemporary Civilization C1101 in the core curriculum of Columbia College; I am grateful to David Johnston, the director of the course, for including it in the course reader, and to the students in my own section who offered useful corrections and suggestions. Susanna Zetzel has offered advice on numerous passages and has improved the introduction immeasurably. Robert Kaster and Gareth Williams generously read a draft of the entire book and have offered many corrections of my Latin, English, and logic. The remaining faults are my own.

This translation was begun during a sabbatical leave in 1993 and completed during a research leave in 1997–98 aided by a Fellowship from the John Simon Guggenheim Memorial Foundation. I am grateful both to Columbia University and to the Guggenheim Foundation for their support. I received practical assistance of other kinds from my good friends Douglas Kilburn, Robert Phinney, and Scott Decker, who supplied water, heat, and light, without which the revision of this book would have taken far longer to complete.

Introduction

Cicero's Career

Early in December 63 BCE, the consul Marcus Tullius Cicero, having unmasked the conspiracy of Catiline and supervised the execution of several of the leading conspirators, was hailed as Father of his Country and escorted home by a crowd of grateful Romans from all ranks of society; a public thanksgiving was decreed in his honor, the first such award ever made for nonmilitary service to the state. That moment was the summit of a remarkable career: not only had Cicero's consulate been distinguished by signal success and acclaim, but the very fact that he had achieved that office – the chief magistracy in republican Rome – and had done so at the earliest legal age of 42 was itself unusual. Cicero was born in 106 BCE to one of the leading families of the town of Arpinum, some 115 kilometers southeast of Rome; and although the town had had Roman citizenship since 188, no one in Cicero's family had ever held public office at Rome. Ties of friendship between Cicero's family and some of the leading aristocrats of Rome had permitted him to learn the ways of Roman politics and law under the tutelage of the leading orator (Lucius Licinius Crassus) and jurists (Quintus Mucius Scaevola the Augur and his cousin Quintus Mucius Scaevola the Pontifex) of the 90s and 80s; but in the first half of the first century BCE it was rare for a "new man" – the first in his family to achieve high office – to become consul. Recruitment to the ranks of the Roman aristocracy in Cicero's day was real, but it usually took several generations to reach the highest offices; more rapid elevation was generally the result of military rather than oratorical talent. Cicero rose to eminence as a public speaker and as a supporter of moderate reform within the traditional social order based on landed wealth and hierarchical deference; his early speeches attack corruption and abuse of power within the system rather than the system itself. His success was based in part on his rhetorical and political skills, in part on his reassuring conservatism at a time of extraordinary military and social upheaval. Elected as a safe alternative to Catiline, the bankrupt and unsavory aristocrat whose electoral failure drove him to conspiracy and revolution, he managed very briefly to unite the discordant elements of Roman society in the face of the genuine danger posed by Catiline: the honors and acclaim that he received were well earned.

The actions that deserved honor, however, were the source of a downfall even more rapid than his rise. Legitimate fear of armed insurrection led Cicero to execute citizens in 63 on the basis of a resolution of the senate, without a formal trial. In the violent factional politics of the late 60s and early 50s, his actions in 63 left Cicero vulnerable to his enemies; the coalition which he had created against Catiline dissolved in the face of mob violence and rampant corruption; and he was sent into exile in 58 at the instigation of the tribune Publius Clodius Pulcher – only to be recalled eighteen months later when political circumstances changed. Cicero relied on his own abilities at a time when the possession of money and armed troops had far more political effect than eloquence, decency, or parliamentary skill; although honored for his eloquence and expertise, he remained without real influence through the turbulence that preceded the civil war between Pompey and Caesar; and having half-heartedly chosen to support Pompey, he had virtually no place in public life under Caesar's dictatorship in the 40s. Only at the end of his life, after the assassination of Caesar on 15 March 44, did Cicero regain some measure of power, leading the senate in its support of Brutus and Cassius against Antonius. But in the bewildering military and political circumstances of 44–43, Cicero's mistaken judgment that he could control and use the young heir of Caesar (then Gaius Iulius Caesar Octavianus, eventually to become Augustus) had fatal consequences: at the formation of the Second Triumvirate (Antonius, the young Caesar, and Marcus Lepidus) in November 43, he was proscribed. After he was killed on 7 December, his head and hands were cut off and placed on the Rostrum in Rome, a sign of the ruthlessness of the triumvirs and a symbol of the end of traditional republican politics.

Cicero the philosopher

By the 90s, when Cicero came to Rome as a teenager, young men of wealth and standing were beginning to be educated in more than the traditional elements of law and public speaking. In the dialogue *On the Orator* written in 55 BCE (with a dramatic date of 91), Cicero documents the growing acquaintance of Roman senators with Greek philosophy and rhetoric: by 100, it was not unusual for magistrates on their way to govern eastern provinces to stop in Athens to listen to philosophers explain the simpler dialogues of Plato; Cicero himself, when he found it politically prudent to leave Rome in the early 70s, went to Rhodes to study philosophy and rhetoric. That encounter with Greek learning had a lasting effect. More than many of his generation, he studied those subjects seriously. He listened to the lectures of Philo, the head of the skeptical Academy, and to his successor Antiochus of Ascalon, who turned the Academy away from skepticism towards an interest in ethics closer to that of Plato and his immediate successors. For many years, he provided a home for the blind Stoic philosopher Diodotus, and although his own philosophical allegiance remained with the skeptical Academy, he read and studied widely in Greek philosophy at large. He was equally adept in the rhetoric and poetry of Hellenistic Greece, writing while still in his twenties a treatise on the first of the traditional elements of rhetoric, *inventio* (selection of arguments), and translating at about the same time the *Phaenomena* of Aratus, a third-century poem on astronomy the immense popularity of which in antiquity remains something of a puzzle to modern readers. His speeches reveal, while in traditional Roman fashion disclaiming, a deep and extensive knowledge of Greek philosophy, poetry, history, and art; and although his philosophical works often proclaim distrust of Greek learning for its own sake, he consistently attempted to shape it to the needs and values of Roman society.

By the time he returned from exile in 57 to his frustratingly powerless position in Rome, therefore, it is not altogether surprising that he turned from political action to writing. The 50s were a time of extraordinarily broad and complex engagement with Greek ideas in Rome: Pompey's vast conquests in the Greek east in the 60s encouraged what Sulla's brutal siege of Athens in 88 had begun, an exodus of leading Greek intellectuals to Rome. Some came willingly to the new financial, military, and now cultural capital of the Mediterranean; others, like Virgil's Greek teacher Parthenius, came as enslaved prisoners of war. The Epicurean Philodemus of Gadara, many of whose copious writings have been unearthed in the excavations of Herculaneum, was the house Greek of Cicero's enemy Piso (one of Caesar's fathers-in-law) and was well known to Cicero, who also defended in 62 the Roman citizenship of the elderly Greek poet Archias from Syrian Antioch. The invasion of Greek intellectuals had a powerful effect on Roman letters beginning in the 50s: both Catullus, writing learned poetry in the manner of the Alexandrians, and Lucretius, expounding Epicureanism in Latin verse, were the beneficiaries of Greek learning and exercised an immense influence on Latin poetry in the next generations.

In this cultural climate, and with his extensive knowledge of Greek rhetoric and philosophy, Cicero was similarly moved to adapt the learning of Greece to the traditional culture of Rome. In the period between 55 and his reluctant departure to govern the province of Cilicia in the spring of 51, Cicero wrote three dialogues (the first works of the kind written in Latin) in imitation of Plato: *On the Orator* adapted and replied to the *Gorgias* and *Phaedrus*; *On the Commonwealth* (*De re publica*) is his version of the *Republic*; and *On the Laws* (*De legibus*) – which was left incomplete – is modeled on Plato's *Laws*. After the Civil War, his literary production increased in speed and diminished in elegance: two more works on rhetoric and a long series of studies, which Cicero himself claimed (falsely) were simply transcripts of Greek works, on epistemology, ethics, and religion. While in these dialogues Cicero adapted his models through the use of Roman examples and issues, it was only after the death of Caesar, at the same time that he wrote the *Philippics* attacking Antony, that he returned to writing about the immediate concerns of Roman public life: the treatise *On Duties* written at the end of 44 was for centuries his most widely read and influential work.

A Roman Plato

Although in all his philosophical works Cicero made extensive use of the writings of Hellenistic philosophers, above all the Stoics and Peripatetics (the school of Aristotle), and in the dialogues written after the Civil War he generally employed the form of Aristotelian dialogue – set speeches expounding different philosophical points of view rather than Socratic conversation – it was Plato to whom he was first attracted as a literary and stylistic model, even though (or perhaps because) he found Plato's views on rhetoric and government both wrong and unrealistic. The use of strongly characterized speakers of divergent views in a fully realized dramatic setting – particularly true of the Platonic dialogues Cicero most extensively employed, *Gorgias*, *Phaedrus*, *Republic*, and *Laws* – was eminently suitable for Cicero's project in the 50s, an attempt to transpose Greek ideas about public life into a Roman context and to provide a more rigorous philosophical model for Roman public behavior and institutions than had previously existed. *On the Orator* was placed in the dramatic setting of 91 BCE, just before the outbreak of the war between the Romans and the Italians (the Social War), using as speakers figures whom Cicero had known as a young man. In the dialogue, he combined a technical discussion of rhetoric with a broader exposition of the civic and practical value of the true orator, arguing (against Plato and others) not only that rhetoric was itself an *ars* (Greek *technê*: a discipline with rational rules capable of being taught and transmitted) but also that it was the master art to which philosophy, at least ethics, should be subordinated; furthermore, he transposed the notion of *ars* itself from the schoolroom to the forum: the consummate orator becomes a figure capable of transmitting to society the ethical and social values learned through both study and practical experience.

In *On the Orator* there are clear indications of Cicero's larger concerns with the political context of ethical values and with the importance of the orator as the true statesman; above all, it displays Cicero's belief that it is through the character and political wisdom of particular individuals – in *On the Orator* seen as an element of rhetoric itself – that the larger goals of society can best be fostered and maintained. In *On the Commonwealth*, which he began to write less than six months after the earlier work, he attempted to give a fuller account of the values and nature of public life. Cicero's correspondence gives some indications of the process of composition and of his ideas about its contents: he first describes it as *politika* (Greek: concerning public life), then as "about the best commonwealth and the best citizen" before settling on the title *On the Commonwealth*. The original plan was for a nine-book work set in 129 BCE at the home of Scipio Aemilianus; when a friend criticized this as limiting the opportunities for comment on current affairs and appearing too improbable (the conversation takes place twenty-three years before Cicero's birth), he considered turning it into a dialogue with himself as the main speaker, but rapidly thought better of that and returned to the original setting, but in six books.

The choice of characters and the dramatic moment of the conversation were important for Cicero. Publius Cornelius Scipio Aemilianus Africanus, twice consul and censor, adoptive grandson of the elder Scipio Africanus (the conqueror of Hannibal) and himself the destroyer of Carthage in the Third Punic War in 146 BCE and of Numantia in Spain in 133, was a man whom Cicero greatly admired as not only a great general and orator but as someone renowned for his intellectual accomplishments as much as his success in public life. A friend of the Greek historian Polybius (whose account of the Roman constitution Cicero used extensively in the first two books of *On the Commonwealth*) and the Stoic philosopher Panaetius as well as of the Roman poets Terence and Lucilius, Scipio emerges in Cicero's presentation as an ideal example of the successful fusion of public action and educated thought, someone who could well be imagined to have offered an explanation, as he is made to do in the dialogue, of the philosophical underpinnings of Roman government. The conversation is imagined to have taken place early in 129, during a political crisis: Scipio was leading the conservative attempt to eviscerate the law for agrarian reform passed by his cousin Tiberius Gracchus as tribune of the plebs four years earlier. That legislation and the concomitant violence and upheaval had resulted in the murder of Gracchus by a mob led by another of Scipio's relatives, Scipio Nasica Serapio; and the tribunate of Gracchus was regarded by Cicero and his contemporaries as the beginning of social upheavals which lasted into their own time. The dialogue envisages Scipio as the one person whose stature and abilities could halt such developments; but it takes place only a few days before the real Scipio died suddenly and mysteriously. His death may have been natural, but Cicero believed that he had been murdered by supporters of the Gracchan laws. As in *On the Orator*, which takes place a few days before the sudden death (of a stroke or heart attack) of the protagonist Crassus and the outbreak of the Social War, *On the Commonwealth* represents a very precise moment, during a political crisis the deleterious effects of which could have been halted by the protagonist had it not been for his sudden death. In that respect, both Scipio and Crassus represent Roman equivalents for the Socrates of the *Phaedo*, speaking inspired words at the very end of their lives.

The other participants in the conversation are also carefully selected. Scipio's principal interlocutor (at least in the surviving text) was his closest friend in real life, Gaius Laelius, a man of considerable learning in his own right; he is portrayed as an ironic and practical man, who repeatedly returns the conversation from the higher philosophical flights of Scipio to the real world of Roman life. He is accompanied by his two sons-in-law, Quintus Mucius Scaevola (the Augur) and Gaius Fannius; the former (one of Cicero's teachers) appears in Book 1 of *On the Orator* as an elder statesman and expert on law. Another figure of the younger generation is Publius Rutilius Rufus, who is said by Cicero to have been his source for the conversation: a man of Stoic beliefs and rectitude, he was exiled unjustly in the 90s for extortion and spent the rest of his life at Smyrna, in the province of Asia which he was convicted of having mistreated. Quintus Aelius Tubero, Scipio's nephew, was also a Stoic and a man of serious scholarly attainments; his career was cut short because he refused to compromise his philosophical beliefs in order to win election. Three other figures fill out the cast: Spurius Mummius, whose brother Lucius destroyed Corinth in the same year that Scipio destroyed Carthage, is presented as a hardened defender of aristocratic privilege; Lucius Furius Philus, one of Scipio's closest friends, was a public figure of great integrity and learning, who is made unwillingly to argue the case for injustice against justice; and Manius Manilius, one of the leading legal experts of the second century, was considerably older than any of the other participants and had been Scipio's commanding officer in Africa in 149 at the beginning of the Third Punic War. Taken as a group, the participants in the dialogue represent what Cicero felt to be the highest levels of intellectual and civic accomplishment in the second century, and also represent three generations of Roman eminence: one of the central concerns of *On the Commonwealth* is the way in which knowledge of morality and tradition can be passed on and kept alive; in viewing the conversation, the reader witnesses a living example of the values and social behavior that Cicero most admired.

The dramatic structure and setting of *On the Commonwealth* are deeply influenced by Plato's *Republic*: there too there is more than one generation (the old man Cephalus; Socrates and Thrasymachus as mature men; Cephalus' son Polemarchus and Plato's brothers Glaucon and Adeimantus of the next generation); there too the conversation takes place on a festival; and there too the topic of justice is dealt with both as an internal quality of individual morality and as an element of social order. In Cicero's sequel to *On the Commonwealth*, the unfinished *On the Laws*, a Platonic model is equally evident. In Plato's *Laws*, the main speaker is the Athenian Stranger, generally identified in antiquity – and by Cicero – with Plato himself; it is set on a long summer day with a contemporary date. Cicero's equivalent presents himself as the main speaker, with his brother Quintus and his close friend Atticus as interlocutors; the conversation takes place at Cicero's ancestral home in Arpinum, at an unidentifiable date in the late 50s. The primary difference between the two is that Plato's *Laws* proposes laws not for the ideal commonwealth of the *Republic*, but for a second-best society, while *On the Laws* proposes the laws for the state which is defined as best in *On the Commonwealth*, namely the ideal constitution of Rome of the mid Republic, after the laws of the Twelve Tables of the mid fifth century. If one ignores that difference (as Cicero himself does), then the two pairs of dialogues are precisely parallel: one in the historical past, one in the present; the second a deliberate sequel to the first. In Cicero's view, the combination was meant to provide first a framework for establishing and maintaining an ideal government (which he identifies with Rome) and second the particular legal code and customs that would correspond to that government. It is often suggested, with some plausibility, that the nine-book version of *On the Commonwealth* that Cicero abandoned in October 54 would have included much of the material (if not the precise format of a legal code) now found in *On the Laws*. In revising his plan, he determined to compose two parallel dialogues in imitation of his Platonic model. That model, however, is more formal than substantive: although he quotes Plato frequently, the philosophical and political systems of Cicero's pair of dialogues owe far more to Aristotle and the Stoics than they do to Plato.

On the Commonwealth

Although *On the Commonwealth* seems to have been a canonical text in antiquity and was widely known until the fifth century CE, it cannot be shown to have existed entire after that, and it survives only in fragmentary form. The principal source for it – and the only manuscript copy of most of it – consists of 151 leaves of a palimpsest, a manuscript written in the fourth century but erased and reused for a text of Augustine's *Commentary on the Psalms* at the monastery of Bobbio near Milan in the seventh century. Luckily, it was not erased very carefully, and the lower text is almost entirely legible; it was discovered in 1819 in the Vatican library by Angelo Mai and published for the first time in 1822, making it the last major Ciceronian text to be printed. The surviving portion represents roughly a quarter of the complete text; it contains most of the first two books (except for the opening of Book 1 and the conclusion of Book 2), a small part of Book 3, and a few pages of Books 4 and 5. The reconstruction of the remains of Books 1 and 2 is virtually certain, but it becomes increasingly tentative thereafter. Other sources, however, supplement the palimpsest: not only are there a great many quotations in lexicographic and grammatical handbooks, but *On the Commonwealth* was used extensively by Lactantius in the *Divine Institutes* early in the fourth century and by Augustine in *City of God* in the fifth. At roughly the same date the Neoplatonist Macrobius used the *Dream of Scipio* (the conclusion of *On the Commonwealth*) as the basis for a commentary which expounds the basic tenets of Neoplatonism; his work, to which was attached a text of the *Dream* itself, was widely read in the Middle Ages and is preserved in a great many copies.

The various sources make reconstruction of the argument of *On the Commonwealth* reasonably certain, if not always in great detail. The dialogue was divided into six books; each pair of books was equipped with a preface in Cicero's own voice and represented one day of conversation. The first two books deal with constitutional theory: Book 1 presents a traditional analysis (parts of which appear as early as Herodotus and which is fully realized in Plato's *Statesman* and Aristotle's *Politics*) of constitutions into three types (monarchy, aristocracy, democracy) together with their degenerate counterparts, and argues that the best form of government is in fact the so-called mixed constitution, incorporating elements of the three good simple forms. The second book applies this theory to Rome: Scipio describes the gradual development of the constitution from the time of Romulus to the restoration of republican government after the fall of the Decemvirate in 450/449, arguing that the form of government in place thereafter (perhaps until nearly Scipio's own time) was in fact the best example of the best (mixed) type of constitution.

Up to this point, the argument closely resembles that put forward in Book 6 of Polybius' *Histories*, a work that Cicero knew well by a man whom Scipio himself also knew well. The constitutional theory of both Cicero and Polybius draws on the work of Aristotle's school, notably Dicaearchus and Theophrastus, while the historical material of Book 2 draws on Polybius and, in all probability, on the lost historical work of the elder Cato, the *Origines*. Near the end of Book 2, however, the argument (and philosophical sources) changed at just the point where the manuscript becomes very fragmentary. Two things clearly take place in the dialogue: there is a move from historical arguments about constitutional form to arguments from nature (2.66); and there is similarly a move from considering "good" government in terms of its practical effectiveness and stability to examining it in terms of its moral values (2.69–70).

These topics occupy the second day of the conversation. Book 3 contains what was undoubtedly the most famous section of the dialogue in antiquity, a reformulation of the pair of speeches delivered by the Academic Carneades in Rome in 155 BCE in which he had argued on successive days that justice is essential to civic life and, conversely, that injustice is essential. Cicero presented the arguments in reverse order: first Philus presents the case for injustice in Carneadean terms, and then Laelius advances a very different argument in favor of justice. This speech is unfortunately very fragmentary: but it is clear that Laelius argued in Stoic terms from the existence of natural affection to the existence of natural and permanent moral values, and thus to natural law, defined as right reason and explained as a fundamental feature of the structure of the cosmos itself. From that conclusion Scipio took the next step, applying the idea of natural law to constitutional forms, demonstrating not only that the degenerate forms of government (tyranny, oligarchy, mob rule) are not properly called commonwealths at all, but that only a constitution which embodies a just distribution of rights and authority is legitimately so named, and hence that the Roman constitution itself, as described in Book 2, is the only proper, rather than the best, form of government. In Book 4 the argument becomes too fragmentary for convincing reconstruction; what is clear is that Stoic ideas are again applied, this time as a solution to the problem of maintaining a just government. Scipio apparently argues from the presence of natural morality in humans (as a part of the moral Stoic cosmos) to an equation between the traditional institutions of Rome and the natural moral code, showing that such institutions are shaped and maintained by individuals of exceptional ability who transmit these values to the people at large and foster institutional morality through their example and actions. The final day of conversation (Books 5 and 6) is almost completely lost except for the *Dream of Scipio* with which it ended. It is clear from Cicero's own references to it and from a few fragments that these books were entirely concerned with the training and function of the individual statesman; the last book dealt with the role of the statesman in a crisis (in part, probably, based on Theophrastus' treatise on that subject), thus bringing the conversation back to the initial occasion for the dialogue, the crisis in Rome in 129. The *Dream* at the end provides a vision of the genuine and posthumous rewards that await the true statesman, placing moral government and civic responsibility in a cosmic framework that corresponds to the Myth of Er at the end of Plato's *Republic* but – as Cicero does throughout *On the Commonwealth* – making individual morality contingent on the values of civic life and public service.

When the palimpsest of the first two books of *On the Commonwealth* was discovered in 1819, Cicero's work was criticized for its lack of originality and for its irrelevance as a political theory. Both criticisms have some validity, both because the portion of the text that was discovered is not – and does not claim to be – particularly original (although it is in fact one of the fullest accounts of the theory of the mixed constitution and the earliest extant history of early Rome in Latin) and because by the early nineteenth century the type of political argument that Cicero made in those books had long been out of fashion. Not only had traditional constitutional theory been replaced by arguments from *raison d'état*, but the links that Cicero makes between moral government and individual virtue (less clear because of the condition of the text) were equally out of favor. Had the text been known two or three centuries earlier, it would have taken an honorable place with Cicero's other works of moral politics, particularly the treatise *On Duties*, in Renaissance discussions of civic humanism and republican virtue. As it is, the description of the statesman in the *Dream* and various fragments preserved by Augustine (such as the analogy of musical harmony and social concord at 2.69a) were widely known and cited long before the discovery of the palimpsest.

On the Commonwealth was the first, and perhaps the only, serious attempt by a Roman to analyze the structure and values of republican government and imperial rule. In adapting Platonic and Aristotelian theories based on the small, self-contained, and relatively homogeneous society of the polis to the conditions of the Roman *imperium*, Cicero made use of Stoic ideas of the *cosmopolis* and of natural law to develop a complex and ambitious argument, linking the traditional values and institutions of republican Rome on the one hand to Aristotelian ideas of civic virtue and on the other to the order of the universe itself. Stoic moral theory made it possible for Cicero to construct an image of society ruled not by a Platonic intellectual élite which alone had access to truth through dialectic and the knowledge of the Forms, but by all those whose recognition of their own moral capacities, as a part of a cosmic whole, led them to contribute to the creation and preservation of a society which reflected and incorporated the natural justice of the universe. As the preface to *On the Commonwealth* and the *Dream of Scipio* make clear, Cicero framed the dialogue as an exhortation to public service and an explanation of the goals and rewards of civic life; he rejects Epicurean withdrawal into private life as well as Platonic and Aristotelian ideas of the superiority of contemplation to action. Political institutions, as in Aristotle, serve not only political ends but moral ones; but in Cicero's universe they also provide a necessary link between social order and the natural law. Perhaps the most striking argument in *On the Commonwealth* is Cicero's attempt in Book 4 to explain the traditional institutions of Roman society in terms of Stoic moral theory, giving a philosophical basis to inherited social practices. Similarly, by demonstrating that the traditional Roman constitution was the only moral form of government and grounding it in the ethical structure of the cosmos in Book 3, Cicero offers a philosophical justification for Roman imperialism and claims to universal rule.

In this connection, however, it is important to recognize that Cicero is very far from advancing an argument in favor of Roman nationalism or exceptionalism, any more than the emphasis on the role of the statesman is (as it has sometimes been understood) a call for monarchy. For both national and individual behavior, Cicero's cosmic framework supplies an absolute standard with which to judge the moral worth of actions and, in the case of nations, an indication of whether or not they deserve to survive. Aristotle had argued that good governments are those in which power is exercised in the interest of the governed rather than the rulers; Cicero extends this to include rule over subject peoples as well and gives a moral and political dimension to Aristotle's ideas about natural slavery. It is essential for Cicero that a commonwealth or an empire be above all a moral community; he makes it very clear not only that lapses in moral government will inevitably lead to political collapse, but also that Rome itself, in both its internal government and its conduct of empire, has fallen away from the standard which it once maintained.

Whether or not Cicero actually believed the cosmic and eschatological framework which he constructed in *On the Commonwealth* is unanswerable; his lifelong adherence to Academic skepticism certainly raises doubts. What is clear is that he found it a compelling means to stress the moral values which he undoubtedly felt to be a necessary basis for the conduct of government and which he knew – as is clear from his correspondence and other writings – were sorely lacking in the public life of his time, and the absence of which he believed, with some justification, endangered the survival of republican government. The largely Stoic theory which Cicero developed allowed him not only to provide a respectable philosophical justification for Roman traditional behavior but to use it to reveal how far Rome had declined from its previous virtue.

But if Cicero's cosmology is not presented as an unquestioned justification for Rome's universal rule, neither is his vision of early Roman greatness a sign of simple-minded nostalgia. Although Cicero uses Stoic theory to provide a rational explanation of the sources and structure of traditional Roman government and institutions, he is completely aware of the fact that the rationality and Stoicism are his own contribution, not characteristics of the primitive rulers of early Rome. Laelius in an important comment (2.21–22) points out that Cicero's Romulus is a very unlikely fiction. There is also an inherent tension in combining a teleological account of Rome's rise to perfection with the philosophical explanation of the immanent virtue of Roman government. The very concept of world empire, central to the idea of Roman rule as the representative of cosmic order, is called into question by the *Dream*, in which the description of the universe reveals the physical and chronological limits – and indeed questions the worth – of Rome's power and glory. What is more, the mechanism for preserving republican virtue itself against the pressures of corruption and decline inevitably involves the use of extraconstitutional power to maintain the republican system. Elizabeth Rawson rightly pointed out the similarity between Cicero's solution to the problem of decline and that of Machiavelli in the *Discorsi*: the preservation of a virtuous republic necessarily entails violation of republican procedures.

On the Commonwealth is the last known Roman literary or philosophical work completed before the outbreak of the civil war between Caesar and Pompey which effectively ended republican government at Rome, and Cicero was well aware that the social and political structure which he idealized in his dialogue had collapsed: indeed, he says as much in the preface to Book 5. What he offers in *On the Commonwealth* is less a practical program for political reform than a philosophical rationale for what had been lost, together with an explanation of why it had failed. It is an explanation based not on the economic and social changes in Rome that had in fact placed intolerable stress on the structure of republican government, but on Cicero's belief in the moral obligations of statesmen and of states. It was perhaps an unfashionable (and certainly ineffective) approach to the problems of civic life even when it was written, and the contradictions in Cicero's own account seem to acknowledge that. In the dialogue, Scipio is presented as the sole possible savior of ancestral virtue; his sudden death only days after the dramatic date of *On the Commonwealth* signals Cicero's sense of the impossibility of maintaining the form of government he so admired and his recognition that the ideal presented in the dialogue was, like Plato's *Republic*, an ideal and not reality.

Because the complete text of *On the Commonwealth* was lost between about 600 and 1819, its direct influence on modern political theory is virtually nonexistent. Nonetheless, portions of it, preserved by other writers, were widely known. The *Dream of Scipio* was known and used by eschatological writers (including Dante) throughout the Middle Ages and (together with Macrobius' commentary on it) was an important source for cosmology and astronomy as well. Lactantius' report of the speeches against and for justice from Book 3 in Books 5 and 6 of the *Divine Institutes* was an important source in the Renaissance for knowledge of the skeptical rhetoric of Carneades as well as for the concept of natural law (more fully discussed in *On the Laws*; see below). Augustine's use in *City of God* of Cicero's definition of the commonwealth at 1.39 as "a concern of the people" (*res populi*) based on "agreement on law" (*iuris consensu*) was cited frequently by medieval writers on politics and is echoed as late as the seventeenth century. The significance of *On the Commonwealth*, however, is far greater than its direct influence. Cicero attempted to place Aristotelian ideas about the ethical importance of civic life within the Stoic framework of universal law, and he was the first person to explore the tensions between the temporal limitations of political achievement and the eternal goals to which such achievements aspire. Augustine in *City of God* used Cicero's framework to explain a different politics and a different eternity; had he been able to read it, Machiavelli too would have recognized what Cicero had achieved.

On the Laws

The history of *On the Laws* is in many ways the opposite of that of *On the Commonwealth*. The latter was well known and studied in antiquity but disappeared by the seventh century; *On the Laws* was far less widely read in antiquity but had a great influence in the Middle Ages and later. The origin and early condition of the work are mysterious: alone among Cicero's major philosophical works, it is not mentioned a single time in Cicero's correspondence. It is generally assumed that it was conceived and written in conjunction with *On the Commonwealth*, and in it Cicero makes frequent allusions to the relationship between the two. It is not complete: what survives in the manuscripts is the better part of three books, with a large gap in the text of the third. It is clear, from one of the few ancient quotations of *On the Laws*, that there were at least five books, but there is no certainty at all as to how many were written or how many were intended; a reference to midday in the fragment of Book 5 suggests that Cicero may have planned a work in eight books. Since it is almost certain that most, if not all, of what survives was written before Cicero departed from Rome in the spring of 51 BCE, and since he does not mention *On the Laws* in the catalogue of his philosophical works that introduces Book 2 of his dialogue *On Divination* (completed shortly after the assassination of Caesar in March 44), it is evident that *On the Laws* had not been completed by that time. It is possible, as some have argued, that Cicero worked on the dialogue at the very end of his life, in 43, but there is no correspondence surviving from that period and no compelling internal evidence for revision; there is certainly no reference in the work itself to any event after 52, and if it had been written later one would have expected at least a veiled allusion to Caesar. On the whole, it is safest to believe that Cicero left *On the Laws* incomplete in 51 and never returned to it under the changed political circumstances of the 40s. In that case, it will have been made public shortly after his death: Cornelius Nepos, the historian and protégé of Cicero's friend Atticus, clearly alludes to it in a fragment of his treatise *On Latin Historians*, probably written in the late 30s.

In many respects *On the Laws*, though incomplete, is Cicero's most successful attempt at imitating the manner of a Platonic dialogue. Unlike *On the Commonwealth*, it has no preface in Cicero's own voice: the setting – on Cicero's family estate in Arpinum – is allowed to emerge from the conversation, as often happens in Plato. Although much of the dialogue is composed of long speeches by Cicero himself, it is a far more vivid and realistic conversation than those of *On the Orator* and *On the Commonwealth*, and the descriptions of the locale – Cicero's family home and the landscaped woods and rivers on his property – are compelling. Because there is no preface, the dramatic date is not specified, and in fact there seems to be no possible date on which the three participants could have met at Arpinum. It consists of a conversation on a long summer day (just as in Plato's *Laws*) between Cicero, his younger brother Quintus, and his close friend and correspondent Titus Pomponius Atticus, a very wealthy member of the equestrian order who advised and assisted Cicero in matters political, financial, and literary.

The subject of law emerges from a conversation about Cicero's proposed activities in retirement, should he ever retire from arguing cases in court. The writing of history is one suggestion – and it is clear that Cicero did in fact consider undertaking a historical project – but the alternative idea, the traditional Roman practice of senior statesmen acting as legal advisers to their clients and friends, leads to the criticism of Roman legal knowledge as insufficiently rational in structure and excessively concerned with minor details. At the request of Quintus and Atticus, therefore, Cicero undertakes to expound on the topic of law, starting from first principles and offering an account of a legal system corresponding to the ideal Roman republic described in *On the Commonwealth*. He takes his starting point where Laelius' argument in *On the Commonwealth* Book 3 leaves off, with the doctrine of natural law. Cicero argues that law itself is part of the cosmos; that it is the same as right reason; that humans and gods both possess reason (and therefore right reason) and are thus fellow citizens of the same community – which is the universe itself. The exposition of the idea and implications of natural law in Book 1 is the fullest exposition of Stoic doctrine on the subject that survives, the idea of the *cosmopolis* or world city. In this account positive human law, if it is to be considered true law, must be in accord with the natural law: that is to say, it must embody the principles of reason as reflected in the order of the world. That is, in effect, precisely the argument that Cicero seems to have made in Books 3 and 4 of *On the Commonwealth*, but here it is expressed in general terms rather than with specific relevance to Roman institutions. That is the function of the rest of the dialogue: in Book 2, after a prologue summarizing the philosophical argument of Book 1, Cicero presents the first part of his code of natural law to correspond with the ideal (Roman) government of the earlier dialogue; quite properly, since the Stoic theory of *On the Laws* assumes a community of gods and men, the code begins with religious laws. In Book 3, he continues with the laws concerning magistracies; and in later books, he almost certainly dealt with (or, if he did not complete the work, would have dealt with) further aspects of public law (the capabilities and limits of magisterial power and the administration of justice in particular), laws concerning education (anticipated at 3.29–30) and the family, and the civil law itself, about the organization of which he is so scornful in Book 1. The laws that Cicero presents are written in a style meant to reflect the conservative and archaic language of Roman legislation; some of them are in fact drawn directly from the laws of the Twelve Tables (and are thus a valuable source for early Roman law). They are, however, filled with false archaisms and bogus reconstructions; the peculiarity of the language is one of the reasons why the text of *On the Laws* is extraordinarily corrupt and difficult to understand in many passages.

On the Laws is a puzzling and not altogether satisfactory work. The precise relationship between the natural law itself and the particular laws proposed in Book 2 and later is never made clear; on more than one occasion (concerning the tribunate and ballot laws) it is made explicit that the proposed law is not meant to be ideal but merely the best under prevailing circumstances. Cicero vacillates between presenting his laws as the best absolutely (and thus embodiments of the natural law) and the best possible; between seeing them as universal and seeing them as specifically related to the particular circumstances of Rome. This uncertainty corresponds to the tensions in the argument of *On the Commonwealth* in describing a state that is simultaneously historical and utopian. In the earlier work, the strains of the argument are themselves one of the strengths of the dialogue, which in fact acknowledges the impossibility of attaining perfection in a real society existing in real time; in *On the Laws*, the difficulties are managed with less success. Similarly, the discussion of particular laws, notably in connection with the continuity of family cult and with burial in Book 2, extends far beyond the necessities of presenting an ideal code. One has the sense that Cicero is quite successful in dealing separately with the philosophical underpinnings of justice and the particularities of legislation but is unable to make the two cohere; in this, of course, Cicero is not unique. There is every reason to believe that *On the Laws* was left incomplete not merely because of the turbulent circumstances of Cicero's life but because it is not nearly so satisfying a work as *On the Commonwealth*.

As a result of the disparity between the first book (with the opening of the second) and the remainder of the dialogue, the two parts of *On the Laws* have been influential in very different ways. The discussion of natural law (together with Lactantius' version of the account of natural law in *On the Commonwealth* Book 3) lent itself easily to Christian adaptation, and it plays an important role in Aquinas' analysis of law in the *Summa Theologiae* (First Part of Part II, QQ. 90–97); but although the idea of natural law was of immense importance in later periods, as for Grotius in the seventeenth century, and is still the subject of considerable debate among legal theorists, its basis lies as much in Aquinas' treatment as in Cicero's. In legal writing, on the other hand, the effect of Books 2 and 3 seems to have been considerable. Although Cicero used the Twelve Tables, it is apparent that the order and the structure of his code are far more rational than those of the archaic text; and throughout *On the Laws* his emphasis is on the analysis of legal principles and the establishment of general rules. Prior to Cicero's time, writing on jurisprudence in Rome consisted largely of case law; in *On the Laws* and in some of his speeches, Cicero placed a great deal of emphasis on the principles of law and equity rather than on the casuistic approach dominant in his youth. Cicero was not alone in his day in attempting to rationalize the presentation of law – his eminent contemporary, alluded to but not named in *On the Laws*, Servius Sulpicius Rufus, was similarly inclined – but there can be little doubt that his polemic against the pettiness of the civil lawyers and the simple and relatively clear organization of his model code played a role in the formation of classical Roman law and thus in European legal thinking since his time.

Chronology

This table includes both events mentioned by Cicero (legendary as well as historical) and important dates in Cicero's own life. For early periods the chronology assumed is that of Polybius; for regnal dates the reconstruction of F. W. Walbank is employed. It should be noted that the Polybian chronology does not correspond to the standard version, constructed by M. Terentius Varro at about the time Cicero wrote *On the Commonwealth*, according to which Rome was founded in 754/3 rather than 751/0. Some dates are attested only in Olympiads, which do not correspond to Roman calendar years and hence are double, e.g. 751/0. It should be recognized that many of the early dates (and some of the individuals) are fictional. All dates are BCE. For an account of the different chronological systems of early Roman history, see T. J. Cornell in *Cambridge Ancient History* vol. VII.2 (1989), 347–50; fuller chronological tables can be found in *Cambridge Ancient History* vol. VII.2 (1989), 645–72; vol. VIII (1989), 523–41; and vol. IX (1994), 780–98.

914	Latest date for Homer
884	Legislation of Lycurgus at Sparta
815/4	Foundation of Carthage
776	First Olympic Games
751/0	Foundation of Rome and accession of Romulus
714/3	Death (or immortality) of Romulus
712/1	Accession of Numa
672/1	Accession of Tullus Hostilius
639/8	Accession of Ancus Marcius
615/4	Accession of Tarquinius Priscus

577/6	Assumption of power by Servius Tullius
c.556	Death of Stesichorus and birth of Simonides (Ol. 55)
532/1	Assumption of power by Tarquinius Superbus
529/8	Arrival of Pythagoras in Italy
508/7	Expulsion of Tarquinius; foundation of Republic
498?	First dictatorship (of Titus Larcius)
486	Consulate (and attempted coup) of Spurius Cassius; executed the following year
454	Law of Aternius and Tarpeius on fines and sureties
451–449	Decemvirate; writing of Twelve Tables
449	Consulate of Lucius Valerius Potitus and Marcus Horatius Barbatus; restoration of Republic
445	Canuleian plebiscite on intermarriage between patricians and plebeians
439	Spurius Maelius killed by Gaius Servilius Ahala for aiming at monarchy
430	Law of Iulius and Papirius on fines
391	Exile of Camillus for misappropriating plunder from Veii
387/6	Gallic Sack of Rome; defeat of Gauls by Camillus
304	Aedileship of Gnaeus Flavius; first publication of the legal calendar
280–275	War with Pyrrhus
264–241	First Punic War
218–202	Second Punic War
212	Marcellus' capture of Syracuse; death of Archimedes
168	Defeat of Perseus of Macedon by Lucius Aemilius Paullus at Pydna
155	Carneades in Rome (Philosophers' Embassy)
149–146	Third Punic War
149	Scipio Aemilianus military tribune in Third Punic War; consulate of Manilius
147	First consulate of Scipio Aemilianus
146	Sack of Carthage and of Corinth
140–139	Scipio Aemilianus' eastern embassy
136	Consulate of Furius Philus; inquiry into Mancinus' treaty

134	Second consulate of Scipio Aemilianus
133	Sack of Numantia Tribunate and death of Tiberius Gracchus
129	Dramatic date of *On the Commonwealth* Death of Scipio
123–122	Tribunate of Gaius Gracchus
121	Death of Gaius Gracchus
109	Exile of Lucius Opimius for bribery in Jugurthine War
106	Birth of Cicero
100	Tribunate and murder of Appuleius; exile of Metellus Numidicus for refusing to swear an oath to support Appuleius' agrarian law
99	Tribunate of Titius
91–89	Murder of Livius Drusus, followed by Social War
88	Sulla's march on Rome and departure to fight Mithridates; flight of Marius
87	Marius' march on Rome
86	Death of Marius
83–81	Sulla's return; his dictatorship (82–81) and proscriptions
79–78	Retirement and death of Sulla; Cicero's travels to Greece and Rhodes for study
75–74	Cicero quaestor in Sicily
70	First consulate of Pompey and Crassus; restoration of full powers of tribunate
69	Cicero aedile
66	Cicero praetor
63	Cicero consul; conspiracy of Catiline and execution of conspirators
60	Formation of so-called First Triumvirate (Pompey, Crassus, Caesar)
59	First consulate of Caesar; transfer of Publius Clodius to plebs
58	Tribunate of Publius Clodius; Cicero sent into exile in March
57	Cicero returns from exile in September
56	Renewal of First Triumvirate; Cicero warned not to oppose them
55	Cicero writes *On the Orator*
54–51	Cicero composes *On the Commonwealth* and *On the Laws*

52 Murder of Clodius by Milo; sole consulate of Pompey

51–50 Cicero governor of Cilicia (31 July – 30 June); return to Italy 24 November 50

49 Outbreak of civil war between Caesar and Pompey

48 Defeat of Pompey at Pharsalus; Cicero returns from Epirus to Brundisium

47 Cicero permitted by Caesar to return to Rome in July

46 Defeat of Republicans by Caesar at Thapsus (N. Africa); suicide of Cato

46–44 Cicero composes the bulk of his rhetorical and philosophical works (*Brutus, Orator; Consolation* [lost], *Hortensius* [lost], *Academica, On the Supreme Good and Evil, Tusculan Disputations, On the Nature of the Gods, On Divination, On Fate, On Old Age, On Friendship*)

44 Assassination of Caesar on 15 March; Cicero delivers first Philippic against Antony in September and composes *On Duties*

43 Formation of Second Triumvirate (Antony, Octavian, Lepidus) in November; assassination of Cicero on 7 December

Bibliography

Ancient works

Cicero's works

The Loeb Classical Library includes almost all Cicero's surviving works (in many volumes, with facing Latin and English texts); there are more recent (and better-annotated) translations of many of them. Of those most relevant to *On the Commonwealth* and *On the Laws*, the speeches delivered shortly after Cicero's return from exile may be found in *Cicero: Back from Exile*, translated by D. R. Shackleton Bailey (Atlanta, 1991); the most important of these is *On Behalf of Sestius* delivered in 56. The same translator's version of the *Philippics* (Chapel Hill, 1991) is also excellent. Of Cicero's philosophical and rhetorical works, those most relevant to *On the Commonwealth* and *On the Laws* include *On the Orator, On the Ultimate Good and Evil, Tusculan Disputations, On the Nature of the Gods, On Divination, On Friendship*, and *On Duties*. There is a Penguin translation of *On the Nature of the Gods* by Horace McGregor and two collections of relevant selections from a number of works in *On the Good Life* and *On Government* (translated by Michael Grant; both Penguin). The Aris and Phillips series contains annotated translations (with facing Latin) of *On Friendship* and the *Dream of Scipio* by J. G. F. Powell, of *Tusculan Disputations* Book 1 and Books 2 and 5 by A. E. Douglas, and of *On Stoic Good and Evil* (*De finibus bonorum et malorum* Book 3 and *Paradoxa Stoicorum*) by M. R. Wright. *On Duties*, translated by M. T. Griffin and E. M. Atkins, is published in this series. The complete translation of Cicero's correspondence by D. R. Shackleton Bailey (*Letters to Atticus* and *Letters to His Friends*) has been allowed to go out of print by Penguin in favor of *Selected Letters*; his complete translation of the correspondence with Atticus is available now only in the seven-volume edition (Cambridge 1965–70, with text, translation, and commentary), while *Letters to His Friends* has been reprinted by the American Philological Association (Atlanta, 1988).

Other ancient works

Among Cicero's contemporaries, the works of Lucretius (*De rerum natura* [*On the Nature of Things*]) and of Sallust (*Conspiracy of Catiline* and *Jugurthine War*) are available in Penguin translations (and many others); the biography of Cicero's friend Atticus by Cornelius Nepos is translated with commentary by N. Horsfall in the Clarendon Ancient History Series (Oxford, 1989).

For the philosophical background to *On the Commonwealth* and *On the Laws*, the works of Plato and Aristotle are most important; of the former, particularly the *Republic* (translated by G. M. Grube, revised by C. D. Reeve: Hackett, 1992), the *Statesman* (translated by J. Annas and R. Waterfield: Cambridge Texts in the History of Political Thought, 1995), and the *Laws* (tr. T. Saunders: Penguin, 1970). Of Aristotle, most relevant are the *Politics* (tr. S. Everson: Cambridge Texts in the History of Political Thought, 1988) and the *Nicomachean Ethics* (tr. D. Ross: World's Classics, 1980). There is a valuable translation of Hellenistic philosophical texts in A. A. Long and D. Sedley, *The Hellenistic Philosophers* vol. I (Cambridge, 1987); the Greek text appears in vol. II. There is a careful and well-annotated translation of Macrobius' *Commentary on the Dream of Scipio* by W. H. Stahl (New York, 1952).

Of great importance for the historical and philosophical background to *On the Commonwealth* is the *Histories* of Polybius, particularly Book 6 (constitutional theory and early Roman history) and Book 31 (his conversations with Scipio Aemilianus); aside from the Loeb edition, there is a good translation by E. S. Shuckburgh (London, 1889; repr. Bloomington, 1962). Other accounts of early Rome, parallel to Cicero's narrative in *On the Commonwealth* Book 2, are those of Livy and Dionysius of Halicarnassus. The relevant portions of Livy are available in *The Early History of Rome*, tr. A. De Selincourt (Penguin); for Dionysius the only available translation is in the Loeb Classical Library.

The legal text most relevant to *On the Laws* is the fragments of the Twelve Tables, now available in a new text with translation and full commentary in M. Crawford et al., *Roman Statutes* (London, 1996). The fragments are also available in E. Warmington (ed.), *Remains of Old Latin* (4 vols., Loeb Classical Library), which also includes the fragments of early poetry quoted by Cicero. The notes in this edition give references to the collections of Crawford and Warmington, but it should be noted that in the latter case both the text and the translation often differ considerably.

Modern works

For almost all subjects relevant to the texts in this volume, a brief introduction will be found in *The Oxford Classical Dictionary* (3rd ed., 1996). The bibliography given here excludes almost all works written in languages other than English, but for the study of *On the Commonwealth* and *On the Laws* in particular some of the fundamental tools for research are in German and (since they have been of great use in preparing this volume) must be mentioned here. An essential guide to modern study of *On the Commonwealth* is P. L. Schmidt, "Cicero 'De re publica': Die Forschung der letzten fünf Dezennien," in *Aufstieg und Niedergang der römischen Welt*, ed. H. Temporini and W. Haase, vol. I.4 (Berlin and New York, 1973), 262–333; the same author's study of the dating of *On the Laws*, *Die Abfassungszeit von Ciceros Schrift über die Gesetze* (Rome, 1973), includes a great deal of material extending far beyond the nominal subject. E. Heck, *Die Bezeugung von Ciceros Schrift De re publica* (Hildesheim, 1966), contains the text of all citations of and allusions to *On the Commonwealth* with detailed discussion.

Background

The bibliography on the late Republic and on Cicero in general is immense. A recent useful guide to the political history will be found in *Cambridge Ancient History* vol. IX (2nd ed., 1994), particularly (for Cicero) the chapters by T. P. Wiseman on the period 69–50. The most influential and eloquent modern treatment of the end of the Republic is R. Syme, *The Roman Revolution* (Oxford, 1939); also admirable are the various studies by P. A. Brunt, including *Social Conflicts in the Roman Republic* (London, 1971) and the articles collected in *The Fall of the Roman Republic and Related Essays* (Oxford, 1988). For the actual workings of Roman civic life, there is also the detailed study by C. Nicolet, *The World of the Citizen in Republican Rome* (London, 1980). For the intellectual history of the period, M. Griffin's chapter in *Cambridge Ancient History* vol. IX is an excellent introduction; a detailed study (which omits Cicero himself) is E. Rawson, *Intellectual Life in the Late Roman Republic* (London, 1985). Her articles collected in *Roman Culture and Society* (Oxford, 1991) include many papers on Cicero, including several directly related to *On the Commonwealth* and *On the Laws.* A valuable introduction to the values of Roman public life is D. C. Earl, *The Moral and Political Tradition of Rome* (London, 1967), and many of the ethical issues relevant to *On the Commonwealth* are discussed by A. A. Long in "Cicero's Politics in *De Officiis*," in *Justice and Generosity*, ed. A. Laks and M. Schofield (Cambridge, 1995).

For Cicero himself, the best brief biography, which pays due attention to Cicero's ideas, is that of E. Rawson, *Cicero: A Portrait* (London, 1975); more recent, fuller, and with more annotation is the two-volume life by T. Mitchell, *Cicero: The Ascending Years* and *Cicero: The Senior Statesman* (New Haven, 1979 and 1991). The useful collection of essays in T. A. Dorey (ed.), *Cicero* (London, 1965), contains a brief political biography and introductions to the various aspects of Cicero's writings; an excellent bibliographical essay on recent Ciceronian scholarship is A. E. Douglas, *Cicero* (Greece and Rome New Surveys in the Classics 2, Oxford, 1968; rev. 1978).

Several recent collections of essays contain valuable papers (some of which are mentioned specifically below) on Cicero's philosophical writings and their background: *Philosophia Togata*, ed. M. Griffin and J. Barnes (Oxford, 1989), and *Philosophia Togata II*, ed. J. Barnes and M. Griffin (Oxford, 1997); *Cicero's Knowledge of the Peripatos*, ed. W. Fortenbaugh and P. Steinmetz (New Brunswick, N.J., 1989) (mostly in German); *Cicero the Philosopher*, ed. J. G. F. Powell (Oxford, 1995); and *Justice and Generosity* (full citation above). There are two helpful introductions to the complex world of Hellenistic philosophy: A. A. Long, *Hellenistic Philosophy* (2nd ed., London, 1986), and R. Sharples, *Stoics, Epicureans and Skeptics* (London, 1996). For Stoic political theory, there is the superb study of M. Schofield, *The Stoic Idea of the City* (Cambridge, 1991). There is also an excellent bibliography for both Hellenistic and Roman philosophy in *Philosophia Togata* [I].

On the Commonwealth

Syme in *The Roman Revolution* described *On the Commonwealth* as a book "about which too much has been written," but unfortunately (or not) very little of it until recently has been in English. The introduction to J. Zetzel (ed.), *Cicero: De re publica: Selections* (Cambridge, 1995), provides orientation on the major issues, and the bibliography includes major scholarly treatments and bibliographies; a fuller study of *On the Commonwealth* by the editor is in progress. The survey of Cicero's political ideas by N. Wood, *Cicero's Social and Political Thought* (Berkeley and Los Angeles, 1988) has some useful analyses but many errors; older general treatments still worth reading are those of C. W. Keyes, "Original Elements in Cicero's Ideal Constitution," *American Journal of Philology* 42 (1921), 309–23, and W. W. How, "Cicero's Ideal in his *De re publica*," *Journal of Roman Studies* 20 (1930), 24–42. Two recent articles that deal with central issues in Cicero's political theory are J. G. F. Powell, "The *rector rei publicae* of Cicero's *De Republica*," *Scripta Classica Israelica* 13 (1994), 19–29, and J.-L. Ferrary, "The Statesman and the Law in the Political Philosophy of Cicero," in *Justice and Generosity*.

For the constitutional theories of Book 1, the study of Polybius by K. von Fritz, *The Theory of the Mixed Constitution in Antiquity* (New York, 1954), remains fundamental. More recent studies include the chapter on Polybius Book 6 in F. W. Walbank, *Polybius* (Berkeley and Los Angeles, 1972); D. Hahm, "Polybius' Applied Political Theory," in *Justice and Generosity*; and A. Lintott "The Theory of the Mixed Constitution at Rome," in *Philosophia Togata II*. J. A. North, "Democratic Politics in Republican Rome," *Past and Present* 126 (1990), 3–21, relates constitutional theory to the practice of Roman politics and reviews the recent debate on democratic elements in Roman government, and M. Schofield provides an excellent discussion of Cicero's use of the term *res publica* in "Cicero's Definition of *Res Publica*," in *Cicero the Philosopher*.

A general treatment of Cicero's philosophical models is A. A. Long, "Cicero's Plato and Aristotle," in *Cicero the Philosopher*. More specifically related to *On the Commonwealth* are R. Sharples, "Cicero's *Republic* and Greek Political Theory," *Polis* 5.2 (1986), 30–50, and D. Frede, "Constitution and Citizenship: Peripatetic Influence on Cicero's Political Conceptions in the *De re publica*," in *Cicero and the Peripatos*.

For the political and dramatic setting of the dialogue, there are useful historical discussions in A. E. Astin, *Scipio Aemilianus* (Oxford, 1967), and A. Bernstein, *Tiberius Sempronius Gracchus* (Ithaca, 1978), together with A. Lintott's chapter in *Cambridge Ancient History* vol. IX; for Cicero's approach to historiography (relevant to both dialogues), the most important treatment is that of E. Rawson, "Cicero the Historian and Cicero the Antiquarian," in *Roman Culture and Society*. For the early history of Rome, discussed by Cicero in Book 2 of *On the Commonwealth*, an excellent recent account of what is actually known may be found in Tim Cornell, *The Beginnings of Rome: Italy and Rome from the Bronze Age to the Punic Wars* (London, 1995). J.-L.Ferrary, *Philhellénisme et impérialisme* (Rome, 1988), includes valuable discussions of the debate on justice in Book 3 and on the intellectual world of the second century. A strictly philosophical account of the Carneadean debate and its relationship to Stoic ethics may be found in Gisela Striker, "Following Nature: A Study in Stoic Ethics," *Essays on Hellenistic Epistemology and Ethics* (Cambridge, 1996), 221–80. On the debate on justice and its influence, see also J. Zetzel, "Natural Law and Poetic Justice: A Carneadean Debate in Cicero and Virgil," *Classical Philology* 91 (1996), 297–319. There is no single study devoted to the later use (direct or indirect) of *On the Commonwealth*, but there are an excellent analysis of Renaissance Ciceronianism (including some uses of *On the Commonwealth*) in Richard Tuck, *Philosophy and Government 1572–1651* (Cambridge, 1993), 1–64, and valuable observations on some particular passages in Maurizio Viroli, "Machiavelli and the Republican Idea of Politics," in G. Bock, Q. Skinner, and M. Viroli (eds.), *Machiavelli and Republicanism* (Cambridge, 1990), 143–71.

The *Dream of Scipio* has long been treated as a separate text as a result of its separate transmission. A valuable recent study is J. G. F. Powell, "Second Thoughts on the Dream of Scipio," *Papers of the Leeds International Latin Seminar* 9 (1996), 13–27; also worth reading (although too inclined to see Pythagorean influences) is R. G. C. Coleman, "The Dream of Cicero," *Proceedings of the Cambridge Philological Society* n.s. 10 (1964), 1–14. The fundamental study of the sources and philosophical origins of the *Dream* remains P. Boyancé, *Etudes sur le Songe de Scipion* (Paris, 1936); his articles on Cicero, collected in *Etudes sur l'humanisme cicéronien* (Brussels, 1970), contain much of value on Ciceronian philosophy as a whole.

On the Laws

Far less has been written about *On the Laws* than about *On the Commonwealth*, and less about the dialogue as a whole than about particular portions of it. A new commentary by A. Dyck is in preparation. The fundamental introduction to most of the major critical issues is E. Rawson, "The Interpretation of Cicero's *De Legibus*," in *Roman Culture and Society*. Recent articles of value for general interpretation include S. Benardete, "Cicero's *De Legibus* I: Its Plan and Intention," *American Journal of Philology* 108 (1987), 295–309, and W. Goerler, "Silencing the Troublemaker: *De Legibus* 1.39 and the Continuity of Cicero's Skepticism," in *Cicero the Philosopher*.

On the concept of natural law and its history before Cicero, see above all M. Schofield, *The Stoic Idea of the City* (Cambridge, 1991); of value also are his article "Two Stoic Approaches to Justice," in *Justice and Generosity*, and G. Striker, "Origins of the Concept of Natural Law," *Essays on Hellenistic Epistemology and Ethics* (Cambridge, 1996), 209–20. A good recent review of the subject is P. Mitsis, "Natural Law and Natural Right in Post-Aristotelian Philosophy: The Stoics and Their Critics," *Aufstieg und Niedergang der römischen Welt*, part II, vol. XXXVI.7 (Berlin and New York, 1994), 4812–50. There are a good translation of the relevant texts of Aquinas and much material on the modern history of natural law in P. Sigmund, *St. Thomas Aquinas on Politics and Ethics* (New York, 1988).

For the context of *On the Laws* in the development of Roman jurisprudence, there is much relevant material in B. Frier, *The Rise of the Roman Jurists: Studies in Cicero's "Pro Caecina"* (Princeton, 1985); basic introductions to the development of Roman law will be found in F. Schulz, *Roman Legal Science* (Oxford, 1946), and H. F. Jolowicz and B. Nicholas, *Historical Introduction to the Study of Roman Law* (3rd ed., Cambridge, 1972). The religious laws of Book 2 are closely related to Cicero's discussions of Roman religion in *On the Nature of the Gods* and *On Divination*; two useful introductions to various aspects of these texts are P. Brunt, "Philosophy and Religion in the Later Republic," in *Philosophia Togata*, and J. Linderski, "Cicero and Roman Divination," *Parola del Passato* 36 (1982), 12–38.

Text and Translation

The translation of *On the Commonwealth* is based on C. [K.] Ziegler (ed.), *M. Tullius Cicero: De re publica* (7th ed., Leipzig, 1969), and (for the continuous portions of the palimpsest and the *Dream of Scipio*) J. Zetzel (ed.), *Cicero: De re publica: Selections* (Cambridge, 1995). The translation of *On the Laws* is based on K. Ziegler (ed.), *M. Tullius Cicero: De legibus* (3rd ed., rev. by W. Goerler: Heidelberg, 1979). Most departures from these editions are indicated in the notes. It should be noted that a new critical edition of both texts is being prepared by J. G. F. Powell for Oxford Classical Texts.

On the Commonwealth differs in the format of the dialogue from *On the Laws* in that the latter is pure dialogue, with no narrator, and changes of speaker are marked (by convention) with the name of the speaker followed by a colon, as in dramatic texts; in *On the Commonwealth*, by contrast, there is a narrator, and in the Latin text speakers are often introduced by phrases such as "Then Scipio said." To avoid extremely stilted translation, these phrases have been replaced here by the same dramatic convention as is used in *On the Laws.*

With respect to the order and presentation of the fragments of *On the Commonwealth*, there have been many departures from Ziegler's text. His numbering of the sections has been maintained (with the addition of lower-case letters to indicate separate fragments grouped under one section), although many of them have been moved; an index of fragments will be found at the back of the book. In printing the fragments, the following conventions have been employed:

1 Verbatim quotations given without context have the source of the

citation in parentheses at the end of the fragment; the sign + indicates that the source assigns the fragment to a specific book.

2 Fragments quoted with context or consisting largely of paraphrase are given with the source of the citation at the beginning of the fragment. Paraphrase or loose citation is given in italics, and words or phrases that are, or are very close to, Cicero's own are in roman type.

Although this is occasionally cumbersome, it is important in many cases (particularly in quotations in Lactantius and Augustine) to be able to distinguish carefully the words of Cicero from the often tendentious context in which they appear. And in dealing with a fragmentary text, it is crucial for the reader to be able to assess the degree of accuracy of any given citation. It should also be noted that the beginnings and ends of sections of the manuscript of *On the Commonwealth* are marked by an asterisk (*), and that editorial supplements are enclosed in angle brackets (< >).

Notes on terminology

The terminology of Cicero's political and legal theory is not always precise, and is almost never capable of being transferred into English with complete consistency. The following words deserve particular notice; the translations given in parentheses are those used in this volume and do not cover the possible range of meanings in other contexts.

***Res publica* (commonwealth, government, public undertaking, public career, public affairs, public life)**

Literally, *res publica* means "public thing," and Cicero defines it (*On the Commonwealth* 1.39 and elsewhere) as *res populi*, "the people's thing," here always translated as "the concern of the people" in order to emphasize its connection with ideas of property as well as of government. *Res publica* is used idiomatically in a number of phrases (notably *rem publicam adire* or *gerere*, lit. "to approach" or "to perform the public thing") that simply mean participation in the work of government and holding office, and they are translated variously as the context requires. Most often in *On the Commonwealth*, however, *res publica* is a technical term for Cicero, used to translate Plato's and Aristotle's *politeia*, and here translated in every appropriate case as "commonwealth." That is perhaps not a term of current constitutional language except in the British Commonwealth (which is not parallel) or in the commonwealths of Massachusetts and Virginia (which are), but its very lack of modern specificity makes it useful, as the meaning of *res publica* itself varies considerably in Cicero: it can be used (as in Book 1) for any constitutional form of government; it can be limited to some form of participatory republic and contrasted with monarchy (as at 6.9); it can denote a morally legitimate constitution only (as in Book 3.43ff.). In almost all cases in *On the Commonwealth*, it refers to the constitutional aspect of a state, the way in which power is structured internally.

***Civitas* (state, government, civic affairs)**

There are many occasions in which *civitas* is a synonym for *res publica*, but in general it emphasizes the corporate collection of individuals (derived from *civis*, "citizen") that make up a society rather than the constitutional structure in which they are organized. Frequently the phrase *status civitatis*, "organization/condition/form of the state" is a synonym for *res publica*. The translation "state" is used here (in all but a few idiomatic usages) not because *civitas* is equivalent to the modern notion of the nation-state but as a relatively neutral term that implies nothing about legitimacy or structure.

***Consilium* (counsel, judgment, plan, planning, policy, deliberation, deliberative function, deliberative responsibility, council)**

Consilium is an extraordinarily flexible term, of considerable importance in *On the Commonwealth*. It represents both the necessary intelligence needed to guide a commonwealth, whether in a single person or a group (and hence shades into *concilium*, "council"), and also the specific virtue of aristocratic government (at least in the aristocrats' self-presentation at 1.51–52). Cicero also employs it at 1.60 to identify an aspect of the mind that mediates between reason and passion.

***Prudens; prudentia; providere* (prudent, man of foresight; prudence, foresight, judgment; to foresee, see ahead, look into the future)**

Cicero emphasizes the etymology of *prudens* from the verb *providere*, to look ahead. *Prudentia* is the essential quality of the good statesman, the ability to understand circumstances and to deal with them in advance. He uses it as the equivalent of the Aristotelian virtue of *phronesis*, practical knowledge; but it is also used more cynically by Philus in Book 3 of *On the Commonwealth* (particularly 3.28) to contrast with decency and honorable behavior. It should also be noted that *prudentia* is carefully distinguished from *sapientia*, "wisdom," which translates Greek *sophia* (theoretical wisdom in Aristotle; "knowledge of things divine and human" for the Stoics).

Auctoritas (authority)

Auctoritas is a term particularly associated with the Roman senate: it is, among other things, a technical term for something voted by the senate, its advice and recommendation. The important point is that the senate had no legislative powers: it could only advise and could not command. Cicero's extension of senatorial power is one of the more significant changes from Roman practice made in *On the Laws* Book 3. Hence "authority" here does not connote a legal right to direct behavior; it connotes strong influence and the right to command respect for one's views.

Lex (law, legislation, rules, proviso)

In these two works, *lex* has a single very specific meaning which is significantly extended in one important respect. A *lex* in *On the Commonwealth* and *On the Laws* is a written rule approved by a body (or person) with the constitutional right to make such rules, that is, a statute or set of statutes. The one occasion on which it is translated "rules" is Cicero's equation (*On the Laws* 2.39) of musical and societal "laws," and in other contexts it can be used of binding contracts as well as of statutes, as at *On the Commonwealth* 1.38, where it is translated "proviso." The one important extension is the "law of nature" at *On the Commonwealth* 3.33 and in the first two books of *On the Laws*, where Cicero makes an explicit analogy (and contrast) between the usual meaning of *lex* as positive law and its larger significance as the binding if unwritten statute that governs the behavior of all rational beings, equated with "right reason" and the intention of the divine ruler of the cosmos.

***Ius* (law, justice, right, rights, procedures of justice, just behavior, court, regulations, power, authority)**

The range of meanings of *ius* (from which are derived *iustus*, "just," *iustitia*, "justice," and *iniuria*, "wrong, injury, crime") is far broader than that of *lex*. The two words are in some contexts equivalent: almost all *leges* are *iura*, but the converse is not true. *Ius* can refer to varieties of rules (e.g. pontifical law) that are not statutory but are nonetheless binding; to the rights, powers, and responsibilities that are part of a magistrate's capacities; to all the aspects of a legal system (legal procedure, courts, magistrates' decisions, the civil law taken as a whole, the principles of law and jurisprudence) that extend beyond and around the texts of statutes. *Ius* also has the connotation of "justice" – that is, the broader principles of equity or morality which a legal system is supposed to embody.

***Aequitas; aequabilitas; aequabilis* (equity; equality, balance and fairness; equitable, balanced)**

The fundamental distinction in Cicero's usage (particularly in *On the Commonwealth*) is that *aequitas* can only mean fairness or equity, not equality, while *aequabilitas* can mean either. Equity (roughly equivalent to proportional equality in Aristotelian language) is an essential characteristic of a balanced constitution, but the conflict between proportional and arithmetic equality is crucial to the aristocratic argument at 1.53, which blurs the distinction between (arithmetic) equality and (proportional) equity in order to disparage democratic ideals. Cicero uses *aequalitas*, "equality," in the philosophical discussions of *On the Laws* Book 1 (38, 49); he does not use it in the political analysis of *On the Commonwealth*.

***Optimates; optimus quisque* (optimates, aristocracy, aristocrats, "the best people"; every responsible citizen, the best people)**

Optimate (which has been taken over in English) is the favorable term for the Roman aristocracy, derived from *optimus*, "best" – itself the Latin equivalent of the Greek *aristos*. In *On the Commonwealth* Book 1 and Book 3, there is some question raised as to whether the aristocracy is in fact "best" or whether they have simply arrogated that term to themselves. In Roman political language, the negative equivalent for *optimates* was *factio* – which is the term that Cicero uses to designate "oligarchy." In real life, the two could refer to the same people or groups from opposite points of view, while in *On the Commonwealth* they refer to the good and bad forms of government by the few. Cicero himself, both here and even more in the speech for Sestius of 56 BCE, attempted to portray his supporters (and the supporters of the traditional Roman government) as "the best" – either *optimates* or *optimus quisque*, "each best person" – whether they were optimates in the traditional sense or members of other social classes. The use of these words is tendentious; it should be noted that Cicero himself is as tendentious in their use as the advocates in *On the Commonwealth* of various political positions.

Otium (peace, peace and quiet, calm, ease, leisure, relaxation, tranquillity, free time)

Otium has two meanings, one personal and one social. In personal terms, it is the opposite of *negotium*, "business, busyness"; as such it can connote either a well-deserved holiday and relaxation (as for the speakers of *On the Commonwealth*) or simple laziness and the failure to take part in the public world (as in Cicero's view of the Epicureans). In social terms, it denotes "domestic tranquillity" or "law and order," to be contrasted with civil upheaval and disorder on the one hand, and with *pax* (the absence of external disturbance and war) on the other. One of Cicero's political slogans in the mid 50s was *otium cum dignitate*, "calm with honor," which, like all slogans, has numerous meanings, depending on which meaning of *otium* one chooses.

Synopsis

On the Commonwealth

Book 1

47–50	The argument for democracy
51–53	The argument for aristocracy
54–55	The virtues of the three forms; Scipio's preference for monarchy
56–64	Arguments for monarchy: the government of the gods and the universe (56–57); historical evidence (58); the structure of the mind (59–60); the analogy of the household (61); the need for unitary control in crisis (62–63); the love for a good king (64)
65–69	The instability of the simple forms; their corruption; the virtues of a mixed constitution
70–71	Conclusion: Rome as the best form of government; transition to Book 2

Book 2

1–3 PREFACE: COMPARISON OF ROME TO GREEK CONSTITUTIONS AND PLATO

4–20 ROMULUS

4	Birth and early life
4–9	Choosing the site for a city
10–11	Foundation of Rome
12–13	Rape of the Sabines; joint rule with Titus Tatius
14–16	Romulus' institutions: senate and auspices
17–20	Deification of Romulus; excursus on Romulus and Greek chronology

21–22 EXCURSUS ON METHOD: PLATO, THE PERIPATETICS, AND SCIPIO

23–30 NUMA

23–24	Interregnum; elective and hereditary monarchy
25	Election of Numa
26–27	Numa's reign
28–30	Numa and Pythagoras

Book 3

26–38a	We are not always just through fear of consequences: people cheat and kill if they can get away with it
27–28	Conclusion: the disadvantages of being just

32b–41 LAELIUS: THE ARGUMENT FOR JUSTICE

32b–32a	Introductory conversation
39a–39b	Human affections are natural, and hence so is morality
40b–3 inc. 5	The soul is immortal; the rewards of virtue are not material
33	True law is right reason and is eternal and universal
4.1c–37a	To be unjust is to cease being human; the rule of the just over the unjust is as natural as the rule of mind over body and reason over passion
34a–41	Unjust rule and unjust war are fatal to a state; the unjust actions of Tiberius Gracchus endanger Rome's survival

42–48 SCIPIO: JUST GOVERNMENT

42	Praise of Laelius
42–45	Unjust governments are not true commonwealths
46–48	Examples of just forms of simple constitutions
[missing]	Even the good forms of simple constitution do not distribute rights and responsibilities justly; the only true commonwealth is the mixed constitution of Rome

Book 4

1a–1f PREFACE: BODY AND MIND

2 THE PROPRIETY OF THE ORDER OF ROMAN SOCIETY

3a–14 ROMAN SOCIAL INSTITUTIONS

3a–4	The regulation of the young
4–5c	Criticism of Plato
6c–6f	The regulation of women
6a–7a	The censorship; proper behavior of adult males
9a–14	The theater and music
8a–8f	The function of law in society

Book 5

1–2b PREFACE: MORALITY, INSTITUTIONS, AND THE STATESMAN

3–11d CHARACTERISTICS OF THE STATESMAN

3	The statesman as lawgiver
4–5	The statesman as a person of general understanding
6–8b	The statesman as moral arbiter and guide
9–11d	The virtues of the statesman

Book 6

1a–2e SEDITION AND THE TRUE STATESMAN; THE DEMAGOGUE

8–29 SCIPIO'S DREAM

8	The rewards of the statesman: Scipio Nasica
3–6	Contrast between Scipio's dream and the Myth of Er in Plato
9–10	Scipio and Masinissa
11–12	Prophecy of Scipio's life and death
13–16	The afterlife of statesmen; the duty of human souls
17–19	The structure of the cosmos
20–25	The limits of earthly glory; celestial rewards
26–28	The immortality of the soul
29	Service to the commonwealth is the noblest way of life

On the Laws

Book 1

1–16 INTRODUCTORY CONVERSATION

1–5	Poetic truth and historical truth
5–10	Proposal that Cicero write history; weaknesses of Roman historiography
10–12	Cicero as a legal expert
13–16	Choice of a subject: the laws for the best commonwealth, modeled on Plato's *Laws*

17–35 THE BASIS OF LAW IN NATURE

17–18	Universal law and civil law

18–20	Origins of law in nature; law as right reason
21–27	The community of gods and men through shared reason and law; nature's gifts to humans
28–35	The similarity of all humans for good and ill; the universality of reason and law; friendship

36–57 JUSTICE AND VIRTUE

36–39	The idea of the good in post-Aristotelian philosophy
40–42	Fear of punishment, utility, and human law are not the basis of justice
42–46	The standard of justice and of all virtue is nature and is universal
47	Disagreements on justice and virtue result from human failings
48–52	Justice and the other virtues are desirable on their own account
52–57	Digression: philosophical disputes about the highest good are primarily verbal, not substantive

58–63 CONCLUSION: THE PRAISE OF PHILOSOPHY

Book 2

1–7 INTRODUCTORY CONVERSATION: DOUBLE CITIZENSHIP

8–14 RESUME OF PREVIOUS DISCUSSION: NATURAL LAW AND HUMAN LAW

14–18 INTRODUCTION TO THE LAW CODE: THE PRAISE OF LAW

19–22 CICERO'S LAW CODE, PART I: RELIGIOUS LAWS

19	How, where, and what gods to worship
19–20	Rituals and the calendar
20–21	Priestly functions
21–22	Offenses against religion
22	Rituals for the dead and burial regulations

23–68 COMMENTARY ON THE LAWS

23–24	Introduction

Book 3

On the Commonwealth

Book 1

Fragments of the preface[1]

1 [4.7f Ziegler]. Augustine, *Epist.* 91.3: *Take a brief look at that book* On the Commonwealth, *from which you drank up that attitude of a patriotic citizen, that* there is for good men no limit or end of looking out for one's country.[2]

2 [fr. 1a]. Thus, since our country provides more benefits and is a parent prior to our biological parents, we have a greater obligation to it than to our parents. (+Nonius 426.8)

3 [fr. 1d]. From which those people[3] call <us> away. (+Arusianus 7.457.14K).

4 [fr. 1b]. Pliny, *Natural History, praef.* 22: *Cicero is honest: in* On the Commonwealth *he announces that he is Plato's companion.*

5 [fr. 1c]. Pliny, *Natural History, praef.* 7: *There is also a kind of public rejection of the learned. Even Cicero uses it, although his genius is beyond all doubt; more surprising is that he does so through a spokesman:* "and not for the very learned: I don't want Persius to read this, I do want Iunius Congus to."[4] *If Lucilius, the creator of verbal wit, thought that he had to speak this way, and Cicero thought that he had to borrow it, especially when*

[1] More than half the preface is lost; the few extant fragments show that C. discussed the obligation to serve one's country, referred to Plato's *Republic* as his model, and emphasized the greater importance of experience and action than of philosophical expertise both in general and in the dialogue itself.

[2] The rest of this quotation will be found at 4.7f.

[3] The Epicureans.

[4] Lucilius 633–34 Warmington. The text is corrupt, but it is clear that the first person named is a very learned person, while Iunius Congus is the ideal (moderately learned) audience. For the identification of proper names, see the biographical notes.

writing about the commonwealth, how much more do I have a reason to defend myself from some judge?

6 [fr. 1e]. Lactantius, *Inst.* 3.16.5: *They do not seek utility but pleasure from philosophy, as Cicero attests:* In fact, although all the writings of these people[5] contain the richest sources for virtue and knowledge, if they are compared to the actions and accomplishments of the others I am afraid that they seem to have brought less utility to men's activities than enjoyment to their leisure.

7 [fr. 1f]. Nor would Carthage have had so much wealth for nearly six hundred years without judgment and education. (+ Nonius 526.8)

[1] <If they had not preferred virtue to pleasure . . .> would <not> have freed Rome from the attack <of Pyrrhus>;[6] Gaius Duilius, Aulus Atilius, and Lucius Metellus would not have freed Rome from the terror of Carthage. The two Scipios would not have put out with their own blood the rising flames of the Second Punic War; when it flared up with greater force Quintus Fabius Maximus would not have weakened it or Marcus Marcellus crushed it or Scipio Africanus torn the war from the gates of Rome and forced it back within the enemy's walls.[7] Marcus Cato, an unknown man of no pedigree – a man who serves as a model of industry and virtue to all of us who share his goals – could have remained at Tusculum, a healthy spot and not far off, enjoying peace and quiet;[8] but that madman (as some people[9] think), under no compulsion, chose to be tossed in the waves and storms of public life to an advanced old age rather than live a happy life in peace and calm. I leave out countless men who one and all contributed to the safety of this state; I will not mention those of recent times, so that no one will object that he or someone in his family was omitted. I make this one assertion: nature has given men such a need for virtue and such a desire to defend the common safety that this force has overcome all the enticements of pleasure and ease.

5 Philosophers in general; "the others" are statesmen. Lactantius does not refer the quotation to a specific work, and it is sometimes ascribed to the lost *Hortensius*.

6 The manuscript begins in the middle of a sentence; for other possible supplements cf. J. Zetzel (ed.), *Cicero: De re publica* (Cambridge, 1995), *ad loc*. The opening paragraph is part of a polemic against the rejection of public life.

7 C. lists in chronological order three wars (against Pyrrhus and the First and Second Punic Wars) of the third and second centuries BCE and their heroes.

8 Tusculum (in the hills SE of Rome) was Cato's home; C. and other wealthy Romans had villas there.

9 Epicureans; the language of storm and calm is typically Epicurean.

[2] Furthermore, virtue is not some kind of knowledge to be possessed without using it: even if the intellectual possession of knowledge can be maintained without use, virtue consists entirely in its employment;[10] moreover, its most important employment is the governance of states and the accomplishment in deeds rather than words of the things that philosophers talk about in their corners.[11] Philosophers, in fact, say nothing (at least nothing that may be said decently and honorably)[12] that does not derive from the men who established laws for states. What is the source of piety and religion? of international or civil law? of justice, good faith, and equity? of modesty and moderation, the avoidance of shame, and the desire for praise and honor? of courage in toil and danger? Surely they derive from the men who established such things through education and strengthened some by custom and ordained others by law. [3] They say that Xenocrates, a very distinguished philosopher, was once asked what his pupils achieved; he answered that they learned to do of their own free will what the laws would compel them to do. And therefore that citizen, who through his formal authority and the punishments established by law compels everyone to do what philosophers through their teaching can persuade only a few people to do, is to be preferred even to the teachers who make those arguments. What is so remarkable about their teaching that it should outrank a state that is well established through public law and customs? For my own part, just as I think "great and powerful cities" (as Ennius calls them)[13] better than villages and forts, so too I think that the men who lead these cities by their counsel and authority should be considered far wiser than philosophers who have no experience at all of public life. We are strongly drawn to try to increase the resources of the human race, and we are eager to make human life safer and better by our plans and efforts; it is the spur of nature herself that goads us on to this pleasure.[14] Therefore, let us keep to the course that has always been that of every responsible citizen;[15] let us not listen to

[10] Cf. also *On Duties* 1.19, 2.19; the idea of virtue as active is Aristotelian.

[11] For the image see Plato, *Gorgias* 485d; C. used it previously at *On the Orator* 1.57, a passage closely parallel to this one.

[12] Again, an attack on Epicureanism.

[13] *Varia* 21 Warmington.

[14] C. uses Epicurean terminology to rebut Epicurean views.

[15] *Optimus quisque*: "men of good standing," i.e. supporters of the traditional (plutocratic) structure of Roman government. On the meaning of *optimus* (best) and optimate cf. the excursus on optimates in *On Behalf of Sestius* 96–131; see also "Text and Translation" above.

the trumpet that sounds the retreat, to summon back even those who have already gone forward.

[4] These arguments, certain and lucid though they are, are rejected by those who take the contrary position. They cite first the labors which must be undergone in defending the commonwealth – a minor burden for an alert and vigorous man, and one to be scorned not only in major matters but even in lesser desires or duties, or even in business. They add the dangers to one's life, confronting brave men with a disgraceful fear of death, men who generally think it far more miserable to be worn away by nature and old age than to be given an occasion to lay down for their country a life that would in any case have to be surrendered to nature. On this score, they think that they are particularly eloquent when they collect the disasters of great men, the injuries inflicted on them by ungrateful fellow citizens.[16] [5] They list the familiar examples of this among the Greeks: Miltiades, the conqueror of the Persians, before the honorable wounds that he received in his great victory had healed, gave up in the chains placed on him by his fellow citizens the life that had survived the enemy's weapons; Themistocles was driven in fear from the country he had freed and took refuge not in the harbors of Greece that he had saved but in the barbarian lands which he had defeated. There is no shortage of examples of the fickleness of the Athenians and their cruelty towards their greatest citizens. They say that this practice, which began and became common among the Greeks, has spread from them even to our more responsible state: [6] they mention the exile of Camillus and the attack on Ahala; the hatred of Nasica, the expulsion of Laenas, and the condemnation of Opimius; the exile of Metellus or the most bitter disaster of Gaius Marius < . . . >[17] the slaughter of leading citizens, or the deaths of many people which soon ensued. They even include my own name; I suppose that because they think that they were preserved in a life of peace by my counsel and danger they make even stronger and more affectionate complaints about what happened to me. But I would be hard put to say why, when they themselves go overseas for study or tourism *

[one leaf missing]

[16] A standard criticism of the Athenian democracy; cf. particularly Plato, *Gorgias* 515b–517a.

[17] There is a gap in the text. C. refers (as also at *On the Orator* 3.8) to Marius' flight from Sulla and his violent return and revenge after Sulla's departure to the Mithdradatic War.

[7] * I had taken an oath (and so did the Roman people) in a public meeting on the day that I completed my term as consul that <the commonwealth> was safe, I would easily have been recompensed for the worry and burden of all the injuries to me.[18] And yet my misfortunes had more honor than hardship and incurred less difficulty than glory; and I reaped greater joy from the sympathy of respectable citizens than pain from the happiness of the wicked. But as I said, if things had worked out differently, how could I complain? Nothing unforeseen happened to me, nothing worse than I expected considering how much I had done. I had always been the sort of person who could achieve greater rewards from my leisure than other people because of the varied delights of the studies in which I had immersed myself from childhood; and if something painful happened to everyone, then my misfortune would be no greater than that of others. Even so, I did not hesitate to subject myself to the greatest tempests, even thunderbolts, of fate for the sake of saving my fellow citizens and for creating through my own individual dangers a peace shared by all. [8] Our country did not give us birth or rearing without expecting some return from us[19] or thinking that while herself serving our convenience she should provide a safe refuge for our relaxation and a quiet place for rest; but she did so with the understanding that she has a claim on the largest and best part of our minds, talents, and judgment for her own use, and leaves for our private use only so much as is beyond her requirements.

[9] Furthermore, we should pay no attention at all to the excuses people advance in order more easily to enjoy their ease. They say that for the most part those who are active in public life are completely worthless men: to be paired with them is low, and to fight against them, especially when the mob is stirred up, is wretched and dangerous. Therefore, they say, a wise man should not take the reins when he cannot curb the insane and uncontrollable impulses of the crowd, nor should a free man endure blows or await injuries unendurable to a wise man in struggling with foul and disgusting opponents – as if for good and brave men of great spirit there could be any more suitable reason for taking part in public life than not to be subject to wicked men or allow them to ravage the commonwealth while they themselves are incapable of bringing aid, even if they should wish to.

[18] When prohibited from speaking to the assembly on the last day of his consulate by the tribune Metellus Nepos, C. instead swore an oath that he had saved the commonwealth and the city; cf. *Against Piso* 6.

[19] See above, Book 1 fr. 2.

[**10**] Who, moreover, can be convinced by this proviso, that they say that the wise man will take no part in public affairs unless the necessity of a crisis compels him? As if there could be any greater necessity than happened to me; but how could I have done anything if I had not been consul at the time? And how could I have been consul if I had not from my childhood held to a course of life which took me from my origins in the equestrian order to the highest rank in the state? There is, then, no possibility of bringing aid to the state, however great the dangers that oppress it, at a moment's notice or when you want to, unless you are in a position that permits such action. [**11**] And I am particularly amazed by this feature of the philosophers' argument, that people who admit their incapacity for steering in calm weather – because they have never learned how or wanted to know – these same people offer to take the helm in the greatest storms. They make a habit of saying openly, and even boasting, that they have neither studied nor taught anything about the methods of organizing and preserving commonwealths, and they think that such knowledge belongs not to wise and learned men but to men of practical experience in these areas. But then what is the sense of promising their aid to the commonwealth under the pressure of necessity when they have no idea of how to guide a commonwealth when there is no such necessity, something that is much easier to do? For my own part, even if it were true that a philosopher should not willingly lower himself to take part in civic affairs, but should not refuse to do so under the compulsion of a crisis, still I would think that the knowledge of public administration is something that philosophers should by no means neglect, because they ought to prepare in advance whatever they might need, even if they do not know whether they actually will.

[**12**] I have said all this at length because my goal in this work is a discussion of public affairs; and in order to avoid its being pointless, I was obliged to eliminate doubts about taking part in public life.[20] But anyone who is moved by the authority of philosophers should pay attention for a short time and listen to the ones who have the greatest authority and fame among learned men; I believe that even if they did not hold office, they performed a public function because they did much research and writing about government. Those seven men whom the Greeks named "wise," I

[20] Both "public affairs" and "public life" translate *res publica*; for its meanings see "Text and Translation."

observe, were almost all deeply involved in public affairs.[21] And there is nothing in which human virtue approaches the divine more closely than in the founding of new states or the preservation of existing ones.

[13] In such matters, since I have had the occasion both to achieve something memorable in my public career and to have a certain capacity for explaining the principles of civic life not only from my experience but from my desire to learn and to teach < . . . >[22] I should be an authority, since some earlier figures were skilled in argument but performed no public actions, while others were admirable in their deeds but poor at exposition. In fact, the argument that I will expound is neither new nor discovered by me; instead, I will recall the memory of a discussion of the greatest and wisest men in our state of a single generation, which was described to you and me in our youth by Publius Rutilius Rufus when we were with him for several days at Smyrna; I think that nothing of any significance for these matters has been omitted.

[14] For when Publius Africanus the younger, the son of Paullus, had determined to spend the Latin holidays in the consulate of Tuditanus and Aquilius on his estate,[23] and his closest friends had said that they would visit him frequently during those days, on the first morning of the holiday the first to arrive was his sister's son Quintus Tubero. After Scipio had greeted him warmly and said that he was glad to see him, he asked, "What are you up to so early, Tubero? The holiday gave you a welcome opportunity for study."

TUBERO: I have all the time in the world free for my books – they are never busy. But to find you at leisure is truly remarkable, especially during the present public disturbances.

SCIPIO: Well, you have found me, but at leisure more in body than mind.

TUBERO: You should relax your mind as well; as agreed, there are many of us ready, if you find it convenient, to make full use of this leisure with you.

[21] The importance of the Seven Sages as practical politicians was emphasized by the Peripatetic Dicaearchus, one of C.'s sources in the first two books; the only one not active in public life was Thales of Miletus. The list of the seven varies; Plato (*Protagoras* 343a) includes Thales, Pittacus, Bias, Solon, Cleobulus, Myson, and Chilon.

[22] There is a gap in the sense, and a verb is missing.

[23] The Latin holidays (*Feriae Latinae*) took place early in the calendar year (129 BCE); Scipio's estate was in the Campus Martius, just outside the formal boundary of the city of Rome.

SCIPIO: That's fine with me, so long as at some point we learn something of substance.

[15] TUBERO: Then since you seem to invite it and give me hope of your attention, shall we first consider (before the others arrive) what the meaning is of the second sun which has been reported in the senate?[24] The witnesses are neither few nor frivolous, so that it isn't so much a question of believing them as of explaining it.

SCIPIO: How I wish our friend Panaetius were here! He conducts the most scholarly research into the heavens as well as everything else. But, Tubero, to give you my honest opinion, I don't completely agree with our friend in this sort of thing: he makes such definite statements about things the nature of which we can scarcely guess, that he seems to see them with his eyes or even touch them with his hands. I am inclined to think Socrates all the wiser for having given up all concerns of this sort and for saying that research into natural philosophy seeks either things greater than human understanding can follow or things that have nothing at all to do with human existence.

[16] TUBERO: I don't know, Africanus, why people say that Socrates rejected all discussions of this kind and was concerned only with human life and morality. Plato is the fullest source we have about him, and in his books Socrates frequently speaks in such a manner that when he discusses morals, virtues, and even public life he seeks to link them in the manner of Pythagoras with numbers and geometry and harmony.

SCIPIO: True enough; but I'm sure that you have heard, Tubero, that after Socrates' death Plato traveled first to Egypt for the sake of study, then to Italy and Sicily to learn the discoveries of Pythagoras; and that he spent a great deal of time with Archytas of Tarentum and Timaeus of Locri, and purchased the papers of Philolaus; and that since at that time Pythagoras had a great reputation in that region, he devoted himself to the Pythagoreans and their studies. And so, since he loved Socrates above all others and wanted to attribute everything to him, he wove together the wit and subtlety of Socratic conversation with the obscurity of Pythagoras and the weight of his varied erudition.[25]

[17] When Scipio had said this, he saw Lucius Furius approaching

[24] Parhelion ("sun-dogs") is an atmospheric phenomenon caused by the refraction of light through ice crystals; its occurrence in 129 was seen (in hindsight) as an omen of Scipio's death, which took place shortly after the dramatic date of the dialogue (cf. *On the Nature of the Gods* 2.14).

[25] This is the earliest reference to Plato's Egyptian travels; C.'s interpretation of Plato as a synthesis of Socrates and Pythagoras may have been drawn from Dicaearchus.

unannounced; and after greeting him, he grasped him affectionately and placed him on his own couch. And since Publius Rutilius (our informant about this conversation) arrived with him, he greeted him too and told him to sit next to Tubero.

PHILUS: What are you up to? Has our arrival interrupted your conversation?

SCIPIO: Not at all. You regularly give careful attention to the kind of question that Tubero had just raised; and in fact our friend Rutilius even under the walls of Numantia itself used to discuss this kind of thing with me.[26]

PHILUS: What is the subject?

SCIPIO: About those two suns; and I would like to know, Philus, what you think about it.

[18] He had just finished speaking, when a slave announced that Laelius was coming to visit and had already left his house. Then Scipio put on his shoes and outdoor clothes and left the bedroom, and when he had walked in the portico for a little while he greeted Laelius on his arrival and the men who came with him: Spurius Mummius, of whom he was particularly fond, and Gaius Fannius and Quintus Scaevola, Laelius' sons-in-law, young men of learning and already of an age to become quaestors.[27] When he had greeted them all, he took a turn in the portico and placed Laelius in the middle. There was something like a law between them in their friendship, that Laelius would treat Africanus almost as a god when they were on campaign, because of his extraordinary military glory, and that in Rome Scipio treated Laelius as a parent because he was the elder. When they had talked together a little during a few turns up and down the portico, and Scipio had expressed his pleasure and delight at their arrival, it was agreed that they should sit in the sunniest spot of the meadow, as it was still winter. As they were about to do so, Manius Manilius arrived, a man of wisdom whom they all knew and loved. When he had been greeted warmly by Scipio and the rest, he sat down next to Laelius.

[19] PHILUS: I don't think that we need to find a new subject because these people have arrived, but we should discuss it more carefully and say something worthy of their ears.

LAELIUS: What was the subject? what conversation did we interrupt?

[26] Rutilius was a military tribune at the siege of Numantia in Spain in 134–133.

[27] The minimum legal age for the quaestorship was 30.

PHILUS: Scipio had asked me what I thought about the two suns that have been seen.

LAELIUS: Is that so, Philus? Are we so well informed about the things that concern our homes and the commonwealth that we are asking questions about what is going on in the sky?

PHILUS: Don't you think it is relevant to our homes to know what is going on at home? Our home is not the one bounded by our walls, but this whole universe, which the gods have given us as a home and a country to be shared with them.[28] And if we are ignorant of this, then there are many important things of which we must also be ignorant. And indeed, Laelius, the investigation of such things itself brings pleasure to me, and as it does to you too and to all those eager for wisdom.

[**20**] LAELIUS: I make no objection, especially since it is a holiday; but is there something left to hear, or have we come too late?

PHILUS: We have discussed nothing yet, and since it is not yet begun, I would happily yield so that you can speak about it.

LAELIUS: No, we would rather hear you, unless Manilius perhaps thinks that he should compose an interdict between the two suns, that each should possess the sky as it did before.[29]

MANILIUS: Must you continue, Laelius, to make fun of that branch of learning in which you are yourself an expert and without which no one can know what is his own and what is someone else's? But we can come back to that; now let us listen to Philus, whose opinion, I see, is sought on greater topics than mine or that of Publius Mucius.

[**21**] PHILUS: I have nothing new to offer you, and nothing that I have thought up or discovered myself. I remember that when this same sight was reported before, Gaius Sulpicius Galus (a great scholar, as you know) happened to be at the house of Marcus Marcellus, who had been his colleague as consul.[30] He had the celestial globe brought out, the one that Marcellus' grandfather had taken home as his only booty from the capture of Syracuse, a very rich city filled with beautiful things.[31] I had

[28] The Stoic idea of the universe as the shared home of gods and men is central to the moral argument of *On the Commonwealth*; it also underlies the argument about natural law in *On the Laws*.

[29] A joke based on Manilius' eminence as a legal scholar. The interdict in question was an injunction against disturbing possession of disputed property pending adjudication; for the text cf. Gaius, *Institutes* 4.160.

[30] In 166 BCE. Galus also wrote a book about solar eclipses.

[31] Marcus Claudius Marcellus captured Syracuse in 212 BCE, during the Second Punic War; Archimedes was killed in the siege.

often heard about this globe because of the fame of Archimedes, but its appearance was not particularly marvelous: the other globe made by Archimedes, which the elder Marcellus had placed in the temple of Virtue, had greater beauty and fame in the public eye.[32] [**22**] But when Galus with his great learning began to explain the workings of this device, I decided that Archimedes had more genius than human nature seemed capable of possessing. Galus said that the invention of the other globe, the solid one, was old; it had first been made by Thales of Miletus and then was marked out with the fixed celestial stars by Eudoxus of Cnidus, who he said was a pupil of Plato's. Many years later, Aratus brought out a verse description of its ornamentation, drawn from Eudoxus, not using any astronomical knowledge but through his ability as a poet.[33] But this new kind of globe included the motions of the sun and moon and the five stars that are known as "planets" or "wandering," something that could not be achieved in the solid globe. The discovery of Archimedes was all the more remarkable, because he had discovered how a single turning action could preserve these unequal orbits with their different speeds. When Galus moved this globe, the moon followed the sun by as many revolutions of the bronze globe as it does by days in the sky itself; the result was that the same eclipse of the sun occurred on the globe, and the moon then fell into the space which was in the shadow of the earth, when the sun from the region *

[probably four leaves missing]

[**23**] SCIPIO: * was . . . because I was fond of the man myself and knew that he was highly respected and loved by my father Paullus.[34] I remember that when I was in my teens, when my father was consul in Macedonia and I was with him on campaign, the army was shaken by religious fear because on a clear night the bright full moon suddenly disappeared.[35] Galus was there as a legate about a year before he was elected consul; the next day he had no qualms about explaining openly in the camp that it was no omen, but that it had happened then and would always happen in

[32] The Temple of Virtue was vowed by Marcellus (the conqueror of Syracuse) after the battle of Clastidium in 222 BCE and built by his son (also Marcus Marcellus, consul in 196 and father of the consul of 166). The globe dedicated in the temple was a solid celestial sphere; the one kept by Marcellus was clearly an orrery.

[33] C. himself as a young man translated Aratus' poem, the *Phaenomena*; a large portion of the translation survives.

[34] Scipio distinguishes between his natural father, Lucius Aemilius Paullus, and his adoptive father, Publius Cornelius Scipio.

[35] 21 June 168 BCE (3 September in the Roman calendar of that date; cf. Livy 44.37.5–9).

the future at fixed times when the sun was so placed that its light could not reach the moon.

TUBERO: Really? Was he able to teach that to simple countryfolk, and did he dare to say such things before uneducated people?

SCIPIO: He did indeed, and with great <success> *

[probably one leaf missing]

[**24**] SCIPIO: * neither inappropriate bravado nor a speech that was inconsistent with the character of a very authoritative man: he accomplished something great in dispelling the empty religious fear of men who were terrified.

[**25**] During the great war which the Athenians and Spartans waged so bitterly against one another, Pericles, the leading man of his state in authority, eloquence, and judgment, is said to have taught his fellow citizens something similar: when there was a sudden darkness and the sun disappeared,[36] the Athenians were seized by intense fear, and he taught them what he had learned from his teacher Anaxagoras, that such things necessarily take place at specific times when the whole moon passes below the disk of the sun; and that while it does not happen at every new moon, it can only happen at the time of the new moon. In giving a scientific lecture, he freed the people from fear: at that time this was a new and unknown explanation, that the sun is eclipsed by the interposition of the moon. They say that Thales of Miletus was the first to recognize this, but later on it was known even by our own Ennius; as he writes, in roughly the three hundred and fiftieth year after the foundation of Rome, "on the fifth of June moon and night blocked the sun."[37] Astronomical knowledge is so precise that from the date which is indicated in Ennius and the Great Annals,[38] previous eclipses of the sun have been calculated back to the one which took place on the seventh of July in the reign of Romulus. During that darkness, even if nature snatched Romulus to a human death, his virtue is still said to have carried him up to the heavens.[39]

[**26**] TUBERO: Do you see then, Africanus, what seemed otherwise to you a little while ago, that <learning> *

[36] 4 August 431 BCE.

[37] Ennius, *Annales* 166 Warmington. The correct astronomical date is 21 June 400 BCE, 350 years after the Polybian date (used by C.) for the foundation of Rome, 751/0.

[38] The *Annales Maximi* was an annual record kept by the pontifex maximus, including eclipses and other portents.

[39] On the deification of Romulus see below 2.17 and 6.24.

[one leaf missing]

SCIPIO: * let others see.[40] But what element of human affairs should a man think glorious who has examined this kingdom of the gods; or long-lived who has learned what eternity really is; or glorious who has seen how small the earth is – first the whole earth, then that part of it which men inhabit? We are attached to a tiny part of it and are unknown to most nations: are we still to hope that our name will fly and wander far and wide? [27] The person who is accustomed neither to think nor to name as "goods" lands and buildings and cattle and huge weights of silver and gold, because the enjoyment of them seems to him slight, the use minimal, and the ownership uncertain,[41] and because the vilest men often have unlimited possessions – how fortunate should we think such a man! He alone can truly claim all things as his own, not under the law of the Roman people but under the law of the philosophers; not by civil ownership but by the common law of nature, which forbids anything to belong to anyone except someone who knows how to employ and use it. Such a man thinks of military commands and consulates as necessary things, not as desirable ones, things that must be undertaken for the sake of performing one's duty, not to be sought out for the sake of rewards or glory. Such a man, finally, can say of himself the same thing Cato writes that my grandfather Africanus used to say, that he never did more than when he did nothing, that he was never less alone than when he was alone.[42] [28] Who can really think that Dionysius accomplished more by seeking in every way to deprive his citizens of liberty than did his citizen Archimedes, while seeming to accomplish nothing, in creating that globe we spoke about just now? Or that men who have no one with whom to enjoy conversation in the crowded forum are not more alone than men who, even when no one else is present, can converse with themselves or are somehow present in a meeting of the most learned men, whose discoveries and writings give them pleasure? Who would think anyone wealthier than the man who lacks nothing of what nature requires, or more powerful than the man who achieves all that he seeks, or more blessed than the man who is freed from all mental disturbance, or of more

[40] Scipio's first speech anticipates themes taken up later in the dialogue, notably in the preface to Book 3 and in the *Dream*. It also has close connections with Aristotle's lost *Protrepticus* (fr. 10a Ross).

[41] There is an extended play on the technical terminology of Roman property law, which distinguished sharply between ownership and possession.

[42] Cato, *Origines* fr. 127 Peter, but the location is doubtful. C. cites the same aphorism (in slightly different words) at *On Duties* 3.1.

secure good fortune than the man who possesses, as they say, only what he can carry with him out of a shipwreck? What power, what office, what kingdom can be grander than to look down on all things human and to think of them as less important than wisdom, and to turn over in his mind nothing except what is eternal and divine? Such a man believes that others may be called human, but that the only true humans are those who have been educated in truly human arts. [**29**] I think that the saying of Plato (or whoever else said it) is elegant:[43] when a storm drove him from the sea to an unknown land on a deserted shore, when his companions were afraid because of their ignorance of the place, they say that he noticed that some geometrical shapes were drawn in the sand; when he saw them, he exclaimed that they should be of good spirits: he saw human traces. He clearly inferred that not from his observation of sown fields, but from the signs of learning. And therefore, Tubero, learning and educated men and your own studies have always been a source of pleasure to me.

[**30**] LAELIUS: I don't dare respond to that, Scipio, nor <do I think that> you or Philus or Manilius are so *

[one leaf missing]

LAELIUS: * there was a model in his own father's family for our friend Tubero here to imitate,

superbly stout-minded man, wise Sextus Aelius[44]

who was – and was called by Ennius – "superbly stout-minded" and "wise" not because he looked for things he could never find, but because he gave opinions which relieved his questioners of care and trouble. In his arguments against Galus' studies he always used to quote Achilles' famous lines from the *Iphigenia*:[45]

What's the point of looking at astronomers' signs in the sky
when goat or scorpion or some beast's name arises –
no one looks at what's in front of his feet; they scan the tracts of the sky.

He also used to say (I listened to him frequently and with great pleasure) that Pacuvius' Zethus was too hostile to learning; he preferred Ennius' Neoptolemus, who said that "he wanted to be a philosopher, but only a little; it didn't please him totally."[46] But if Greek learning pleases you

[43] The anecdote is in fact normally connected to Aristippus, not Plato.

[44] Ennius, *Annals* 326 Warmington.

[45] Ennius, *Plays* 249–51 1Warmington.

[46] Ennius, *Plays* 400 Warmington. The same two passages are similarly juxtaposed at *On the Orator* 2.156. The contrast between the brothers Zethus and Amphion as men of action and learning respectively derives from Euripides' *Antiope* (adapted by Pacuvius) and is used by Callicles in Plato, *Gorgias* 485e–486a, to demonstrate the folly of philosophers.

that much, then there are other studies, more suitable to free men and more widely applicable, that we can bring to the needs of everyday life or even to public affairs. If studies of your kind have any value, it is this: they sharpen a little and seem to tickle the minds of boys, so that they can learn greater things more easily.[47]

[31] TUBERO: I don't disagree with you, Laelius, but I want to know what you understand to be "greater things."

LAELIUS: I will indeed speak, although I may earn your scorn, since you are asking Scipio about those things in the sky, while I think that the things before our eyes are more worth asking about. Why, I ask you, is the grandson of Lucius Aemilius Paullus, with an uncle like Scipio here, born into the most noble family and in this glorious commonwealth, asking how two suns could have been seen and not asking why in one commonwealth there are two senates and almost two peoples? As you see, the death of Tiberius Gracchus and, before that, the whole conduct of his tribunate have divided one people into two parts. Scipio's enemies and opponents, starting from Publius Crassus and Appius Claudius, but no less after their deaths, control one part of the senate that opposes you under the leadership of Metellus and Publius Mucius; although the allies and the Latins are stirred up, the treaties are broken,[48] and a treasonous land commission is daily starting revolutionary actions, they do not permit this man, the only capable person, to remedy such a dangerous situation. [32] Therefore, my young friends, if you listen to me, you should have no fear of that second sun: either it is nothing at all, or – granting that it is as it appeared, so long as it isn't causing trouble – we can know nothing about such things, or, even if we knew all about them, such knowledge would make us neither better nor happier. But it is possible for us to have one senate and one people, and if we don't we are in very deep trouble; we know that things are not that way now, and we see that if it can be brought about, then we will live both better and happier lives.

[33] MUCIUS: Well then, Laelius, what do you think that we need to learn in order to accomplish what you demand?

LAELIUS: The skills that make us useful to the state: that, I think, is the most outstanding task of philosophy and the greatest evidence and function of virtue. Therefore, so that we may devote this holiday to

47 Also drawn from Callicles, *Gorgias* 485cd; imitated previously by C. at *On the Orator* 3.58.
48 See also 3.41 below.

conversations that will be most useful to the commonwealth, we should ask Scipio to explain to us what he thinks the best organization of the state to be. After that, we will investigate other subjects, and when we have learned about them I hope that we will arrive directly at these present circumstances and will unravel the significance of the current situation.

[34] When Philus and Manilius and Mummius had expressed their strong approval *

[one leaf missing]

LAELIUS: * This is what I wanted to happen, not only because a leader of the commonwealth should be the one to talk about the commonwealth, but also because I remembered that you frequently used to discuss this with Panaetius in the presence of Polybius – possibly the two Greeks most experienced in public affairs. Your argument was that by far the best condition of the state was the one which our ancestors had handed down to us.[49] And since you are better prepared to speak about this subject, you will do us all a great favor (and I will speak for the others too) if you explain your ideas about the commonwealth.

[35] SCIPIO: In fact, I cannot say that I pay closer or more careful attention to any subject than the one which you, Laelius, are proposing to me. I observe that artisans who are outstanding in their own crafts think and plan and worry about nothing except the improvement of their own skill; and since this is the one craft handed down to me by my parents and my ancestors – the service and administration of the commonwealth – would I not be admitting that I am less attentive than some workman, if I exerted less effort in the greatest craft than they do in trivial ones? [36] Moreover, although I am not satisfied with what the greatest and wisest men of Greece have written about this subject, I am also not bold enough to prefer my own opinions to theirs. Therefore, I ask you to listen to me in this way: as someone neither completely ignorant of Greek learning nor deferring to the Greeks – particularly on this subject – but as one Roman citizen, reasonably well educated by the care of his father and inflamed from childhood with the desire for learning, but educated much more by experience and home learning than by books.[50]

[49] This sentence has often been used as evidence for C.'s use of Panaetius as a major source for *On the Commonwealth*. In fact, it says the opposite: the argument that follows was Scipio's, not Panaetius'. Polybius was clearly one of C.'s sources in Books 1, 2, and 4 (at least); there is no evidence that he made use of Panaetius, although it is not unlikely.

[50] Crassus makes a similar disclaimer at *On the Orator* 1.111, as does C. himself at *On Fate* 4 and probably in the preface to this dialogue: cf. fr. 5 above.

[37] PHILUS: I have no doubt at all, Scipio, that no one surpasses you in talent, and in terms of experience in important public affairs you also easily outdo everyone; but we also know the kind of intellectual activities in which you have always been engaged. Therefore if, as you say, you have addressed the study of public affairs (almost a science in itself), then I am very grateful to Laelius. I expect that what you will say will be richer than all the books of the Greeks.

SCIPIO: You arouse very great expectations of what I will say – a very heavy burden for someone about to speak on an important topic.

PHILUS: The expectation may be great, but you will surpass it, as you usually do: there's no danger that your eloquence will fail you as you discuss the commonwealth.

[38] SCIPIO: I will do what you want to the best of my ability, and I will begin my discussion with this proviso – something that speakers on every subject need to use to avoid mistakes – namely that we agree on the name of the subject under discussion and then explain what is signified by that name; and when that is agreed on, only then is it right to begin to speak.[51] We will never be able to understand what sort of thing we are talking about unless we understand first just what it is. And since we are looking into the commonwealth, let us first see what it is that we are looking into.

When Laelius agreed, SCIPIO said: In talking about such a well-known and important subject, I will not begin by going back to the origins which learned men generally cite in these matters, starting from the first intercourse of male and female and then from their offspring and family relationships;[52] nor will I give frequent verbal definitions of what each thing is and how many ways it can be named. In speaking to knowledgeable men who have earned great glory through participation in the public life, both military and domestic, of a great commonwealth, I will not make the mistake of letting the subject of my speech be clearer than the speech itself. I have not undertaken this like some schoolteacher explaining everything, and I make no promises that no tiny details will be left out.

LAELIUS: The kind of speech you promise is just what I am waiting for.

[51] The emphasis on the importance of definitions is drawn from Plato, *Phaedrus* 237bc; so also *On the Orator* 1.209–13 and elsewhere.

[52] So, for example, Aristotle, *Politics* 1.2 1252a24–30, 1.3 1253b1–8, and Polybius 6.6.2.

[39a] SCIPIO: Well then: the commonwealth is the concern of a people,[53] but a people is not any group of men assembled in any way, but an assemblage of some size associated with one another through agreement on law and community of interest. The first cause of its assembly is not so much weakness as a kind of natural herding together of men: this species is not isolated or prone to wandering alone, but it is so created that not even in an abundance of everything <do men wish to live a solitary existence> *

[one leaf missing]

[40] Lactantius, *Inst.* 6.10.18:[54] *Others have thought these ideas as insane as they in fact are and have said that it was not being mauled by wild animals that brought men together, but human nature itself, and that they herded together because the nature of humans shuns solitude and seeks community and society.*

[39b] And nature itself not only encourages this, but even compels it (Nonius 321.16)

[41] * what we can call seeds;[55] nor can we find any deliberate institution either of the other virtues or of the commonwealth itself. These assemblages, then, were instituted for the reason that I explained, and their first act was to establish a settlement in a fixed location for their homes. Once they had protected it by both natural and constructed fortifications, they called this combination of buildings a town or a city, marked out by shrines and common spaces. Now every people (which is the kind of large assemblage I have described), every state (which is the organization of the people), every commonwealth (which is, as I said, the concern of the people) needs to be ruled by some sort of deliberation[56] in order to be long lived. That deliberative function, moreover, must always be connected to the original cause which engendered the state; **[42]** and it must also either be assigned to one person or to selected individuals or be

[53] The definition (*est ... res publica res populi*) is virtually untranslatable, playing on the meaning of *res* (lit. "thing") as property. On the meanings of *res publica*, see "Text and Translation." Scipio returns to and modifies the meaning of this definition at 3.43. The account of the origins of society given here is basically Aristotelian.

[54] Lactantius' summary clearly overlaps with the end of sect. 39a; for that reason the quotation from Nonius is placed after it, rather than before as in Ziegler's text. "These ideas" are Epicurean, and Ziegler prints as the first part of this fragment a long selection from Lactantius' summary of Lucretius Book 5. "Others" presumably refers to C. himself.

[55] Presumably "seeds of justice"; the Stoic implication that virtues are naturally implanted in us is taken up more fully in Books 3 and 4.

[56] *Consilium*; see "Text and Translation."

taken up by the entire population. And so, when the control of everything is in the hands of one person, we call that one person a king and that type of commonwealth a monarchy. When it is in the control of chosen men, then a state is said to be ruled by the will of the aristocracy. And that in which everything is in the hands of the people is a "popular" state – that is what they call it. And of these three types any one, even though it may not be perfect or in my opinion the best possible, still is tolerable as long as it holds to the bond which first bound men together in the association of a commonwealth; and any one might be better than another. A fair and wise king, or selected leading citizens, or the people itself – although that is the least desirable – if injustice and greed do not get in the way, may exist in a stable condition.

[43] But in monarchies, no one else has sufficient access to shared justice or to deliberative responsibility; and in the rule of an aristocracy the people have hardly any share in liberty, since they lack any role in common deliberation and power; and when everything is done by the people itself, no matter how just and moderate it may be, that very equality is itself inequitable, in that it recognizes no degrees of status. And so, even if Cyrus the Great of Persia was the most just and most wise of kings, that still does not seem to be a very desirable "concern of the people" (for that is what I called the commonwealth earlier), since it was ruled by the decisions of a single man. Even though our clients the people of Marseilles[57] are ruled with the greatest justice by chosen leading citizens, that condition of the people still involves a form of slavery. And when the Athenians at certain times, after the Areopagus had been deprived of its authority, did nothing except by the decisions and decrees of the people, the state did not maintain its splendor, since there were no recognized degrees of status.[58]

[44] And I say this about these three types of commonwealth when they are not disturbed or mixed but maintain their proper condition. Each of these types is marked by the particular faults which I just mentioned, and they have other dangerous faults in addition: each of these types of commonwealth has a path – a sheer and slippery one – to a kindred evil.[59] Beneath that tolerable and even lovable king Cyrus (to

57 Massilia (Marseilles) was technically independent but was a client state of Rome.

58 The conservative council of the Areopagus was deprived of most of its authority by the radical democracy of the fifth century.

59 For the concept of the "kindred evil" cf. Plato, *Republic* 10.609a; as applied to constitutions, Polybius 6.10.3–4.

pick the best example) there lurks, at the whim of a change of his mind, a Phalaris, the cruelest of all; and it is an easy downward path to that kind of domination. The governance of Marseilles by a few leading citizens is very close to the oligarchic conspiracy of the Thirty who once ruled in Athens.[60] And the Athenian people's control of all things, to look no further, when it turned into the madness and license of a mob was disastrous <to the people itself> *

[one leaf missing]

[45] * most foul,[61] and from that arises a government either of an aristocracy or of a faction, or tyrannical or monarchic or, quite frequently, popular, and similarly from that usually arises another of those which I have previously mentioned. There are remarkable revolutions and almost cycles of changes and alterations in commonwealths;[62] to recognize them is the part of a wise man, and to anticipate them when they are about to occur, holding a course and keeping it under his control while governing, is the part of a truly great citizen and nearly divine man. My own opinion, therefore, is that there is a fourth type of commonwealth that is most to be desired, one that is blended and mixed from these first three types that I have mentioned.

[46] LAELIUS: I know that is your view, Africanus, and I have heard it from you often; but still, if it isn't too much trouble, I would like to know which of these three types of commonwealth you think best. It will be of some use to know *

[one leaf missing]

[47] SCIPIO: * and the character of any commonwealth corresponds to the nature or the desire of its ruling power.[63] And so in no other state than that in which the people has the highest power does liberty have any home – liberty, than which nothing can be sweeter, and which, if it is not equal, is not even liberty. And how can it be equal (I won't speak about monarchy, in which slavery is not even hidden or ambiguous) in those states in which everyone is free in name only? They vote, they entrust commands and offices, they are canvassed and asked for their support,

60 The so-called Thirty Tyrants were the oligarchs installed in Athens by Sparta at the end of the Peloponnesian War.

61 The form of government referred to is probably mob rule rather than tyranny. In what follows, "of a faction" is an emendation; for discussion cf. Zetzel (ed.), *Cicero: De re publica, ad loc.*

62 The "cycle of constitutions" in C. differs from that in Polybius and elsewhere by having no fixed order.

63 In sects. 47–50 Scipio represents the views of an advocate of democracy.

but they give what must be given even if they are unwilling, and they are asked to give what they do not have themselves. They have no share in power, in public deliberation, or in the panels of select judges, all of which are apportioned on the basis of pedigree or wealth.[64] In a free people, as at Rhodes or Athens, there is no citizen who *

[one leaf missing]

[48] * if one or several wealthy men arise from the people, then they say that <these faults> come from their scorn and haughtiness, as the cowardly and weak give way to the arrogance of the wealthy.[65] But if the people holds to its own rights, they deny that there is anything more outstanding, more free, more blessed: they are masters of the laws and the courts, of war and peace, of treaties, of the status and wealth of every individual. They think that this commonwealth (that is, the "concern of the people") is the only one properly so named; and so it is usual for the "concern of the people" to be liberated from the domination of kings and aristocrats, and not for kings or the power and wealth of an aristocracy to be sought by a free people. [49] Furthermore, they say that this type of free people should not be condemned because of the failings of an undisciplined populace: when the people is harmonious and judges everything in terms of its safety and liberty there is nothing more unchanging or more stable. It is easiest, they say, for harmony to obtain in a commonwealth in which everyone has the same interest: from a variety of interests, when different things are advantageous for different people, discord arises.[66] And so, when the senate gains control of affairs, the condition of the state is never stable, and that is all the more true of monarchies: as Ennius said, "there is no holy bond or trust" in a monarchy.[67] And therefore, since law is the bond of civil society, and rights under law are equal,[68] then by what right can a society of citizens be held together when the status of citizens is not the same? Even if equality of property is not appealing, and if the mental abilities of all

[64] The democratic description of aristocratic government here corresponds closely to the workings of the Roman constitution.

[65] I.e. the democrats blame oligarchs for the collapse of truly democratic government.

[66] The democrats assume that "the people" incorporates all citizens; the representatives of aristocracy (and Scipio himself) assume that "the people" does not include the aristocracy.

[67] Ennius, *Plays* 402–3 Warmington, also quoted by C. at *On Duties* 1.26.

[68] Translated as "right is equivalent to law" in Zetzel (ed.), *Cicero: De re publica*. The phrase is very compressed and open to more than one interpretation. There is an extended play on the word *ius*, "right," in this passage.

cannot be equal, certainly the rights of all who are citizens of the same commonwealth ought to be equal. What is a state if not the association of citizens under law? *

[one leaf missing]

[50] * they believe that other commonwealths should not even be given the names that they themselves prefer.[69] Why should I call "king," using the title of Jupiter the Best, a man who yearns for power and sole rule, lording over an oppressed populace, rather than "tyrant"? It is possible for a tyrant to be as merciful as a king can be harsh, so that there is this difference only for their subjects, whether they are slaves to a mild master or a harsh one: it is in any case impossible for them not be to slaves. How could Sparta, at the time when it was thought to have the best-ordered commonwealth, make sure that it had good and just kings, when they had to accept as king whoever was born in the royal family? And who could endure aristocrats, "the best people,"[70] who have taken that name for themselves not by the concession of the people but by their own self-election? How is one of them judged "best"? by learning, skill, education? So you say: but when <has that ever been the criterion for being an aristocrat?> *[71]

[two leaves missing]

[51] * if it <chooses its leaders> by chance, it will be overturned as quickly as a ship that has one of its passengers chosen by lot as helmsman.[72] But if a free people chooses the men to whom to entrust itself (and it will chose the best people if it wants to be safe), then surely the safety of the citizens[73] is found in the deliberations of the best men. That is particularly true because nature has made sure not only that men outstanding for virtue and courage rule over weaker people, but that the weaker people willingly obey the best. But they say that this ideal condition is overturned by men's bad judgments: through their ignorance of virtue (which not only appears in few men but is judged and recognized by few) they think that men of wealth and property, or men of noble birth, are "best." By this common error, when the wealth of a few replaces virtue in control of the commonwealth, those leaders cling

[69] Some scholars believe that this paragraph is the remnant of a speech on behalf of monarchy, but that is very improbable.

[70] "Optimate" (derived from *optimus*, "best") is one of the standard (self-)descriptions of the Roman aristocracy; see "Text and Translation."

[71] The supplement is uncertain, and the text of the last words is probably corrupt.

[72] Sects. 51–53 are spoken by an advocate of aristocracy.

[73] "Citizens" is Kenney's emendation; the manuscript reads "states."

doggedly to the name of "best citizens," but in fact they lack the substance for that very reason. For wealth, or reputation, or resources, if they are empty of prudence and of a method of living and of ruling over others, are filled with disgrace and insolent pride; and there is no uglier form of state than that in which the richest are thought to be the best. [52] But when virtue rules over the commonwealth, what could be more glorious? Then the man who commands others is himself enslaved to no desires when he himself embraces all the things to which he educates and exhorts his citizens, and he imposes no laws on the populace which he does not himself obey but offers his own life as a law to his citizens. If one such person could adequately accomplish everything, then there would be no need of more; if everyone could see what is best and could agree on it, then no one would seek selected leaders. The difficulty of making policy transferred control from a king to a group of people, and the rash folly of popular governments has transferred it from the multitude to the few. In this way, the aristocrats hold the middle ground between the weakness of a single person and the rashness of many. Nothing can be more moderate than this, and when the aristocrats look after the commonwealth then the populace is of necessity most blessed: they are free of every care and thought, having handed over their tranquillity to others who must guard it and must make sure that the people do not believe that their interests are being neglected by their leaders. [53] For legal equality – the object of free peoples – cannot be preserved: the people themselves, no matter how uncontrolled they may be, give great rewards to many individuals, and they pay great attention to the selection of men and honors. And what people call equality is in fact very unfair.[74] When the same degree of honor is given to the best and the worst (and such must exist in any population), then equity itself is highly inequitable. But that is something that cannot happen in states that are ruled by the best citizens. These, Laelius, and others like them, are the arguments adduced by those who particularly favor this kind of commonwealth.

[54] LAELIUS: What do you think, Scipio? Which one of these three forms do you most approve?

SCIPIO: You are right to ask which one of the three I most approve, since I approve of none of them by itself, separately. I prefer to the

[74] The aristocrats deliberately confuse juridical equality and social equality (and thus slide from "equality" to "equity" – compare also Scipio's almost identical statement at 1.43 above), just as the democrats blur the distinction between equal rights and equal power.

individual forms the type that is an alloy of all three.[75] But if I had to express approval of one of the simple forms, then I would choose monarchy . . . is named at this point, the name of king appears almost fatherly, someone looking after his citizens as if they were his children, and preserving them more eagerly than . . . to be supported by the diligence of one man, the best and greatest. **[55]** Here are the aristocrats, who claim that they can do this same job better and say that there is more judgment in the deliberations of several people than of one, but the same equity and honor. And here is the populace shouting loudly that they will not obey one person or a few; that even for wild animals there is nothing sweeter than liberty, and that everyone is deprived of it, whether it is a king or aristocrats to whom they are enslaved. And so kings captivate us by their affection, aristocrats by their judgment, and the people by its liberty, so that in comparing them it is hard to pick the most desirable.

LAELIUS: That makes sense; but the rest of the subject can hardly be explained if you leave this question unanswered.

[56] SCIPIO: Then we should imitate Aratus: in undertaking to speak about great matters he believes that one must begin from Jupiter.[76]

LAELIUS: Why Jupiter? How is this subject anything like that poem?

SCIPIO: Only that we should duly take our starting point from him, whom all men, learned and unlearned, agree is the one king of all gods and men.

LAELIUS: Why?

SCIPIO: Why do you think? The reason is in front of your eyes. The leaders of commonwealths may have thought that it would be useful for civic life that people should believe that there is one king in the sky who turns all Olympus with his nod, as Homer says, and that he is both king and father of all;[77] there is much authority and many witnesses (everyone, in fact) to show that all nations have acquiesced in the decision of their leaders that nothing is better than a king, because they believe that all the gods are ruled by the will of one. On the other hand, it may be that, as we have been taught, this belief is one of the errors of the uneducated and a kind of myth. In any case, we should listen to the common instructors of educated men, who have seen as if with their eyes things that we scarcely know from hearing about them.

[75] The leaf containing the following sentence has lost one corner, and several lines have lost their opening or concluding letters.

[76] Alluding to the opening words of Aratus' *Phaenomena*, which C. had translated into Latin: "Let us begin from Jupiter."

[77] *Iliad* 1.528–30.

LAELIUS: And who are those instructors?

SCIPIO: Men who, through their investigation of the universe, have recognized that this entire world <is ruled> by <a single> mind *[78]

[two leaves missing]

[57b] LAELIUS: And so please bring your speech down from there to things closer at hand (+ Nonius 85.18 = 289.8)

[58] SCIPIO: * But if you like, Laelius, I will give you witnesses who are neither very antiquated nor in any respect barbarians.

LAELIUS: That's the kind I want.

SCIPIO: Do you know that this city has been without kings for fewer than four hundred years?

LAELIUS: Yes, it is less than that.

SCIPIO: Well then: is four hundred years particularly long for a city or a state?

LAELIUS: In fact it's scarcely grown up.

SCIPIO: So within the past four hundred years there has been a king at Rome?

LAELIUS: And a haughty one, too.[79]

SCIPIO: And before that?

LAELIUS: A very just one, and going back all the way to Romulus, who was king six hundred years ago.

SCIPIO: So even he isn't very ancient?

LAELIUS: Hardly, and at a time when Greece was already getting old.

SCIPIO: Tell me: did Romulus rule over barbarians?

LAELIUS: If what the Greeks say is true, that everyone is either a Greek or a barbarian, then I'm afraid that he must have ruled barbarians. But if we use that term of manners rather than languages, then I don't think the Greeks were any less barbarian than the Romans.[80]

SCIPIO: Yet for our present concern we are looking at brains, not nationality. If men who were both intelligent and fairly recent wanted to have kings, then my witnesses are neither very ancient nor inhuman savages.

[59] LAELIUS: I see, Scipio, that you are well equipped with testimony; but for me, as for any good judge, arguments matter more than witnesses.

[78] Philosophers. A passage of Lactantius placed here by Ziegler does not belong. In the missing passage there was presumably some reference to Asiatic monarchies.

[79] Tarquinius Superbus ("the Haughty"), the last king of Rome. His predecessor was Servius Tullius.

[80] "Barbarian" in Greek refers primarily to non-Greek-speakers.

SCIPIO: Then, Laelius, you should use the argument of your own feelings.

LAELIUS: What feelings?

SCIPIO: If you ever by some chance felt that you were angry at someone.

LAELIUS: More often than I would like.

SCIPIO: Well then: at the moment that you are angry, do you let your anger rule your mind?

LAELIUS: No indeed, but I imitate the famous Archytas of Tarentum: when he came to his farm and found nothing done as he had instructed, he said to his overseer, "You wretched man: if I weren't so angry, I would have whipped you to death."

[**60**] SCIPIO: Excellent. So Archytas rightly believed that the rejection of reason by anger was a kind of revolt in the mind, and he wanted it to be settled by sound judgment.[81] To anger add greed, add the desire for power and glory, add lust, and you will see this: if there is a kind of royal power in men's minds, there will be the rule of one element, namely judgment (that is, of course, the best part of the mind); and when judgment rules, there is no place for lust, none for anger, none for rashness.

LAELIUS: True enough.

SCIPIO: Then you approve of a mind so constituted?

LAELIUS: Absolutely.

SCIPIO: So you would not approve if judgment were expelled and desires (which are countless) or angry passions were in complete control?

LAELIUS: I could imagine nothing more wretched than such a mind, or than a man with such a mind.

SCIPIO: So you approve of having all the parts of the mind under the monarchy of judgment?

LAELIUS: I approve.

SCIPIO: Then why are you not sure what to think about a commonwealth? In it, if authority is exercised by several people, then you can understand that there will be no controlling power; and unless power is undivided it is nothing at all.

[**61**] LAELIUS: I would like to know what the difference is between one and several, if the several are just.

[81] The struggle in the mind between passion and reason is ultimately Platonic, but C.'s separation of reason (*ratio*) from judgment (*consilium*) is not. The language here is political, and C. views *consilium* as the necessary attribute of good government (cf. 1.41).

SCIPIO: Since I see that you are not greatly impressed by my witnesses, Laelius, I will continue to use you as my witness to prove what I say.

LAELIUS: Me? How?

SCIPIO: Because I noticed recently, when we were at your villa at Formiae, that you gave firm instructions to your slaves to obey one man.

LAELIUS: My overseer, you mean.

SCIPIO: And what about in Rome? Is there more than one person in charge of your affairs?

LAELIUS: No, only one.

SCIPIO: Well then: is there anyone besides you in charge of your whole household?

LAELIUS: Certainly not.

SCIPIO: Then why don't you admit that the situation in commonwealths is similar, that the rule of a single person, so long as he is just, is best?

LAELIUS: You persuade me, and I am almost willing to agree.

[62] SCIPIO: You will agree even more, Laelius, if I leave out the familiar comparisons, that it is better to entrust a ship to one helmsman and a sick man to one doctor (assuming that they are competent in their professions) than to many people, and instead use more important examples.

LAELIUS: What are your examples?

SCIPIO: Well, don't you see that because of the relentless arrogance of a single man, Tarquinius, the name of king became hated by our people?

LAELIUS: I see it.

SCIPIO: So you see this too (something I expect to say more about as our discussion goes on),[82] that when Tarquinius was expelled, the novelty of freedom made the people amazingly unrestrained in their pleasure: that was when innocent people were driven into exile and many people's property was plundered; annual consuls were established, the fasces were lowered before the people, there was a right of appeal for every kind of crime, there were secessions of the plebs: in short, that was when most things were arranged so that the people had total control.

LAELIUS: All that is true.

[63] SCIPIO: Peace and tranquillity are like a ship or a minor illness: you can be undisciplined when there is no danger. But when the sea gets

[82] See below, 2.53–55.

rough or the disease gets worse, the sailor or the sick man calls for one person's help. So too, at home and in peace, our people give orders to the magistrates themselves – they threaten, refuse to obey, ask for one magistrate's help against another, and appeal to the people; but in war they obey their leaders as they would a king: safety matters more than one's own desires. And in major wars, our people wanted all the power to be in the hands of one individual without a colleague, whose very title indicates the extent of his power: he is called a dictator because he is appointed, but in our augural books, Laelius, you see that he is called "master of the people."[83]

LAELIUS: Yes, I do see that.

SCIPIO: Wisely therefore did the people of old *

[one leaf missing]

[**64**] * but when the people is deprived of a just king, for a long time "desire holds their hearts," as Ennius said after the death of a great king:[84]

> and at the same time
> they speak this way to one another: "Romulus, divine Romulus,
> what a guardian of the country the gods brought forth in you!
> Oh father, oh life-giver, oh blood sprung from the gods."

They did not call those whom they justly obeyed "lords" or "masters," and not even "kings," but "guardians of the country," "fathers," "gods" – and not without reason. What do they add?

> "you brought us into the shores of light."

They thought that life, honor, and glory were given to them by the justice of the king. The same goodwill would have lasted among their descendants, if the kings had retained the same character; but you see that because of the injustice of one of them that entire form of the commonwealth was destroyed.

LAELIUS: I see it and want to learn the patterns of changes not just in our own commonwealth but in all commonwealths.

[83] Both Scipio and Laelius were members of the college of augurs, to which C. himself had recently been coopted, a distinction of which he was very proud; see also *On the Laws* 2.31–33 on the importance of the augurate. On the dictatorship see below, 2.56, and *On the Laws* 3.9.

[84] Ennius, *Annals* 117–20 Warmington.

[65] SCIPIO: When I have said what I think about the type of commonwealth I most admire, I must speak with greater precision about the transformations of commonwealths, even though I think that they will not take place easily in the best type. But the alteration of the monarchic form is the first and the most certain: when a king begins to be unjust, the form is immediately destroyed, and that same person is a tyrant, the worst form, but closest to the best. If the aristocracy gets rid of him (which generally happens), the commonwealth has the second of the three forms; it is almost monarchic, that is, a senatorial council of leaders taking good care of the people. If the people themselves kill or expel the tyrant, the government is reasonably restrained, so long as it is intelligent and perceptive: they rejoice in their accomplishment, and want to protect the commonwealth that they have set up. But when either the people bring force to bear on a just king and deprive him of his throne or even (as happens more frequently) have tasted the blood of the aristocracy and subordinated the entire commonwealth to their own desires, do not make the mistake of thinking that any huge ocean or fire is harder to calm than the violence of a mob out of control. Plato has eloquently described this condition; it is hard to put it into Latin, but I will try to do it anyway.[85]

[66] "When," he says, "the insatiable throats of the people are parched with thirst for liberty, and through the aid of evil ministers have drained in their thirst a pure draught of liberty instead of a moderate mixture, then unless the magistrates and the leaders are very mild and lenient and serve up liberty to them generously, the people persecute, attack, and accuse them, calling them overpowerful kings or tyrants." I think that all this is familiar to you.[86]

LAELIUS: Very familiar.

[67] SCIPIO: What follows is this: "Those who obey the leaders are attacked by the people and called willing slaves; but they shower with praise and give exorbitant honors to magistrates who act like private citizens and private citizens who act as if there were no difference between private citizens and magistrates. In such a commonwealth everything is inevitably filled with liberty: private homes have no master, and this evil extends even to animals; ultimately fathers fear their sons,

[85] What follows is a translation (at times free) of Plato, *Republic* 8.562c–563e. At the end of sect. 68 translation is replaced by loose paraphrase.

[86] "All this" refers both to Plato's description and to the situation described.

sons neglect their fathers, all sense of shame is lost, and they are utterly free. There is no difference between citizen and foreigner, the teacher fears his pupils and fawns on them, pupils scorn their teachers, the young take on the gravity of old men, while old men are reduced to children's games, so as not to be hateful or tiresome. Slaves behave with too much freedom, women have the same rights as their husbands, and even dogs and horses and asses go about so freely in this atmosphere of liberty that people have to get out of their way in the streets. The final outcome of this extreme license," he says, "is that the minds of citizens become so delicate and sensitive that if the least authority is brought to bear on them they are angered and unable to endure it; the result is that they begin to ignore the laws as well, so that they are utterly without any master."

[68] LAELIUS: Your translation of what Plato said is completely accurate.

SCIPIO: To return to my source: he says that this excessive license, which they think the only true liberty, is the stock from which tyrants grow, so to speak. For just as the excessive power of the aristocracy causes their fall, so too liberty itself makes slaves out of this excessively free populace. Anything that is too successful – in weather, or harvests, or human bodies – generally turns into its opposite, and that is particularly true of commonwealths: extreme liberty, both of the people at large and of particular individuals, results in extreme slavery. From this pure liberty arises a tyrant, the most unjust and harshest form of slavery. For from this unruly, or rather monstrous, populace some leader is usually chosen against those aristocrats who have already been beaten down and driven from their place: someone bold, corrupt, vigorous in attacking people who have often served the commonwealth well; someone who buys the people's good will using others' property as well as his own. As a private citizen, he fears for his safety, and so he is given power which is renewed; he is protected by bodyguards, like Pisistratus in Athens; and finally he emerges as tyrant over those very people who promoted him. If, as often happens, a tyrant is overthrown by respectable people, the state is restored; if by men of daring, it becomes an oligarchy, which is just another form of tyranny. The same type of regime can often emerge from a good aristocratic government, when corruption turns the leaders themselves from the right path. In this way, they snatch the government from one another as if it were a ball: tyrants from kings, aristocrats or the people from them, and from them oligarchies or tyrants. No form of commonwealth is ever maintained for very long.

[69] Since that is the case, of the three primary forms my own preference is for monarchy; but monarchy itself is surpassed by a government which is balanced and compounded from the three primary forms of commonwealth. I approve of having something outstanding and monarchic in a commonwealth; of there being something else assigned to the authority of aristocrats; of some things being set aside for the judgment and wishes of the people. This structure has, in the first place, a certain degree of equality, which free people cannot do without for very long; it also has solidity, in that those primary forms are easily turned into the opposite vices, so that a master arises in place of a king, a faction in place of aristocracy, a confused mob in place of the people; and these types themselves are often replaced by new ones. That does not occur in this combined and moderately blended form of commonwealth unless there are great flaws in its leaders. There is no reason for revolution when each person is firmly set in his own rank, without the possibility of sudden collapse.

[70] But I am afraid, Laelius and all you other good and wise friends, that if I continue too long in this vein, I will seem to speak like some instructor or lecturer instead of a fellow inquirer into this subject.[87] So I will turn to something everyone knows, and which we started looking for some time ago. I will state my own opinion and belief and judgment that no commonwealth, in either its organization or its structure or its conduct and training, can be compared to the one our fathers received from their ancestors and have passed on to us. And if you agree, since you want to hear from me what you know yourselves, I will explain both the character and the superiority of our commonwealth. My description of our commonwealth will serve as the pattern to which I will tailor what I have to say concerning the best form of state. If I can carry this out completely, then I will, in my opinion, have thoroughly fulfilled the task which Laelius gave me.

[71] LAELIUS: The task is yours, Scipio, and yours alone. Who could speak about the institutions of our ancestors better than you, who are descended from the most distinguished ancestors? Who could speak better about the best form of the state? And if we ever get such a state, who could be more distinguished in it than you? Who could speak better

[87] See above, 1.36, 38.

about planning for the future, since you, by defeating two terrors that threatened this city,[88] have provided for its future?

Unplaced fragment from Book 1

Together with me, you should certainly recognize this custom, the enthusiasm and manner of speech (+ Nonius 276.6)

[88] Scipio had destroyed in war both Carthage in 146 and Numantia in 133.

Book 2

[1] <When he saw that everyone was>[1] eager to hear him, SCIPIO began to speak as follows: I will tell you something that Cato said in his old age. As you know, I was deeply attached to him and admired him very greatly; following the judgment of both my fathers[2] and my own desire, I devoted myself to him completely from an early age, and I could never get enough of what he said: he had so much experience of public affairs, in which he had taken part with great distinction for a very long time, both in civil and military matters; he was so measured in speaking, mixing wit with seriousness; and he was passionately fond of both learning and teaching. His life was in complete harmony with his speaking style. [2] Cato used to say that the organization of our state surpassed all others for this reason: in others there were generally single individuals who had set up the laws and institutions of their commonwealths – Minos in Crete, Lycurgus in Sparta, and in Athens, which frequently changed its government, first Theseus, then Draco, then Solon, then Clisthenes, then many others; finally, when Athens was drained of blood and prostrate, it was revived by the philosopher Demetrius of Phalerum. Our commonwealth, in contrast, was not shaped by one man's talent but by that of many; and not in one person's lifetime, but over many generations. He said that there never was a genius so great that he could miss nothing, nor could all the geniuses in the world brought together in one place at one time foresee all contingencies without the practical experience afforded by the passage of time. [3] I will therefore follow his model and take my start from the

[1] The opening words (written in red ink) are illegible.

[2] Natural and adoptive.

origin of the Roman people; I am happy to make use of Cato's own word.[3] I will have an easier time in completing my task if I show you our commonwealth as it is born, grows up, and comes of age,[4] and as a strong and well-established state, than if I make up some state as Socrates does in Plato.

[4] When everyone had agreed, SCIPIO said: What beginning of any established commonwealth is so famous and universally known as the foundation of this city by Romulus? His father was Mars (we should allow this much to tradition, because it is not only ancient but wisely passed down by our ancestors that men who have deserved well of the community should be thought to be divine by birth as well as by talent); when he was born, they say that Amulius, the king of Alba, was afraid of the threat to his kingdom and ordered him to be exposed on the bank of the Tiber along with his brother Remus. There, after he was nursed by a woodland beast,[5] shepherds brought him up in the life of a country laborer. When he grew up, they say that his physical strength and fierce spirit[6] were so outstanding that everyone living in the territory where Rome now is readily and freely obeyed him. He became the leader of their forces and (turning from fable to fact) is said to have defeated Alba Longa, a strong city and powerful for those times, and killed King Amulius.[7] [5] On the basis of the glory he achieved, they say, he first thought of founding a city (after taking the auspices)[8] and of establishing a commonwealth.

The location of a city is something that requires the greatest foresight in the establishment of a long-lasting commonwealth, and Romulus picked an amazingly advantageous site. He did not move to the coast, which would have been easy for him with the forces at hand, to invade the territory of the Rutulians or Aborigines or to found a city at the Tiber mouth, where many years later king Ancus founded a colony;[9] with exceptional foresight he realized that coastal positions are not the most advantageous for cities founded in the expectation of long

3 The title of Cato's historical work (which Cicero knew and presumably used in Book 2) was *Origines*. Cato and Plato here represent contrasting explanatory models; a similar contrast (between Plato and the Peripatetics) is made at 2.21–22.

4 The biological model is Aristotelian and is also used by Polybius.

5 The she-wolf is decorously veiled in C.'s account.

6 The reference to Romulus' ferocity alludes to the primitive kingship described by Polybius 6.5.7.

7 C. omits all legendary material prior to the foundation of the city: Alba Longa was said to have been founded by Aeneas' son Ascanius.

8 On the auspices see below, 2.16.

9 Ostia; see below, 2.33.

life and power. In the first place, maritime cities are exposed to dangers that are both multiple and unexpected. [6] If a city is surrounded by land, there are many advance indications of enemies' arrival – almost audible sounds of crashing – not only when they are anticipated but even when they are unexpected: no enemy can suddenly appear by land without our knowing not only that he is there but who he is and where he is from. But an enemy that comes by ship across the sea can arrive before anyone can suspect that he is coming; and when he does come he does not display who he is or where he is from or even what he wants; there is no sign to indicate whether he is friend or foe.

[7] Maritime cities are also subject to corruption and alteration of character.[10] They are exposed to new languages and customs; not only foreign goods are imported, but foreign customs as well, so that nothing of ancestral institutions can remain unaltered. People who live in those cities do not stick to their own homes; they are drawn far from home by eager hopes and expectations, and even when they remain physically, in their minds they are wandering in exile. Nothing did more to weaken gradually, and ultimately to destroy, Carthage and Corinth than this wandering and dissipation of their citizens: through the desire for trade and travel they abandoned the cultivation of fields and of military skill. [8] Piracy and sea trade supply many allurements to luxury that damage states; the very charm of the place itself supplies many enticements to pleasure that are both expensive and debilitating. What I said about Corinth is probably just as true for Greece as a whole: the Peloponnesus is almost entirely on the coast, and only the territory of Phlius does not abut the sea. Outside the Peloponnesus, only Aeniania, Doris, and Dolopia are away from the coast.[11] And of course the islands are surrounded by water and are virtually floating – along with the institutions and customs of their states. [9] And this is only the original territory of Greece; of all the colonies established by Greeks in Asia, Thrace, Italy, Sicily, and Africa, is there one, other than Magnesia, which is not on the water?[12] The coast seems to consist

[10] The excursus on the dangers of maritime locations was drawn, according to a letter of Cicero, from the writings of Dicaearchus. See also Plato, *Laws* 4.704a–705b for a similar discussion of the moral implications of coastal sites.

[11] Phlius lies between Argos and Sicyon in the northeastern Peloponnesus; the other states are all in northern Greece.

[12] Usually identified as Magnesia on the Maeander in Caria in Asia Minor; but it is not impossible that Cicero (or Dicaearchus) was alluding to the name of the imaginary city of Plato's *Laws*: see above, n.10.

of patches of Greece sewn onto the land of the barbarians; while of the barbarians themselves, none were previously nautical except the Etruscans and Phoenicians, the latter for trade, the former for piracy. The obvious reason for the troubles and revolutions of Greece lies in the vices of maritime cities which I just touched on. But among these vices there is one great advantage, that whatever grows anywhere can be shipped to the city where you live, and conversely whatever your own territory produces you can carry or send to any country.

[10] Could anything display divine ability more than Romulus' embrace of the benefits of the coast while avoiding its vices by placing his city on the bank of a large river that flows strongly into the sea throughout the year? In that way, the city could import essentials by sea and export its surplus produce; it could also use the river to receive the necessities of civilized life not only from the sea but carried downriver from inland.[13] Romulus therefore seems to me to have divined that this city would someday be the home and center of the greatest empire; for a city located in any other part of Italy would not so easily have exercised so much power.

[11] As for the natural defenses of the city, who is so inattentive as not to recognize them distinctly? The course and direction of the wall was marked out by the wisdom of Romulus and the other kings, following high and steep hills in every section; the one approach, between the Esquiline and Quirinal hills, was protected by building a huge mound and a deep ditch; the citadel was well fortified with a steep circuit and rested on an almost sheer rock, so that even on the terrible occasion of the Gallic attack it remained safe and unconquered.[14] The site that Romulus chose also abounded in springs and was a healthful spot in a plague-ridden region: the hills not only receive a breeze, but they bring shade to the valleys.

[12] All this he accomplished with great speed: he established a city, which he ordered to be named Rome after his own name; and in order to strengthen his new state he adopted a new and somewhat crude plan, but one that, in terms of bolstering the resources of his kingdom and people, shows the mark of a great man who looked far into the future: he ordered Sabine girls of good family, who had come to Rome for the

[13] An idealized description: the Tiber was not so easily navigable even in C.'s day.

[14] C. is describing the so-called Servian Wall of the fourth century BCE – not ascribed to Romulus even in antiquity. The Gallic sack of Rome took place in 387/6 according to Polybius' chronology, 390 according to Livy and others.

first annual celebration of the Consualia in the circus,[15] to be seized, and he placed them in marriages with the most important families. [13] This led the Sabines to wage war against the Romans; and when the battle was indecisive, he made a treaty with Titus Tatius the Sabine king at the urging of the women who had been seized. By that treaty he admitted the Sabines to citizenship and joint religious rituals, and he shared his rule with their king.

[14] After Tatius died, the entire power returned to Romulus. Together with Tatius, he had chosen leading citizens for a royal council – they were called "Fathers" because of affection – and had distributed the populace into three tribes under his own name and Tatius' and that of Lucumo, an ally of his who had died in the Sabine war, and into thirty *curiae*, which he named after those of the seized Sabine girls who had subsequently been advocates of a peace treaty.[16] Although all this was organized in Tatius' lifetime, after he was killed Romulus ruled with even more reliance on the authority and the judgment of the Fathers.

[15] In doing this he first recognized and approved the same policy that Lycurgus at Sparta had recognized slightly earlier, that states are guided and ruled better under the sole power of a king if the authority of the most responsible citizens is added to the monarch's absolute rule;[17] and so, relying on the support of this quasi-senatorial council, he waged many wars against his neighbors with great success and continually enriched his citizens while taking for himself nothing of the plunder. [16] What is more – a custom that we still maintain to the great advantage of the public safety – he relied extensively on the auspices. He took the auspices himself before founding the city and creating the commonwealth; and for all public undertakings he selected one augur from each tribe to assist him in taking the auspices. He also had the people

[15] In classical times, celebrated on 21 August. Consus was originally a god of the granary (from *condere*, to store), but C. alludes to an alternative derivation from *consilium*, the virtue of good statesmanship.

[16] The significance of the *curiae* is obscure; in C.'s time the curiate assembly (*comitia curiata*) was an antiquarian vestige represented by the magistrates' lictors, the function of which was primarily to ratify adoptions and the election of priests.

[17] While Polybius compares the developed "mixed constitution" of the Republic to the regime of Lycurgus at Sparta, C. compares Romulus' government to Lycurgus'; he thus suggests that Rome's government was mixed (if not "blended" – see 2.42 below) from the very beginning. C. uses "Fathers" for both the proto-senatorial council of Romulus and (as was traditional) for the formal senate of the Republic, but he generally avoids calling Romulus' group a senate, as it had no established constitutional position.

divided up under the protection of the leading citizens (and I will discuss later the utility of this), and he kept them in order not by force or by physical punishments but through the setting of fines in sheep and cattle; at that time wealth consisted of livestock and landed property, the origin of the words *pecuniosi* and *locupletes* to mean "wealthy."[18]

[17] When Romulus had ruled for thirty-seven years[19] and had created these two excellent foundations for the commonwealth, the auspices and the senate, he was so successful that when he did not reappear after a sudden darkening of the sun, he was thought to have become a god; no mortal could ever have achieved that without an extraordinary reputation for virtue. [18] In the case of Romulus that is even more remarkable: all other men who are said to have become gods lived in less sophisticated periods of human history, when such a fiction might be more acceptable, given that the uneducated are more gullible. But Romulus lived less than six hundred years ago at a time when literacy and learning were well established, and all the primeval ignorance of men's primitive existence had been eliminated. For if, as the chronologies of the Greeks demonstrate, Rome was founded in the second year of the seventh Olympiad, then the lifetime of Romulus fell in a time when Greece was already full of poets and musicians, and legends were given less credence unless they concerned events of the distant past. The first Olympiad took place 108 years after Lycurgus undertook to write laws (although some people are confused by the name and believe that the Olympics were founded by the same Lycurgus); the latest date that anyone gives to Homer is some thirty years before the time of Lycurgus. [19] Thus one can see that Homer lived a great many years before Romulus, so that – since men and even the times themselves were educated – there would be little room for making anything up. Ancient times accepted stories that were often crude inventions, but this cultivated age generally ridicules and rejects everything that is impossible. *

[**20**] * Some people say that <Stesichor>us was his daughter's son.[20] He died the same year that Simonides was born, in the fifty-sixth Olympiad; that makes it easier to understand that the story of Romulus'

[18] *Pecunia*, "money," is derived from *pecus*, "cattle"; *locuples*, "rich," from *locus*, "place."

[19] For the dates in this section see the chronological table at the front of the book.

[20] "His" refers to the poet Hesiod, generally believed to be a contemporary of Homer. C. is here denying this genealogy on chronological grounds. Part of a leaf of the manuscript has been torn off, and parts of the opening of this section are restorations.

immortality was believed at a time when civilized life was well established. But in fact Romulus' intelligence and virtue were so great that people believed the story about him told by Proculus Iulius, a farmer, something that for many generations men had believed about no other mortal. Proculus is said to have addressed a public assembly at the urging of the Fathers, who wanted to dispel the suspicion that they had caused the death of Romulus; he said that he had seen Romulus on the hill which is now called the Quirinal; Romulus had told him to ask the people to have a shrine made to him on that hill, and that he was a god and was called Quirinus.[21]

[21] Do you see that the judgment of one man not only created a new people but brought it to full growth, almost to maturity, not leaving it like some infant bawling in a cradle?

LAELIUS: We do see that, and we see that you have introduced a new kind of analysis, something to be found nowhere in the writings of the Greeks. That great man, the greatest of all writers, chose his own territory on which to build a state to suit his own ideas. It may be a noble state, but it is totally alien to human life and customs.[22] [22] All the others wrote about the types and principles of states without any specific model or form of commonwealth. You seem to me to be doing both: from the outset, you have preferred to attribute your own discoveries to others rather than inventing it all yourself in the manner of Plato's Socrates; and you ascribe to Romulus' deliberate planning all the features of the site of the city which were actually the result of chance or necessity.[23] Moreover, your discussion does not wander but is fixed on one commonwealth. So go on as you have begun; I think I can foresee a commonwealth being brought to perfection as you go through the remaining kings.

[23] SCIPIO: And so when Romulus' senate, which consisted of aristocrats whom the king himself had honored by wanting them to be called "Fathers" and their children called "patrician" – when that senate tried after the death of Romulus to rule the commonwealth itself without a king, the people did not accept that; because of their affection for

[21] For this story see also *On the Laws* 1.3; this is the earliest attestation of the identification of Romulus with the god Quirinus. The tradition that Romulus was murdered by the senate is also found in Livy 1.16.4 and elsewhere.

[22] For the criticism of Plato's lack of practicality cf. also *On the Orator* 1.224. "The others" in the next sentence refers to Aristotle and the Peripatetics.

[23] An extremely important comment: C., through Laelius, draws attention to the implausibility of his own account of Roman constitutional development.

Romulus they kept up their demand for a king.[24] At that point the aristocrats prudently came up with a new plan, the institution of an interregnum, something unknown to other nations: until a king had been declared, the state should neither be without a king nor have one long-term king; no one should be allowed to grow used to power and be either too slow in surrendering it or too prepared for maintaining it. [**24**] At that time, the new nation of Rome saw something that had escaped the Spartan Lycurgus, who thought that the king should not be selected (if in fact this was a matter in Lycurgus' control) but accepted, whoever he might be, so long as he was descended from the family of Hercules; our people even then, rustic though they were, saw that virtue and wisdom were the proper qualifications to be looked for in a king, not a royal pedigree.

[**25**] Since Numa Pompilius had an outstanding reputation in this respect, the people themselves passed over their own citizens and summoned him with the approval of the Fathers, calling him from Cures, a Sabine to rule over Rome. When he came here, even though the people by the vote of the curiate assembly had made him king, he himself still had a curiate law passed concerning his power;[25] and as he saw that the men of Rome, under Romulus' instruction, were inflamed with eagerness for war, he thought that that habit should be somewhat curtailed.

[**26**] His first act was to divide among the citizens the territory which Romulus had captured in war;[26] he also taught them that without plunder and spoils they could have through agriculture an abundance of all they needed. He implanted in them a love of tranquillity and peace, through which justice and trust are most easily strengthened, and under the influence of which agriculture and harvests are best defended. Pompilius also created the greater auspices and added two augurs to the original number; he placed five priests chosen from the aristocracy in charge of religious rituals, and by the promulgation of laws (of which we have documentary evidence) he softened through religious ceremonies minds that were inflamed with the habit and the desire for making war.[27] He also added the Flamines, the Salii, and the Vestal Virgins,

[24] C. clearly suggests a premature attempt to advance the constitutional cycle from monarchy to aristocracy.

[25] The formal separation of election to office and conferral of power (*imperium*) is repeated by all the good kings and was a feature of the republican constitution as well.

[26] An evident anachronism: early land division was in the form of colonies, and distribution to individuals is not known before the second century BCE.

[27] A collection of Numa's laws is also referred to at 5.3. The augurs and pontifices were the

and he organized all aspects of religion with great sanctity. [27] He desired the performance of religious rituals to be difficult but the equipment for them to be very simple: he required many things to be learned and performed, but he made them inexpensive; he thus added effort to religious observances but removed the cost. He also began markets and games and all sorts of occasions for gatherings and festivals. By these institutions he restored to humane and gentle behavior the minds of men who had become savage and inhuman through their love of war. So, after ruling for thirty-nine years in great peace and harmony (I am following my friend Polybius, whose chronology is more careful than anyone else's),[28] he died, having strengthened two things that are most important for the long life of a commonwealth, religion and mildness of character.

[28] When Scipio had said this, MANILIUS said: Is the story true, Africanus, that King Numa was a pupil of Pythagoras himself, or at least a Pythagorean?[29] We have often heard this from our elders, and it is commonly believed; but the public records are not sufficiently explicit.

SCIPIO: The whole story is false, Manilius, and not only a fiction but a clumsy and ridiculous one. Lies are particularly intolerable when we can see that they are not only inventions but completely impossible. For Pythagoras is known to have come to Sybaris and Croton and that region of Italy in the fourth year of the reign of Lucius Tarquinius Superbus: the sixty-second Olympiad marks both the beginning of Superbus' reign and the arrival of Pythagoras. [29] From that, it is clear by the computation of regnal years that Pythagoras first reached Italy about 140 years after the death of Numa, and no one who has paid close attention to chronology has ever had any doubt about that.[30]

MANILIUS: Good lord! What huge mistake, and how long it has been believed! But in fact I can happily accept that we were not educated by foreign and imported learning, but by home-grown domestic virtues.[31]

most significant priesthoods in the late Republic; the Flamines (priests of Jupiter, Mars, and Quirinus) had archaic ritual functions, as did the Salii, priests of Mars whose primary obligations involved rites connected with military activity. The Vestal Virgins are the only ones of the second group mentioned who retained any importance in C.'s or Scipio's time.

[28] In other accounts (e.g. Livy 1.21.6) Numa ruled for 43 years.

[29] The story of Numa's Pythagoreanism is old; C. also rejects the chronology at *On the Orator* 2.154 and *Tusculan Disputations* 4.2–3. Scipio's natural father, Aemilius Paullus, claimed descent from Mamercus the son of Pythagoras.

[30] For the chronology see the table.

[31] A frequent theme both in the historical narrative and in C.'s argument. For the arrival of Greek learning see below, 2.34.

[30] SCIPIO: In fact you will recognize that even more clearly if you watch the commonwealth improving and approaching the ideal condition by a natural route and direction; you will decide that this is itself a reason to praise our ancestors' wisdom, because you will recognize how much better they made the institutions borrowed from other places than they had been in the place of origin from which we adopted them; you will see that the Roman people grew strong not by chance but by planning and discipline, if not without some help from fortune.

[31] After King Pompilius died, the people made Tullus Hostilius king in the curiate assembly presided over by an interrex; he followed the example of Pompilius and asked the assembly to approve his power. He achieved great glory as a soldier, and his military exploits were great. From the spoils of war he made the enclosure for the Comitium[32] and built the Senate House, and he established the law governing the declaration of wars; he sanctified this just procedure through the ritual of the Fetiales, so that any war that was not previously announced and declared was to be judged unjust and impious.[33] You should observe how wisely our kings saw that the people should be given some responsibilities (I will have a great deal to say on that score): Tullus did not dare to use the royal insignia without the permission of the people. In order to have the right to have twelve lictors with the fasces precede him *

[one leaf missing]

[32] Augustine, *City of God.* 3.15: *Concerning Tullus Hostilius, indeed, the third king – who was also killed by a thunderbolt – Cicero says in the same book that he was not believed to have become a god after dying in this way, perhaps because the Romans did not wish to cheapen what had been accepted in the case of Romulus by easily awarding it to someone else.*

[33] LAELIUS?: * In the account you are giving, the commonwealth does not creep but flies towards its best form.

SCIPIO: After him the son of Numa Pompilius' daughter, Ancus Marcius, was made king by the people, and he too carried a curiate law confirming his power. After he had conquered the Latins in war, he enrolled them as citizens; he also annexed the Aventine and Caelian hills to the city. He divided up the territory he had captured, and he made all the coastal woods which he had captured public property. He also

32 The original meeting place in the Forum for public assemblies.

33 The fetial law (which governed the declaration and conduct of war) is discussed also in Laelius' speech in Book 3; see below, 3.35a.

founded a city at the mouth of the Tiber and strengthened it with colonists. He died after he had ruled for twenty-three years.

LAELIUS: King Ancus certainly deserves praise, but Roman history is obscure, if we know who the king's mother was but not his father.

SCIPIO: True enough; but for those times little more than the kings' names is well known.

[34] At this point, the state first seems to have become more cultivated by a sort of graft of education. It was no mere trickle from Greece that flowed into the city, but a full river of education and learning. They say that there was a Corinthian named Demaratus, easily the first citizen of his state in distinction and authority and wealth; but that, as he could not endure the Corinthian tyrant Cypselus, he fled with a great fortune and went to Tarquinii, a very prosperous Etruscan city. When he heard that the rule of Cypselus was firmly established, this free and brave man became an exile; he was accepted as a citizen by the people of Tarquinii and set up his home in that state. There he and his Tarquinian wife had two sons, and he educated them in all the arts in accordance with Greek methods *

[one leaf missing]

[35] * he was readily accepted into the state, and because of his amiability and learning he became so close a friend of King Ancus that he was thought to participate in all his plans and to be almost a co-ruler. He was, moreover, extremely affable and extremely generous towards all citizens in giving support, aid, defense, and money. And so at the death of Marcius the people unanimously elected him king under the name of Lucius Tarquinius: that was how he had changed his name from what it had been in Greek,[34] so as to be seen to follow the customs of this people in all respects. After carrying the law concerning his power, he first doubled the earlier number of Fathers, and he called the original ones "from the greater families," whose opinions he asked first, and those he had selected "from the lesser families." [36] He then organized the cavalry in the manner that has been kept until now, although he was unable to change the names "Titienses," "Rhamnenses," and "Luceres," despite his desire to do so, because the distinguished augur Attus Navius did not authorize it.[35] I notice that the Corinthians too paid close

[34] The original name of Lucius Tarquinius was Lucumo, an Etruscan name; it is striking that C. omits all mention of Etruscan influence on Rome.

[35] The names of the three tribes are alluded to at 2.14 above. C. omits the fabulous story of Attus' cutting a whetstone with a razor as proof of his augural ability.

attention to the assignment of public horses and to supporting them by a tax on orphans and widows.[36] In any case, by adding second divisions to the earlier sections of the cavalry he created 1,200 knights and doubled the number. Afterward, he conquered the Aequi, a large and fierce tribe that threatened the Roman people; he also drove the Sabines back from the walls of the city and then routed them with the cavalry and conquered them in war. He is said to have been the first to perform the great games that are called the Ludi Romani; he also vowed during the war with the Sabines to build a temple to Jupiter Optimus Maximus on the Capitol.[37] He died after ruling for thirty-eight years.

[37] LAELIUS: Now the truth of Cato's saying becomes more evident, that the establishment of our commonwealth was not the work of one time or one man;[38] it is very clear how much the stock of good and useful things increased with each king. But the king who follows is the one who seems to me to have had the greatest vision of all in the commonwealth.

SCIPIO: True enough. The next king was Servius Tullius, who is said to have been the first to rule without the vote of the people. They say that he was the son of a slave woman from Tarquinii and that his father was a client of the king; he was brought up among the slaves and served at the king's table, but the spark of talent that was already evident in his childhood did not pass unobserved: his cleverness appeared in all his duties and in what he said.[39] And Tarquinius, whose children were still very small, was so fond of Servius that Servius was commonly held to be his son; he enthusiastically instructed him in all the subjects which he himself had learned in accordance with the best Greek methods. [38] But when Tarquinius was killed by the treachery of the sons of Ancus, Servius (as I said before) began to rule without the formal approval of the citizens, but with their support and acquiescence.[40] When Tarquinius was falsely said to be alive but ill from his wound, Servius administered justice wearing the royal costume; he freed debtors with his own money; and with great affability he declared that he was administering justice by

[36] Not otherwise attested. C. is attempting to link Tarquinius' actions with his origins.

[37] The Great or Roman Games (*ludi Romani*) were connected with the birthday of the Capitoline temple, celebrated on 13 September. For the completion of the temple cf. 2.44 below.

[38] Above, 2.2.

[39] C. rationalizes the "spark," traditionally a halo of fire that appeared around his head as a child.

[40] C.'s account of Servius includes without comment the elements of his accession that in other traditions mark him as an incipient tyrant: his disapproval of Servius' populist tendencies is balanced by his approval of the timocratic constitution generally ascribed to him.

the order of Tarquinius. He did not ask the approval of the Fathers, but after Tarquinius was buried he asked for the approval of the people, and having gained it he carried a law concerning his own powers. His first act was to wage war on the Etruscans to avenge the wrongs they had done; after that *

[one leaf missing]

[**39**] * 18 <centuries> of the highest census rating.[41] Then after separating this large number of the knights from the people at large, he divided the rest into five classes, separating the older from the younger, and he so organized them that the votes were in the control of the wealthy rather than the majority; he made certain (something that must always be secure in a commonwealth) that the greatest number did not have the greatest power. If his division were unknown to you, I would explain it; but as it is, you see the logic of the system: the centuries of the knights, together with the "six voting groups"[42] and the first class – plus 1 century given to the carpenters because of their great utility to the city – make up 89 centuries; if only 8 of the remaining 104 centuries join them, then a voting majority of the people is achieved, and the much greater multitude in the other 96 centuries is neither excluded from voting, which would be arrogant, nor excessively powerful, which would be dangerous. [**40**] In all this he was extremely careful in the choice of words and names: he called the wealthy *assidui* from contributing money,[43] and those who brought to the census either no more than 1,500 *asses* or in fact nothing but their own persons, he called *proletarii*, thus showing that he expected from them only children, that is, the offspring of the state. In any one of those 96 centuries at that time there were almost more people than in the entire first class. And so no one was kept from the right to vote, but the people who had the most power in the voting were those who had the greatest interest in maintaining the state in the best possible condition. In fact, to the auxiliaries, the trumpeters and the horn players, the proletarians *

[41] The account of the Servian constitution is not only fragmentary but concentrates on its timocratic elements and its place in the mixed constitution to such an extent that C. omits the reorganization of the tribes generally connected with it and the military purpose of the centuriate structure. C.'s numbers diverge somewhat from the other accounts, and all versions clearly reflect later reorganizations of the system.

[42] The "six voting groups" (*sex suffragia*) are a vexed problem; they are probably the 6 centuries of the knights as organized by Tarquinius Priscus, to which Servius added 12 more.

[43] *Assidui ab aere dando* (from giving money) is the ancient etymology. The bronze *as* (weighing 1 pound) was the basic unit of early Roman coinage. *Proles* = "children."

[two leaves missing]

[42] * sixty<-five> years older, because it was founded thirty-nine years before the first Olympiad;[44] and Lycurgus in the distant past recognized much the same thing. And so the balance and fairness of this triple form of commonwealth seem to me to be shared by us with those peoples.

But what is specific to our commonwealth, and is a very grand thing, I will try to explain somewhat more carefully, as it is of such a character that nothing similar is to be found in any other commonwealth. The elements that I have explained so far were combined in this state and in those of the Spartans and the Carthaginians in such a way that they were not at all blended.[45] [43] In any commonwealth in which there is one person with permanent power, especially royal power, even if there is also a senate, as there was at Rome in regal times and as in Sparta under the laws of Lycurgus, and even if the people have some rights, as was the case under our kings – even so, the name of king stands out, and such a commonwealth cannot be called, or be, anything but a monarchy. And that type of state is the most unstable because through a single person's fault it can be sent headlong in the most destructive direction. The monarchic form of state itself not only is not to be criticized, but probably should be ranked far ahead of the other simple forms (if I approved of any of the simple forms of commonwealth) – but only so long as it maintains its condition; and its proper condition is that the safety and equality and peace of the citizens be governed by one person's permanent power and justice and one person's wisdom. The people that is ruled by a king lacks a great deal, and above all it lacks liberty, which does not consist in having a just master, but in having none *

[one leaf missing]

[2.53a] . . . and so, after Romulus' superb constitution had remained firm for some 220 years (+ Nonius 526.10)[46]

[44] * they endured. Even that unjust and cruel master was for a certain amount of time attended by good fortune in his actions. He

[44] The reference is to Carthage, traditionally founded in 815/4. Polybius too compares Rome with Carthage and Sparta as examples of the mixed constitution.

[45] While Polybius emphasizes the mixed constitution as a defensive system of checks and balances, C. prefers to see the ideal more positively as one that incorporates elements of all three simple forms.

[46] The 220 years are those of "good" monarchy, before the tyranny of Tarquinius Superbus. Others including Ziegler have altered the number to 240 and seen it as the total length of the monarchy.

conquered all Latium in war, and he captured Suessa Pometia, a rich and prosperous city; with the wealth he acquired through the large booty of gold and silver he paid his father's vow through the building of the Capitolium. He also established colonies, and in keeping with the customs of his nation of origin he send magnificent gifts as an offering from the spoils to Apollo at Delphi.[47]

[45] At this point you will see the political circle turning; you should learn to recognize its natural motion and circuit from the very beginning. This is the essential element of civic prudence (the topic of our entire discussion): to see the paths and turns of commonwealths, so that when you know in what direction any action tends, you can hold it back or anticipate it. The king of whom I am speaking was, in the first place, of unsound mind because he had been stained by the slaughter of the best of kings;[48] and since he was afraid of being severely punished for his crime, he wanted to be feared. In the second place, he reveled in his violence, relying on his victories and his wealth. [46] And so, when his elder son assaulted Lucretia, the daughter of Tricipitinus and wife of Collatinus, and that modest and noble woman sentenced herself to death because of his attack, Lucius Brutus, a man of outstanding talent and virtue, threw off from his fellow citizens the unjust yoke of harsh slavery. Although he was a private citizen, he upheld the whole commonwealth; he was the first in this state to show that in preserving the liberty of citizens no one is a private person. Under his leadership and initiative, the state was roused both by the fresh complaint of Lucretia's father and relatives and by the memory of Tarquin's pride and of the many injuries inflicted by him and his sons; they ordered the king himself, his sons, and the family of the Tarquins to go into exile.

[47] Do you see, then, how a master emerged from a king, and how by one person's fault the form of the commonwealth was altered from a good one to the worst? This lord of the people is the man the Greeks call a tyrant; they want "king" to be the title of the man who looks after his people like a parent and keeps those of whom he is in charge in the best possible condition of life.[49] It is, as I said, a genuinely good form of commonwealth; but it verges on the most terrible type. [48] As soon as

47 An allusion without details to the story of Brutus' participation in the embassy to Delphi and his correct interpretation of a prophecy.

48 Superbus and his wife Tullia had murdered her father, Servius Tullius.

49 As C. repeats at 2.49, Greek distinguishes between a good "king" and a bad "tyrant," while in Latin the word "king" itself implies tyrannical behavior.

this king turned to a more unjust form of mastery, he immediately became a tyrant; no animal can be imagined that is more awful or foul or more hateful to gods and men alike.[50] Although he has the appearance of a human, through the viciousness of his character he outdoes the most destructive beasts. Who could rightly call "human" someone who desires no bond of shared law, no link of human nature with his fellow citizens or indeed with the whole human race? But there will be a more suitable moment for us to speak about this type of government when the occasion leads us to condemn those men who have sought domination even in a freed state.

[49] There you have the first origin of a tyrant. That is the name that the Greeks wanted to give an unjust king; our own people have used "king" to refer to everyone who had sole and perpetual power over their people. And so Spurius Cassius and Marcus Manlius and Spurius Maelius were said to have wanted to seize monarchic power; and more recently *[51]

[one leaf missing]

[50] * he called <elders> at Sparta; they were too few, only twenty-eight, whom he wanted to serve as the highest council, while the king kept the executive power. Following his example, our people had the same purpose; they translated his terms, and called "senate"[52] the men he had called "elders"; in selecting the "Fathers," Romulus had already done the same thing. Even so, the force, power, and name of king stands out and dominates. Grant the people some power, as did Lycurgus and Romulus: you will not give them enough liberty but you will set them on fire with the desire for liberty, while only giving them the opportunity for a taste. And always the fear will loom over them that the king, as frequently happens, may become unjust. The fortune of a people is fragile that rests, as I said before, on a single person's wishes or character.

[51] Therefore, let this be the first shape and appearance and origin of a tyrant, which we have discovered in the commonwealth which Romulus founded after taking the auspices, not in the one which, as Plato writes, Socrates designed in that elegant[53] conversation: how Tarquinius, not by the acquisition of new power but by the unjust use of power that

50 In C.'s account (here as at 2.62–63) below, a change of constitution from good to bad need not imply a change of ruler: a king can become a tyrant, and aristocrats can become oligarchs. For beasts in human guise see below, 4.1d (before 3.36 in this edition).

51 A reference to Tiberius Gracchus (who was accused of monarchic tendencies at the time) clearly followed.

52 *Senatus* is derived from *senex*, "old man."

53 *Perpolito* is an emendation; the text is corrupt.

he already had, entirely overturned monarchic government. Let there be opposed to this man another, who is good and wise and knowledgeable about the interests and the reputation of the state, almost a tutor and manager of the commonwealth; that, in fact, is the name for whoever is the guide and helmsman of the state. Make sure you recognize this man; he is the one who can protect the state by his wisdom and efforts. And since this concept has not yet been treated in our conversation,[54] and we will often have to consider this type of man in our remaining discussion *[55]

[six leaves missing]

[2.63c] . . . when Lucius Quinctius was named dictator (Servius on Vergil, *Georgics* 3.125)[56]

[52] * he sought . . . and he created a state more to be desired than expected; one as small as possible, not one that could exist, but one in which the principles of civic organization could be discerned. But if I can do it, I will try to use the same principles that he observed, not in the shadowy image of a state but in the greatest commonwealth, so as to appear almost to touch with my pointer the cause of each public good and ill.

The monarchy lasted slightly longer than 240 years, including the interregna;[57] after Tarquinius was expelled, the Roman people hated the name of king as much as they had loved it after the death, or rather departure, of Romulus. Then they were unable to do without a king; at the expulsion of Tarquinius they were unable even to hear the name of king . . . *

[eight leaves missing]

[2.63b] Cicero, *Letters to Atticus* 6.1.8: *You ask a historical question concerning Gnaeus Flavius, the son of Annius. He certainly was not earlier than the decemvirs, since he was curule aedile, an office that was not instituted*

54 Less probably "in our language."

55 Before the lengthy gap, C. begins the first extensive discussion of his ideal citizen, who is given a number of different labels, combining Roman political terminology with the "royal" or "political" man at Plato, *Statesman* 268c. C.'s ideal leader has often been misconstrued as a monarch; in fact, the role described is temporary (Lucius Brutus is the first great example) and can be filled by any one of the many qualified statesmen available. The passage should be read in connection with C.'s description of his own public service at 1.10–11. When the manuscript returns, C. is describing Plato's *Republic*.

56 Lucius Quinctius Cincinnatus was named dictator for the second time in 439 in connection with the attempted coup of Spurius Maelius. The location of the fragment is uncertain, but it has plausibly been connected to the discussion of the ideal citizen.

57 From 751/0 to 508/7 on C.'s chronology.

until many years after the decemvirs. What was the effect of his publication of the official calendar? They think that that document was concealed at one time, so that the days for public actions would have to be sought from a few people. And quite a few sources say that Gnaeus Flavius the scribe made the calendar public and composed the forms of action; so don't think that I or rather Africanus (he is the speaker) made it up.[58]

[**53c**] * that whole law was repealed.[59] In this state of mind, our ancestors at that time threw out Collatinus, although he was innocent, through suspicion arising from his relationship to Tarquinius; they expelled the rest of the family of the Tarquinii through hatred of the name. In the same state of mind Publius Valerius was the first to order the fasces to be lowered when he began to speak in an assembly; he also moved his house to the foot of the Velia after he recognized that the people were becoming suspicious when he began to build higher on the Velia on the same spot where King Tullus had lived.[60] He too – an action in which he most embodied his cognomen "Publicola"[61] – proposed a law to the people, the first which was passed by the centuriate assembly, that no magistrate should execute or whip a Roman citizen without his having the right of appeal to the people. [**54**] The pontifical books state, and our augural books indicate, that the right of appeal also existed under the kings.[62] Similarly, many laws in the Twelve Tables show that there was the possibility of appeal from every judgment and penalty: the fact that the decemvirs who wrote the laws are said to have been elected without the right of appeal is a sufficient proof that there was a right of appeal from other magistrates; and the consular law of Lucius Valerius Potitus and Marcus Horatius Barbatus,[63] men who were wisely democratic for the sake of harmony, ordained that no magistracy should be created without the right of appeal. And in fact the Porcian laws, three laws as

[58] Gnaeus Flavius was aedile in 304 BCE. C.'s comment shows that he must have mentioned Flavius before his account of the Decemvirate; otherwise Atticus would not have raised the chronological issue. For Nonius 526.10 (placed here by Ziegler) see 2.42–44 above. Augustine, *City of God* 5.12 (placed here but considered spurious by Ziegler), is not from C.

[59] A law permitting the family of Tarquinius to take their possessions into exile.

[60] The Velia is the northeast spur of the Palatine Hill.

[61] C. wrongly considers *publicola* to be derived from *populum colere*, "to cultivate the people."

[62] This section is an antiquarian excursus on the origins of *prouocatio*, the right of appeal to the people. The issue was one of personal interest to C., whose exile resulted from his execution of the Catilinarian conspirators in 63 withut giving them the opportunity to appeal the sentence.

[63] The consuls of 449 BCE, after the restoration of the Republic at the overthrow of the decemvirs.

you know named after three members of the Porcian family, added nothing new other than a penalty for violations.[64] [55] And so Publicola, after carrying the law on appeal, immediately ordered the axes to be taken out of the fasces; on the next day he presided over the election of his new colleague Spurius Lucretius, and he ordered his lictors to be transferred to Lucretius because he was the elder. Publicola first established that the lictors should precede one consul at a time in alternate months, so that there would be no more symbols of power in a free republic than there had been in the monarchy. To my understanding, Publicola was a man of no average talent: by giving a moderate amount of liberty to the people, he more easily maintained the authority of the aristocracy. Nor am I now reciting such old and outworn things to you without a reason: I want to set up examples of men and actions using famous people and events, to serve as the basis for the rest of my argument.

[56] This was the condition in which the senate maintained the commonwealth at that time:[65] considering that the people were free, a few things were to be done through the people, but more by the authority of the senate and by custom and precedent; the consuls were to have power that lasted only for one year but was in form and law like royal power. They held very firmly to what may have been the most important element in maintaining the power of the nobles, that votes of the people should not be held valid unless the senate voted to approve them.[66] This period also saw the appointment of the first dictator, Titus Larcius, some ten years after the first consuls;[67] this new form of power seemed very close to that of a king. But in any case everything was in the hands of the aristocracy: they had the greatest authority, and the people gave way to them. Great actions were performed in war in those days by brave men holding supreme power as dictators or consuls.

[57] Nature[68] itself, however, required that, as a result of their having been freed from monarchy, the people should claim rather more rights for themselves; that took place not much later (about sixteen years) in the consulate of Postumus Cominius and Spurius Cassius.[69] This development was perhaps not completely rational, but the nature of commonwealths often overcomes reason. You must bear in mind what I said at the

64 The only reference to there having been three Porcian laws; C. elsewhere knows only one.

65 After the overthrow of tyranny comes the aristocratic stage of the constitution, which lasts until the decemvirs become oligarchic (below, 2.62–63).

66 Not altered until 339 BCE.

67 In 498 according to Dionysius of Halicarnassus and (probably) C.; 501 according to Livy.

68 "Nature" and "the nature of commonwealths" below must be the same thing.

69 493 BCE; the secession traditionally began in the preceding year.

outset: if there is not an equitable balance in the state of rights and duties and responsibilities, so that there is enough power in the hands of the magistrates and enough authority in the judgment of the aristocrats and enough freedom in the people, then the condition of the commonwealth cannot be preserved unchanged. [58] Now when the state was disturbed as a result of the problem of debt, the plebs seized first the Sacred Mount and then the Aventine.[70] Not even the discipline of Lycurgus was able to keep firm hold of the reins in dealing with Greeks: even at Sparta, in the reign of Theopompus, the five ephors (as they are called at Sparta; in Crete they are the ten *cosmoi*) were established as a check on the kings' strength, just as the tribunes of the plebs were established against consular power.[71]

[59] Our ancestors could perhaps have had some method for healing the problem of debt; Solon the Athenian had found one not long before, and somewhat later our senate did too, when because of the passion of one individual all citizens then in debt bondage were freed and the use of debt bondage was discontinued.[72] At all times when the plebs was being crushed by the burden of debt because of a public calamity, some relief and cure has been sought for the sake of the common safety. At that time, however, no such plan was employed, and that gave the people a reason to revolt and create two tribunes of the plebs, in order to diminish the power and authority of the senate. This remained, however, very great: the wisest and bravest men, both in warfare and in directing the government, were protecting the state; their influence remained very strong, because they greatly surpassed their fellow citizens in distinction but were less influenced by their pleasures and were not much wealthier. The virtue of each of them in public affairs was all the more appreciated because in private they took great pains to protect individual citizens by their efforts, advice, and wealth.

[60] While this system of government prevailed, a quaestor accused

70 The Sacred Mount is some 5 km from Rome, across the river Anio. Which of the two places was occupied in the various secessions of the plebs was disputed in antiquity.

71 C. considers the Spartan ephorate to be a popular element in the constitution, although others thought it tyrannical. Theopompus was king in the eighth century.

72 Solon's remission of debts (the *seisachtheia*, "shaking off of burdens") is traditionally dated to 594/3, although C. and some other Roman sources seem to make it a generation later. The Poetelian law of 326 BCE (313 in some sources) ended debt bondage (*nexum*) at Rome; for the wickedness of the usurer Papirius that occasioned the law cf. Livy 8.28. C.'s point here (and elsewhere) is that intelligent individual action by the statesman should modify strict legalism.

Spurius Cassius, a man of great popularity among the people, of seeking to establish a monarchy; as you have heard, when his father said that he knew that Spurius was in fact guilty, with the permission of the people he put him to death. Some fifty-four years after the establishment of the republic, the consuls Spurius Tarpeius and Aulus Aternius carried in the centuriate assembly a popular law concerning penalties and trial bonds; twenty years later, because Lucius Papirius and Publius Pinarius as censors had, through the imposition of fines, transferred a great many cattle from private to public ownership, a law of the consuls Gaius Iulius and Publius Papirius established a low cash equivalent for cattle in fines.[73]

[**61**] But some years earlier, while the senate still had the highest influence and the people endured and obeyed, a plan was initiated according to which the consuls and the tribunes of the plebs would resign from office and a board of ten would be elected with supreme authority and without the right of appeal from their decisions.[74] These men were to have the chief power and were to write the laws. When they had written ten tables of laws of great equity and prudence, they had a second board of ten elected in their place for the following year, who have not been praised for comparable honor or justice. Among this board,[75] Gaius Iulius deserved particular praise. He said that he had been present when a corpse was dug up in the bedroom of a nobleman, Lucius Sestius; and although as a decemvir from whom there was no appeal he had the supreme power, he still allowed Sestius to post bail because he said that he would not violate the excellent law that forbade any capital verdict on a Roman citizen to be rendered by other than the centuriate assembly.

[**62**] The third year of decemviral rule followed; the decemvirs stayed the same and refused to have others elected in their place. In this condition of the commonwealth (which as I have said frequently could not last for long, as it was not equitable towards all orders of the state) the

[73] Spurius Cassius was consul in 486; what he did and the legal problems surrounding his trial and execution in 485 are very unclear. The same is true of the two laws mentioned here (of 454 and 430 respectively): they clearly mitigated the harsh Roman law of debt, but exactly how is a matter for speculation.

[74] The first ("good") Decemvirate was in 451; the second ("bad") Decemvirate, in 450–449. For C., this represents the change from aristocracy to oligarchy, while the overthrow of the second Decemvirate and the restoration of the Republic under the consuls Valerius and Horatius in 449 marks the transition to the mixed constitution.

[75] The first Decemvirate, not the second.

entire commonwealth was in the control of the aristocrats, led by the ten noble decemvirs; there were no tribunes of the plebs to oppose them, and no other magistrates at all; there was no right of appeal to the people left against execution or whipping. **[63]** And so from the injustice of these men suddenly arose a great disturbance and an alteration of the entire commonwealth. They added two tables of unjust laws to the previous tables; they ordained by a most inhumane law that there should be no right of marriage between plebeians and patricians, something that is often enough granted to unrelated peoples; that law was later reversed by the Canuleian plebiscite.[76] In all their public actions they ruled the people greedily and violently and with an eye to their own passions. The story is well known and famous through many works of literature:[77] how a certain Decimus Verginius, because of the intemperateness of one of those decemvirs, killed his own daughter in the forum by his own hand; how in grief he fled to the army that was then on Mount Algidus; how the soldiers abandoned the war in which they were engaged and first occupied the Sacred Mount (as they had done before in similar circumstances) and then the Aventine *[78]

[four leaves missing]

* I judge that our ancestors both approved of most highly and preserved most wisely.

[64] After Scipio had said this, and the others were waiting in silence for the rest of his speech, TUBERO said: Since my elders here are not asking anything of you, Africanus, I will tell you what I find lacking in your speech.

SCIPIO: Please do.

TUBERO: You seem to me to have praised our commonwealth, although Laelius had asked you not about our commonwealth but about commonwealths in general. Nor did I learn from your speech by what training or customs or laws we can establish or preserve that very commonwealth which you praise.

[76] Of 445 BCE; Livy gives a full account of Canuleius' speech and law at 4.1–6.

[77] C.'s is the earliest extant account; for a later one (drawing on earlier sources) cf. Livy 3.44–49.

[78] The missing passage included C.'s account of the end of the secession and the restoration of the Republic. Like Polybius, he ended his account of constitutional development with the passage of the Valerio-Horatian laws (including the restoration of the right of appeal) in 449; C. appears to have thought that the constitution remained stable almost until the tribunate of Tiberius Gracchus in 133.

[**65**] SCIPIO: I think that we will shortly have a more suitable occasion, Tubero, for discussing the establishment and preservation of states;[79] but I believed that I answered Laelius' question about the best condition of the state adequately. First, I defined the three admirable types of states and the equal number of corresponding vicious ones; I showed that no one of these is best, but that a state that is properly blended from the first three types is better than any of them. [**66**] As to my use of our state, that was not in order to define the best condition – I could do that without any illustration – but so that we might see concretely in the greatest state just what sort of thing I was describing in my argument. But if you are looking for the type of the ideal state without the example of any specific people, then we must make use of an image given by nature, since you [think] this image of the city and people is too *[80]

[probably two leaves missing]

[**1.34b**] . . . there is no example to which we should prefer to compare the commonwealth (Diomedes 1.365.20K).

[**67**] SCIPIO: * <whom> I have long been looking for and whom I am eager to reach.

LAELIUS: Are you by any chance seeking the man of foresight?[81]

SCIPIO: The very one.

LAELIUS: There is a fine supply of them among those present; you might even begin from yourself.

SCIPIO: If only the proportion in the whole senate were the same![82] But in fact the man of foresight is one who, as we often saw in Africa, sits on a huge and destructive creature, keeps it in order, directs it wherever he wants, and by a gentle instruction or touch turns the animal in any direction.

LAELIUS: I understand; when I was your legate I often saw it.[83]

SCIPIO: So that Indian or Carthaginian keeps this one creature in order, one that is docile and used to human customs; but what hides in human spirits, the part of the spirit that is called the mind, has to rein in

[79] Laws and institutions are the subject of Book 4 in particular.

[80] The manuscript becomes too fragmentary at this point to follow the argument with any certainty. The "image given by nature" is almost certainly the cosmos itself.

[81] *Prudentem*, a term almost impossible to translate, as it incorporates both Aristotelian *phronesis*, "practical wisdom," and its Latin etymological sense of foresight, from *prouideo*. See also 2.51 and "Text and Translation" above.

[82] For the failings of the actual senate see also *On the Laws* 3.27–32.

[83] In Africa during the Third Punic War (147–146 BCE).

and control not just one creature or one easy to control, and it is not often that it accomplishes that task. For he must control that fierce *

[two leaves missing]

[68a] . . . which is fed on blood, and which rejoices so greatly in savage cruelty that it can scarcely be satisfied by men's merciless deaths (+Nonius 300.29)[84]

[68b] . . . for a greedy and grasping man, who is filled with lusts and wallows in pleasures (+Nonius 491.16)

[68c] . . . and the fourth is worry, which is inclined to grief; it is mournful and always troubling itself (+Nonius 72.34)

[68d] . . . are pains, if afflicted with misery or cast down by fear or cowardice (+Nonius 228.18)[85]

[3 fr. inc. 1] . . . there is something unruly in every individual which either rejoices in pleasure or is broken by difficulties (Nonius 301.5)[86]

[68e] . . . just as an untrained charioteer is dragged from the chariot, flattened, mangled, and crushed (+Nonius 292.38)

[2.41] . . . the best-organized commonwealth, moderately blended from the three primary types (monarchic, aristocratic, and democratic), which does not provoke by punishment the wild and savage mind . . . (+Nonius 342.39)[87]

[69a] SCIPIO: * can be said.

LAELIUS: Now I see what kind of responsibilities you are placing in the charge of that man I have been waiting for.

SCIPIO: There is really only one, because practically all the rest are contained in this one alone: that he never cease educating and observing himself, that he summon others to imitate him, that through the brilliance of his mind and life he offer himself as a mirror to his fellow citizens. In playing the lyre or the flute, and of course in choral singing, a degree of harmony must be maintained among the different sounds, and if it is altered or discordant a trained ear cannot endure it; and this harmony, through the regulation of very different voices, is made pleas-

[84] This and the following three fragments are the remains of a catalogue of passions that affect the mind; the first one is probably anger, although it has been suggested that this is a description of the tyrant and belongs in the gap after 2.44.

[85] The text of this fragment is corrupt.

[86] The location of this fragment is uncertain (the book number is missing), but it seems to belong in the catalogue of passions.

[87] This fragment is generally placed at 2.41; Büchner suggested placing it after 2.69, but in fact the combination of constitutional and psychological theory that it contains makes it fit better as part of the conclusion of 2.68.

ing and concordant. So too the state, through the reasoned balance of the highest and the lowest and the intervening orders, is harmonious in the concord of very different people. What musicians call harmony with regard to song is concord in the state, the tightest and the best bond of safety in every republic; and that concord can never exist without justice.[88]

[probably eleven leaves missing]

[69c] Augustine, *City of God* 2.21: *And when Scipio had spoken more broadly and fully on this topic, the value of justice for the state and the damage caused by its absence, Philus (one of the participants in the discussion) took up the subject and demanded that it be treated more thoroughly and that more should be said about justice because of the common belief that a republic cannot be ruled without injustice.*[89]

[3.11b] . . . justice looks outward; it is entirely directed abroad and stands out (+ Nonius 373.30)[90]

[3.11c] . . . the virtue which beyond all others is completely devoted to and concerned with the interests of others (+ Nonius 299.30)

[3.9a] . . . to give an answer to Carneades, who often mocks the noblest causes through his vicious cleverness (+ Nonius 263.8)[91]

[70] PHILUS: * filled with justice.

SCIPIO: I agree completely, and I state to you that we should consider all that has been said so far about the commonwealth to be as nothing, and that we can go no further without establishing not only the falseness of the statement that the commonwealth cannot function without injustice but also the profound truth of the idea that the commonwealth cannot possibly function without justice. But if you agree, we have said enough for one day, and we should postpone what is left (and there is quite a lot) until tomorrow.

When everyone agreed, they brought the day's discussion to a close.

[88] The last part of this paragraph is preserved only by Augustine, *City of God* 2.21. The fragment placed here by Ziegler is of doubtful authenticity and will be found at the end of Book 2.

[89] The remainder of Augustine's summary of the end of Book 2 corresponds to 2.70 below.

[90] This and the following two fragments have frequently been placed in Book 3 despite explicit attribution to Book 2; they make sense as part of the preparation for the debate on justice that is to follow.

[91] Carneades' speeches in 155 BCE for and against justice are the model for the debate in Book 3; for a description see 3.9b below.

Doubtful fragment

[**69b**] . . . the lyre should be struck gently and calmly, not with violence and force. (Ossolinski MS 458)[92]

[92] This fragment and another (found in this translation at the end of Book 4) are attested only in nineteenth-century quotations by A. Bielowski from lost manuscripts in Poland; they are of very dubious authenticity.

Book 3

Augustine, *City of God* 2.21:[1] *The discussion of this topic was put off to the next day, when it was the subject of a heated debate in Book 3. Philus himself undertook to give the argument of those who believe that the conduct of public affairs is impossible without injustice, while making a strong plea not to be taken to believe this himself. He gave a careful presentation of the case of injustice against justice: he tried to show by plausible arguments and examples that the former is useful to the state, while the latter is useless. Then Laelius at the request of everyone took up the defense of justice and asserted as strongly as possible that there is nothing so dangerous to a state as injustice, and that in fact a state cannot exist or be maintained without a high degree of justice.*

When this subject had been discussed to everyone's satisfaction, Scipio returned to the previous topic; he recalled and commended his brief definition of the commonwealth, in which he had said that it was the concern of the people and that the people was not any large assemblage, but an assemblage associated with one another by agreement on law and community of interest.[2] *He then showed how useful definitions are in argument, and from these definitions of his he drew the conclusion that a commonwealth (that is the concern of the people) then truly exists when its affairs are conducted well and justly, whether by a single king, or by a few aristocrats, or by the people as a whole. But when there is an unjust king (whom in the manner of the Greeks he called a tyrant) or unjust aristocrats (whose conspiracy he called a faction), or when the people itself is unjust – and here he was not able to find*

[1] This summary of Book 3 (unnumbered in Ziegler) does not include the preface and is sometimes placed after 3.7. [2] Cf. 1.39.

any familiar name other than to call the people itself a tyrant – then there is not a flawed commonwealth, as had been argued on the previous day, but (the logical conclusion from his definitions) no commonwealth at all: there is no "concern of the people" when a tyrant or a faction has seized hold of it, nor is the people itself still a people if it is unjust, because it is no longer a multitude associated with one another by agreement on law and community of interest, as the people had been defined.

[four leaves missing]

[**1a**] Augustine, *Against Julianus 4.12.60: In the third book of his* Commonwealth *Cicero likewise says* that man is sent out into life by nature not as if by a mother but as if by a stepmother: his body is naked, frail, and weak; his spirit is troubled by distress, groveling in times of fear, weak in the face of toil, prone to lust; but there is still within him a sort of smothered divine spark of genius and of mental capacity.[3]

[**3**] * <Human reason overcame> slowness through the use of vehicles, and after encountering the crude and confused sounds with disorganized noises made by humans, it divided and organized them; and by attaching words, like some kind of signs, to things, it bound together through the pleasing mutual bond of language men who had previously been isolated. A similar act of reason invented a few marks by which the apparently infinite sounds of the voice were expressed by signs through which conversations could be held with absent people and indications of desires and memorials of past events be preserved. To this was added number, something not only necessary for life but also the one unchanging and eternal thing; number was first to direct our gaze up to the sky, to make us observe the motions of the stars purposefully, and through the calculation of nights and days *[4]

[four leaves missing]

[**4**] * whose minds raised themselves higher, and were able to create or invent something worthy of the gift (as I said before) of the gods. Therefore we should consider those who have discussed the proper conduct of human life to be great men (as indeed they are); let them be

[3] Another paraphrase of the same passage appears in Ambrose, *On the death of Satyrus* 2.29 [Ziegler 1b]: *What is more wretched than we are? We are tossed out into this life like people stripped naked, with weak bodies, treacherous hearts, and a feeble spirit; we are worried by cares, lazy in the face of toil, prone to pleasures.* Ziegler includes here also a passage from Lactantius which is less likely to come from this passage; here it is printed at the end of Book 3.

[4] There are similar arguments repeatedly in Balbus' exposition of Stoic beliefs in *On the Nature of the Gods* Book 2, e.g. at 153.

considered learned men, masters of truth and virtue. But this too should be something deserving of considerable respect (as in fact it is): the study of civil society and the organization of peoples – whether it was discovered by men who had experience in the range of forms of commonwealth, or was the object of study in the leisure time of philosophers – a study which brings about in good minds now, as often in the past, the development of an incredible, divine virtue.[5] **[5]** If anyone has thought to add learning and a fuller knowledge of affairs to the mental apparatus which he acquired through nature or civil institutions, such as the men who took part in the conversation recorded in this work, then everyone ought to consider them the best of all. What, after all, can be more glorious than the conjunction of practical experience in great affairs of state with the knowledge of these arts acquired through study and learning? What can be imagined more perfect than Publius Scipio or Gaius Laelius or Lucius Philus? In order to achieve the highest glory of great men, they added to the traditional knowledge of their own ancestors the imported philosophical knowledge of the Socratic school. **[6a]** The person who has had the will and capacity to acquire both – that is, ancestral institutions and philosophical learning – is the one who I think has done everything deserving of praise. But if it should be necessary to choose one path of learning or the other, even if the tranquil pattern of life devoted to study and learning may seem more blessed, nevertheless civic life is both more praiseworthy and more glorious: this life endows the greatest men with honor, such as Manius Curius, "whom no one could overcome with either steel or gold,"[6] or *

[three leaves missing]

[6b] Seneca, *Moral Letters* 108.33: *Then he [the grammarian] gathers verses by Ennius, and particularly those written about Africanus:*[7] "to whom no one, neither citizen nor enemy, will be able to render full reward for his actions." *From this he said that he understood that the word* ops *in early times means not only "aid" but "action."*

[7] * great wisdom existed, but there was this difference between the two approaches, that one group cultivated the principles of nature through words and through learning, the other through institutions and laws. This single city has brought forth many, if not philosophers (since

5 This passage continues and elaborates the argument of the preface to Book 1; see in particular 1.3, 12.

6 Ennius, *Annals* 209 Warmington.

7 Ennius, *Epigrams* 5–6 Warmington. Scipio Africanus, grandfather of Scipio Aemilianus and conqueror of Hannibal in the Second Punic War.

this term is used so narrowly by them),[8] then at least men worthy of the greatest praise, because they cultivated the precepts and discoveries of the philosophers. And if we take the praiseworthy states which exist and have existed (since the foundation of a state capable of lasting for a long time takes greater judgment than anything in the world), and if we count one person to each state, then how great a multitude we will find of excellent men! If in Italy we consider Latium, or the Sabine and Volscian nations, or Samnium, Etruria, and Magna Graecia, and add to them the Assyrians, Persians, Carthaginians, if these *

[six leaves missing]

[8] * PHILUS: What a marvelous case you give me, asking me to undertake the defense of wickedness.

LAELIUS: As if you need to worry about seeming to believe the usual arguments against justice that you speak! You are yourself almost the only true example of ancient honesty and faith; and we know your custom of speaking on both sides of the question in order to arrive at the truth most easily.[9]

PHILUS: Oh well, I will go along with you and cover myself with filth deliberately. If people who look for gold don't object to it, then we who are searching for justice, something far more valuable than all the gold in the world, should not shirk any difficulty.[10] But I wish that, just as I will use someone else's arguments, I could use someone else's mouth too! As it is, Lucius Furius Philus is compelled to say things that Carneades, a Greek and one accustomed <to expressing> whatever seemed useful *

[two leaves missing]

[9b] Lactantius, *Inst.* 5.14.3–5: *Anyone who does not know about Carneades the Academic philosopher – his power in speaking, his eloquence, his sharpness – can learn about him from the praise of Cicero or of Lucilius, in whose writings Neptune in discoursing on a very difficult subject shows that it could not be explained "not even if Hell should send back Carneades himself."*[11] *When Carneades was sent as an ambassador of the Athenians to Rome, he gave an eloquent speech about justice in the hearing of Galba and Cato the*

8 C. uses *sapiens* to translate the Greek *philosophos*; the model for such wise men is the Seven Sages; see above, 1.12.

9 Speaking on both sides of a question with equal conviction was the basic method used by academic skeptics (including Carneades) to prove to their hearers and to themselves the impossibility of certain knowledge of anything.

10 Cf. Plato, *Republic* 1.336e.

11 Lucilius, fr. 35 Warmington. It is quite possible that C. was Lactantius' source for the quotation.

Censor, the greatest orators of the time. But on the next day Carneades overturned his own speech with one arguing the opposite, and destroyed the justice which he had praised on the day before. He did not employ the seriousness of a philosopher (whose opinion ought to be fixed and stable) but rather the style of the oratorical exercise of arguing on both sides of a question; he did this regularly in order to be able to refute his opponents, whatever position they took. In Cicero Lucius Furius recalls the argument in which Carneades overturned justice; I think that he did so because he [Cicero] was discussing the commonwealth in order to introduce the defense and praise of justice, without which he thought that a commonwealth could not be administered. Carneades on the other hand, in order to refute Aristotle and Plato the defenders of justice, in his first speech gathered all the arguments used on behalf of justice so that he could overturn them, as he did.

[21a] Lactantius, *Inst.* 5.16.2–3: *Therefore Carneades, because the assertions of the philosophers were weak, had the daring to refute them, because he understood that they could be refuted. The gist of his argument was as follows:* that men ordain laws for themselves in accordance with utility, that is to say they vary in accordance with customs and have frequently been altered by the same people in accordance with the times; there is no such thing as natural law. All men and all other animate creatures are drawn to their own utility under the guidance of nature; and furthermore, either there is no justice at all, or if there is any, it is the highest stupidity, since it would harm itself in looking after the interest of others.

[12] PHILUS: * in order to find and defend <justice>, the other filled four quite large books about justice itself.[12] I looked for nothing grand or magnificent from Chrysippus, who speaks in his own fashion, looking at everything in terms of the significance of words, not the substance of things. It was the task of those heroes to take that virtue, which is the one that is most generous and liberal (if it exists at all), which loves all people more than itself, which is born for others rather than for itself,[13] and to rouse it up from where it was lying and to place it on the divine throne not far from wisdom. **[13]** They lacked neither the will – what other plan or reason for writing did they have? – nor the genius, in which they stood above everyone; but the case itself overcame their will and their capacities. The justice we are considering is something civil and not natural at all. If it were natural, then – like hot and cold and bitter and sweet – just and unjust things would be the same for everyone.

[12] The damaged first clause describes Plato's *Republic*; the second, Aristotle's lost dialogue *On Justice*.

[13] Cf. Aristotle, *Nicomachean Ethics* 5.1 1130a2–13.

[14] But now, if someone "riding on a chariot of winged snakes" (to use Pacuvius' phrase)[14] were able to look down on and inspect the many varied races and cities, he would see first among the Egyptians, the most uncorrupted of races, which has consigned to writing the memory of many generations and events, that a bull is considered a god, which the Egyptians name Apis, and that many other monstrosities and creatures of every sort have been consecrated as gods by this same people. Then in Greece (as here), that magnificent temples have been consecrated with human statues, which the Persians thought sacrilegious: for that one reason, Xerxes is said to have ordered the temples of the Athenians to be burned, because he thought that it was sinful for the gods, whose home is this whole world, to be shut in by walls. [15] Later on, Philip (who planned it) and Alexander (who waged it) used this excuse for making war on the Persians, namely to avenge the shrines of Greece – shrines which the Greeks did not think should even be rebuilt, so that their descendants would have before their eyes eternal evidence of the crime of the Persians. How many people, like the Taurians in the Black Sea, like Busiris the king of Egypt, like the Gauls and the Carthaginians, have thought it both pious and highly pleasing to the immortal gods to sacrifice human beings! Human customs are so far apart that the Cretans and the Aetolians think it honorable to be a bandit, and that the Lacedaemonians asserted that all territory belonged to them which they could touch with a spear. The Athenians used to swear a public oath that all land was theirs that bore either olives or grain; the Gauls think it disgraceful to raise crops with their own hands, and so they harvest others' fields under arms. [16] We ourselves, the most just of peoples, do not permit the tribes on the other side of the Alps to grow olives and vines, so that our olive groves and vineyards may be more valuable. In so doing, we are said to behave with prudence but not with justice: this will show you the difference between fairness and wisdom. Even Lycurgus, the discoverer of the best laws and the most equitable justice, entrusted the lands of the rich to be cultivated by the common people as if they were slaves.

[17] If I wished to list the types of law, institutions, customs, and behaviors not only in their varieties among the races of the world but in one city, even in this one, I would show that they were changed a thousand times, so that our friend Manilius here, the interpreter of the

[14] *Plays* fr. 242 Warmington.

law, would recognize one set of laws now concerning legacies and inheritances of women, but when he was a young man used to recognize something quite different before the passage of the Voconian Law.[15] And that law itself, which was passed in the interest of men's utility, is highly injurious to women. Why should a woman not have money? Why should she be heir to a Vestal Virgin but not to her own mother? Why, if the point was to set a limit to women's wealth, could the daughter of Publius Crassus, if she were an only child, receive a million sesterces without breaking the law, while my daughter could not have three hundred thousand? *

[one leaf missing]

[18] * would have established laws for us, and we would all use the same, and the same people would not use now one set, now another.

But I ask you, if it is the part of a just and good man to obey the laws, which ones should he obey? Whatever there are at a given moment? But virtue does not allow inconsistency, nor does nature permit variation; our laws are observed because of punishments, not because of our justice. Justice, therefore, is not natural at all; and that leads to the conclusion that no people is naturally just. Or do they say that there is variation in laws, but that good men naturally follow true justice, not that which is thought to be justice? It is the part of a good and just man to give to each person what is worthy of him.[16] [19] Well then, what shall we first give to the dumb beasts? It was no average men, but the greatest and most learned, Pythagoras and Empedocles, who claimed that one justice applied to all animate beings, and they assert that inexpiable penalties await those who harm an animal. Therefore it is a crime to harm a beast, and the person who wants <to avoid> this crime *

[nine leaves missing]

[23] PHILUS:[17] * all those who have the power of life and death over a people are tyrants, but they prefer themselves to be called kings, using

[15] The Voconian Law of 169 BCE prohibited wealthy men from naming women as heirs but allowed them to leave legacies to women up to a certain percentage of the estate. The difference between what Crassus' daughter and Philus' can receive is a function of the value of their estates. Vestal Virgins (considered to be men for legal purposes) had the right both to make wills and to inherit.

[16] Distributive justice; cf. Plato, *Republic* 1.331e, and Aristotle, *Nicomachean Ethics* 5, particularly 5.3 1131a10–b24.

[17] There is clearly a gap in the argument here: the argument against carnivorousness will have ended by showing that it is utility rather than altruism that governs human behavior; in what follows, Philus is showing that the rule applies to states as much as to individuals and that governments are based on the self-interest of the ruling class.

the title of highest Jupiter.[18] Furthermore, when certain individuals because of their wealth or family or other resources control the commonwealth, it is a faction, but they call themselves "the best people."[19] And if the people has the greatest power and everything is done by its decision, that is called liberty but is in fact license. But when each fears another, both individuals and classes, then because no one is sure of himself, there is a kind of bargain made between the people and the magnates, and out of this arises that combined form of state which Scipio praised; and indeed neither nature nor our wishes is the mother of justice: weakness is. When it is necessary to make a choice among three possibilities, to do injury and not receive it, both to do it and to receive it, or neither, the best is to act without penalty if you can, the second best is neither to do nor to receive injury, and far the worst is always to be fighting in the arena both giving and receiving injuries.[20] Therefore those who can achieve the first *

[four leaves missing]

[**20a**] Lactantius, *Inst.* 6.9.2–4:[21] *If someone ignorant of divine law wishes to follow justice, he will embrace the laws of his own people as if they were true justice, but in fact it was utility rather than justice that discovered them. Why have different and various laws been established throughout the world, if not because each people ordained for itself what it thought useful for its own affairs? The Roman people teaches us the distance between utility and justice: by declaring war through the fetials and by causing injury under the guise of law, by constantly desiring and seizing others' property, they obtained possession of the entire world.*

[**24b**] PHILUS: * remember. Wisdom orders us to increase our resources, to enlarge our wealth, to extend our boundaries – what else is the reason for the praise carved on the tombs of the greatest generals that "he extended the boundaries of the empire" if something had not been added from others' territory? – to rule over as many people as possible, to enjoy pleasures, to be powerful, to rule, to be a lord; but justice instructs us to spare everyone, to look after the interests of the human race, to render to each his own, to keep hands off things that are sacred or public or belong to someone else. What will be the result if you obey wisdom? Wealth, power, resources, offices, commands, rule, whether by individuals or

[18] Compare 1.50 above. [19] Compare 1.51–52 above.

[20] Cf. Plato, *Republic* 2.358e–359b.

[21] This passage presumably summarizes part of Philus' argument, although the reference to "divine law" shows Lactantius' different perspective.

nations. But since we are talking about the commonwealth, and since things that are done in public are more perspicuous, and since the reasoning underlying law is the same for both, I think that I should speak about the wisdom of nations. And to set other peoples aside: our own people, whose history from the beginning Africanus discussed in yesterday's conversation, whose rule now controls the whole world – do you think that it was through justice or wisdom that it grew from a tiny nation to the <greatest> of all? *

[ten leaves missing]

[**24a**] For when he was asked what crime drove him to ravage the seas with one galley, he replied, "the same one that drove you to ravage the whole world." [Nonius 125.12, 318.18, 534.15][22]

[**21b**] Lactantius, *Inst.* 5.16.4: *He made use of the following arguments:* All successful imperial powers, including the Romans themselves who have gained possession of the entire world, if they should wish to be just – that is to say to return property that belongs to others – would have to go back to living in huts and languishing in want and wretchedness.[23]

[**25**] PHILUS: * except the Arcadians and Athenians; and in my opinion, because they were afraid that at some time this injunction of justice would be served on them, they pretended that they arose from the earth like these mice from the field.[24]

[**26**] The reply to these arguments comes first from those who give the least-dishonest response;[25] they have all the more weight in this case because in the search for a good man, whom we want to be both open and straightforward, they are not tricky or artificial or deceitful in their arguments. They deny that the wise man is good because goodness and justice are automatically or in themselves pleasing to him, but because the life of good men is one free from fear, care, worry and danger, while

[22] The same anecdote about Alexander the Great and the pirate is also taken from C. by Augustine, *City of God* 4.4.

[23] Similarly in Lactantius, *Epitome* 51(56).3 [not in Ziegler]: "If all the peoples who hold empires, including the Romans themselves who control the whole world, should wish to follow justice and return to everyone the possessions which they have taken through force of arms, they would return to huts and to poverty. If they did that, one would have to judge that they were just but stupid in their effort to help others by harming themselves." A briefer summary in Augustine, *City of God* 19.21 (below, 3.36).

[24] Both the Arcadians and the Athenians claimed to be autochthonous and are hence (in this argument) the only people who can claim original possession of their land. The argument here probably alludes to Roman property law: ownership (as opposed to possession) can only be proven by tracing title back to an original mode of acquisition – known as *probatio diabolica* (the Devil's proof) in the Middle Ages because of its virtual impossibility.

[25] The Epicureans.

there is always some uneasiness clinging to the minds of the wicked, and they always have before their eyes the prospect of trials and torture: there is no advantage or reward derived from injustice that is so great that you should always be afraid, that you should always think that some penalty or loss is in the offing or hanging over you *

[four leaves missing]

[29] Lactantius, *Inst.* 5.16.5–13: *Then he*[26] *moved from generalities to particulars:* "If a good man," *he said*, "has a fugitive slave or an unhealthy and contaminated house, and he alone knows of these defects, and advertises them for sale, will he admit that he is selling a fugitive slave or a contaminated house, or will he conceal it from the buyer? If he admits it, he will be judged to be good because he is not deceptive, but he will still be judged stupid, because he will sell it at a low price or not at all. If he conceals it, he will be intelligent in looking after his property, but he will also be wicked, because he is deceptive. Again: if he finds someone who thinks that he is selling brass when it is in fact gold, or lead, when it is really silver, will he keep quiet to buy it at a low price, or will he reveal it and pay a high price? It seems obviously stupid to prefer to pay the high price." *He wanted it to be understood from this that the just and good man is stupid, and the smart one is wicked. And yet it is possible for men to be content with poverty without any danger.*

[30] *Therefore, he turned to larger issues, in which no one could be just without risk to his life. He said:* "It is just not to kill a man, and not to lay hold of someone else's property. So what will the just man do if he happens to be shipwrecked, and a weaker man has got hold of a plank? Won't he push him off and get on himself and use it to escape – especially since there are no witnesses in the middle of the ocean? If he is smart, he will do it: he will have to die if he doesn't, and if he prefers to die rather than lift a hand against someone else, then he will be just but stupid in losing his own life while sparing another's. Likewise, if in battle his own side is routed and the enemy is pursuing, and the just man gets hold of a wounded man on a horse, will he spare him at the cost of his own death, or will he knock him off the horse so that he can escape the enemy himself? If he does so he is smart but wicked, and if he doesn't he is just but stupid." [31] *And so, after dividing justice into two parts, one civil and the other natural, he overturned both by showing that what is called civil justice is wisdom but not justice, while natural justice is indeed justice but is*

[26] Carneades. The quotation from Lactantius extends through 31.

unwise. These arguments are clever and venomous, and Cicero could not refute them: for when he made Laelius reply to Furius and speak on behalf of justice, he left these arguments unanswered and avoided them like a trap, with the result that Laelius appears to have defended not natural justice, which had been charged with stupidity, but civil justice, which Furius had admitted to be wisdom but shown to be unjust.[27]

[38a] Cicero, *On the Supreme Good and Evil* 2.59:[28] If you knew, said Carneades, that a poisonous snake was hiding somewhere and that an incautious person from whose death you would profit was about to sit on top of it, you would behave wickedly if you did not warn him not to sit down, but you would not be punished for it: who could prove that you knew?

[27] PHILUS:[29] I ask you: if there should be two people, of whom one is the best of men, the fairest, the most just, the most honorable, and the other of outstanding criminality and boldness; and if the state should be so wrong as to think the good man to be wicked, criminal, and evil, and to consider the wicked man to be utterly honorable and honest; and that as a result of this opinion of all the citizens the good man should be harassed and attacked, his hands cut off and his eyes put out – that he should be condemned, put in chains, tortured, and sent into exile in poverty, so that in strict law he should appear to all to be the most wretched of men, while on the other hand the wicked man should be praised, cultivated, and cherished by all, that all offices and powers and wealth should be conferred on him, and that he be considered by universal belief to be the best of men and worthy of every good thing – what person will ever be so crazy as to have any doubt as to which he would prefer to be?

[28] What applies to individuals also applies to nations: there is no state so stupid that it would not prefer to rule unjustly than to be enslaved justly. I will not go far for proof: when I was consul, I was in charge of the investigation of the Numantine treaty, and you were in my council.[30] Who did not know that Quintus Pompeius had made a treaty

[27] Lactantius' inference about Laelius' speech is – as his own quotations from it show – wrong: he is unwilling to acknowledge a non-Christian defense of natural justice.

[28] The second half of this quotation concerns Laelius' speech and appears on p. 70.

[29] Sect. 27 is quoted by Lactantius, *Inst.* 5.12.5–6; the second half of the section is preserved in the palimpsest as well. The argument is drawn from Plato, *Republic* 2.361a–d.

[30] After a particularly disastrous battle in the war against Numantia in 137, the consul Hostilius Mancinus made a disadvantageous treaty to save his army. The senate, at Scipio's suggestion, repudiated the treaty; Mancinus was, with his own approval, turned over to the Numantines as compensation. Quintus Pompeius had made a similar treaty after being defeated in 140 but repudiated it himself with the senate's approval. Many

and that Mancinus was in the same situation? One of them, an extraordinarily good man, spoke in favor of the bill that I proposed on the advice of the senate, and the other defended himself as strongly as possible. If you are looking for decency, honor, and trustworthiness, Mancinus had them; but if you want calculation, planning, and prudence, Pompeius stands out. Which *

[a large and uncertain amount is missing; the next leaf begins at 41]

[**32b**] But he is certainly not to be listened to by our young people: if his beliefs match what he says, he is a terrible man; if not (as I prefer to believe), his speech is still appalling. [+Nonius 324.15 + 323.18]

[**32a**] It would not disturb me, Laelius, if I did not think that these people desired it, and if I did not myself want you to take some part in our conversation, especially as you said yourself yesterday that we would have too much of your speaking. That is impossible, and we all ask that you not give us too little. [Aulus Gellius, *Attic Nights* 1.22.8][31]

[**39a**] Cicero, *Letters to Atticus* 7.2.4: *I am happy that you are enjoying your little daughter and that you approve of the idea that love of one's children is something natural.* In fact, if that is not true, then there can be no natural link between one man and another, and if that is removed all social bonds are destroyed. "Just fine!" says Carneades in a disgusting fashion; but he is smarter than our friend Lucius and Patro.[32] They make self-interest the only standard and think that nothing is done for someone else's sake; and in saying that a man ought to be good in order to avoid trouble, not because it is naturally right, they don't recognize that they are speaking of a clever person, not about a good man. *But all this, I think, is to be found in the book which you give me heart by praising.*[33]

[**38a**] Cicero, *On the Supreme Good and Evil* 2.59: It is clear that if equity, faith, and justice do not derive from nature, and if all these things are measured by utility, then it is impossible to find any good man. *Laelius said quite enough on this score in* On the Commonwealth.

[**38b**] Cicero, *Letters to Atticus* 10.4.4: *And if, as you remind me, I stated correctly in that book* that there is nothing good except what is honorable, and nothing bad except what is disgraceful . . .

[**39b**] In this respect I agree that justice that is troubled and in danger is not appropriate to a philosopher. [Priscian 2.399.13K]

Romans thought this procedure dishonorable; the Numantines were also not amused.

31 Gellius wrongly assigns the quotation to Book 2.

32 Both Epicureans.

33 This and the next two quotations appear to give the starting point of Laelius' argument on behalf of justice.

[40b] Augustine, *City of God* 22.4: *When Cicero asserted that Hercules and Romulus became gods, he said:* "It was not their bodies that were taken up to the sky; nature would not permit what is derived from the earth to stay anywhere but on the earth."

[40a3] What riches will you put in the path of this man? What military commands? What kingdoms? Such things he believes to be human, but judges his own goods to be divine.[34] [+ Lactantius, *Inst.* 5.18.4]

[40d] I suppose that Fabricius did not have access to the generosity of Pyrrhus, or Curius to the wealth of the Samnites.[35] [+ Nonius 132.17]

[40e] We have heard from our good friend Cato himself that when he went to his home in the Sabine country he used to go to see his [sc. Curius'] hearth – where he sat and rejected the gifts of the Samnites, once his enemies and later his clients. [+ Nonius 522.26]

[40a1–2, 4–5] Virtue desires honor, and virtue has no other reward. But it accepts this reward without bother and does not demand it harshly. And if either the ingratitude of the whole people or the hostility of many or powerful enemies despoil virtue of its rewards, then it has many consolations to give it pleasure, and it sustains itself above all by its own dignity. [+ Lactantius, *Inst.* 5.18.4, 6, 8][36]

[3 inc. 5] . . . unless someone wants to raise up[37] Mount Athos from its base as a monument. But what Athos or Olympus is big enough . . . [+ Priscian 2.255.9K]

[33] True law is right reason, consonant with nature, spread through all people. It is constant and eternal; it summons to duty by its orders, it deters from crime by its prohibitions.[38] Its orders and prohibitions to good people are never given in vain; but it does not move the wicked by these orders or prohibitions. It is wrong to pass laws obviating this law; it is not permitted to abrogate any of it; it cannot be totally repealed. We cannot be released from this law by the senate or the people, and it needs no exegete or interpreter like Sextus Aelius. There will not be one law at Rome and another at Athens, one now and another later; but all nations at all times will be bound by this one eternal and unchangeable law, and the god will be the one common master and general (so to speak) of all

[34] Compare Scipio's speech at 1.26–29.

[35] Generals of the early Roman republic who were not attracted by the wealth of their opponents.

[36] Lactantius breaks up a single passage of C. in the course of his discussion of it. His own comments are omitted here. For the ideas, compare C.'s comments on his own exile at 1.7 above.

[37] Text uncertain.

[38] The definition of law here is Stoic; it is elaborated more fully in *On the Laws* 1.22ff.

people. He is the author, expounder, and mover of this law; and the person who does not obey it will be in exile from himself. Insofar as he scorns his nature as a human being, by this very fact he will pay the greatest penalty, even if he escapes all the other things that are generally recognized as punishments. [+ Lactantius, *Inst.* 6.8.6–9]

[4.1c] There is no one who would not rather die than be transformed into the shape of an animal while still having a human mind; all the more miserable is it to have a beast's mind in a human body. That seems to me as much worse as the mind is more noble than the body. [Lactantius, *Inst.* 5.11.2]

[3 inc. 4] The notorious Sardanapalus, much uglier in his vices than in his name. [+ Scholiast on Juvenal 10.362]

He [Sardanapalus] ordered this to be carved on his tomb. [Arusianus Messius 7.487.16K][39]

Cicero, *Tusculan Disputations* 5.105: . . . from this we can recognize the mistake of Sardanapalus, the wealthy king of Syria. He ordered this to be carved on his tomb: "I possess all the things I have eaten and all that my sated lust has enjoyed; the many other wonderful things lie abandoned." What else, says Aristotle, would you carve on the tomb of a cow rather than a man?

[4.1d] Augustine, *Against Julianus* 4.12.59: He did not think that what is "good" for a ram is good for Publius Africanus.

[36] Augustine, *City of God* 19.21: *There is a very strong and vigorous argument in* On the Commonwealth *against injustice on behalf of justice.* In the earlier argument, for injustice against justice, it was said that a commonwealth could not survive and grow without injustice; and the strongest statement was that it is unjust for men to be enslaved to masters. But if an imperial state, a great commonwealth, does not subscribe to that injustice, then it cannot rule over provinces.[40] The answer made by justice is that empire is just because slavery is useful for such men and that when it is rightly done, it is done on their behalf, that is, when the right to do injury is taken away from wicked people: the conquered will be better off, because they would be worse off if they had not been conquered. In order to bolster this reasoning, Cicero supplies a

[39] This and the following fragment are omitted by Ziegler but clearly belong here. The presence of the introductory formula in this fragment makes it clear that C. quoted the epitaph itself here as well as in the later *Tusculan Disputations*, and it is likely that the context in the two works was very similar. The example of Sardanapalus was taken from Aristotle's lost *Protrepticus*.

[40] A summary of part of Philus' argument above, 3.20a and 3.21b.

noble illustration drawn from nature, and says:[41] "Do we not see that the best people are given the right to rule by nature herself, with the greatest benefit to the weak? Why then does god rule over man, the mind over the body, reason over desire, anger, and the other flawed portions of the mind?"[42]

[37b] There is a kind of unjust slavery when people who could be independent belong to someone else; but when they are slaves . . . [43]
[+ Nonius 109.2]

[37a] The different types of rule and slavery must be recognized. The mind is said to rule over the body, and is also said to rule over desire; but it rules the body the way a king rules his subjects or a parent his children, while it rules desire the way a master rules his slaves, in that it subdues and controls it. The rule of kings and generals and magistrates and fathers and nations directs their citizens and allies in the same way that the mind rules bodies, while masters subdue their slaves in the same way that the best part of the mind, wisdom, subdues the flawed and weak parts of that same mind, such as desires, anger, and other disturbances.[44]
[+ Augustine, *Against Julianus* 4.12.61]

Augustine, *City of God* 21.11:[45] *Cicero writes that there are eight legal forms of punishment:* fines, chains, whipping, compensation in kind, loss of status, exile, death, and slavery.

[34a] Augustine, *City of God* 22.6: *In the third book of Cicero's* On the Commonwealth, *unless I am mistaken, it is argued* that no war is undertaken by a good state except on behalf of good faith or for safety.

[35a] Isidore, *Etymologies* 18.1.2–3: *There are four types of war: just, unjust, civil, and more than civil.*[46] *A just war is one that is first declared and then waged to recover stolen property or to fight off enemies. An unjust war is one that is started out of madness rather than for a legitimate cause. About this Cicero says in* On the Commonwealth: "Those wars are unjust which are undertaken without cause. For aside from vengeance or for the sake of fighting off enemies no just war can be waged." *And a little later he adds:* "No war is considered just unless it is announced and declared and unless it involves recovery of property."

[41] Part of the quotation is preserved only by Augustine's fuller citation at *Against Julianus* 4.12.61. [42] Compare the discussion of reason and the passions above at 2.67–68.

[43] Compare the argument for natural slavery at Aristotle, *Politics* 1.5–6 1254a17–1255b15.

[44] A refinement of the argument in favor of monarchy above at 1.59–60.

[45] Also in Isidore 5.27.4; not included by Ziegler.

[46] "More than civil" is an allusion to the opening words of Lucan's first-century-CE epic on the Roman Civil War: he refers to war between relatives.

[35b] But our nation has gained control of the entire world through defending its allies [+ Nonius 498.16]

[34b] Augustine, *City of God* 22.6: *What he means by "safety,"*[47] *or what safety he wants to be understood, he shows elsewhere:* "But many individuals escape by a speedy death from these punishments which are felt by even the most stupid of people – want, exile, chains, and whips. For states, however, death itself *is* the punishment, death, which frees individuals from punishment. For the state ought so to be established as to be eternal, and therefore there is no natural death of a commonwealth as there is for a man, for whom death is not only necessary but at times desirable. When a state is removed, destroyed, extinguished, it is somehow similar (comparing small to great) to the death and collapse of the entire cosmos."

[41] LAELIUS: * . . . Asia . . . Tiberius Gracchus, who was persistent in support of the citizens but neglected the rights and treaties of the allies and the Latins.[48] If that license should become customary and spread more widely and should transform our power from right to might,[49] so that those who are now our willing subjects should be held by terror, even if those of us who are getting on in years have almost finished our watch, I am still concerned about our descendants and about the immortality of the commonwealth, which could be eternal if our life were conducted in accordance with ancestral laws and customs.[50]

[42a] When Laelius had finished speaking, all those present indicated their great delight with what he had said, but SCIPIO above all seemed positively ecstatic: You have defended many cases, Laelius, so well that I would not <hesitate to compare> you to our colleague Servius Galba,[51] whom during his lifetime you declared the best orator of all; and I would not even compare any of the Attic orators to you in sweetness or . . .

[six leaves missing]

[47] Cf. 34a above.

[48] The reference to Asia must allude to Tiberius' attempt to use the money derived from the bequest to Rome of his kingdom and fortune by Attalus III, the last king of Pergamum, in 133, to pay for the settlement of poor citizens on public land. As noncitizens (allies and Latins) were not eligible for these land distributions and were being expelled from public land which they had long used, Laelius' description is reasonably accurate. In 140 as consul, Laelius himself had proposed an agrarian law but had withdrawn the proposal because of senatorial opposition; he had not suggested the displacement of allies and Latins.

[49] The two Latin words, *ius* and *uis*, are visually almost identical.

[50] This fragment is preserved in the manuscript and was the very end of Laelius' speech. The next paragraph follows immediately.

[51] Galba was also a member of the college of augurs.

[**42b**] <He said> that he lacked two things, confidence and a good voice, which kept him from speaking to a crowd or in the forum.[52] [+Nonius 262.24]

[**42c**] The bull bellowed with the groans of the men shut inside it.[53] [Scholiast on Juvenal 6.468]

[**43**] SCIPIO: * bring back.[54] So who would call that state a "concern of the people," that is a commonwealth, at the time when everyone was crushed by the cruelty of one man and there was no single bond of law or agreement or association of the group, which is what is meant by "people"? The same applies to Syracuse. That great city, which Timaeus says is the greatest of the Greek cities and the most beautiful of all cities – its glorious citadel, its harbor that flows into the center of the town to the foundations of the city itself, its broad streets and porticoes and temples and walls – none of these made it any more of a commonwealth at the time when Dionysius controlled it: nothing belonged to the people, and the people itself belonged to a single man. And so where there is a tyrant, then it is wrong to say, as I did yesterday, that there is a flawed commonwealth: the logic of the argument compels me to say that it is no commonwealth at all.

[**44**] LAELIUS: You're completely right, and I see the direction of your argument.

SCIPIO: So you see that a state that is completely controlled by an oligarchy also cannot truly be called a commonwealth.

LAELIUS: That is my opinion.

SCIPIO: And you are right. What was the "concern of the Athenians" at the time when, after the great Peloponnesian War, the Thirty Tyrants ruled that city with great injustice?[55] Did the ancient glory of the city, or its beauty, or the theater, gymnasia, porticoes and gateways, or the citadel and the marvelous works of Phidias, or the great harbor of Piraeus make it into a commonwealth?

LAELIUS: Hardly, since there was no "concern of the people."

SCIPIO: What about at Rome, when the decemvirs ruled in their third

[52] The person referred to is the fourth-century Athenian rhetorician Isocrates.

[53] The sixth-century-BCE Sicilian tyrant Phalaris is said to have punished people by shutting them in a hollow bronze bull and heating it, so that their screams seemed to be the bellows of the bull.

[54] Scipio is still speaking, arguing that Agrigentum when ruled by Phalaris cannot be considered a true republic. "Bring back" may refer to the fact that Scipio, after the destruction of Carthage, returned the bull of Phalaris (which had been captured by the Carthaginians) to Agrigentum.

[55] See 1.44 above.

year without any right of appeal to the people, and liberty had lost its guarantees?[56]

LAELIUS: There was no "concern of the people" – and in fact the people acted to recover its "concerns."[57]

[45] SCIPIO: I come now to the third type, where there may seem to be difficulties. When everything is said to be done through the people and everything is said to be in the people's power, when the crowd punishes anyone it wants, when they snatch and seize and hold and scatter whatever they want: can you deny, Laelius, that that is a commonwealth? Everything belongs to the people, and we want the commonwealth to be the "concern of the people."

LAELIUS: But there is no state that I would more quickly deny to be a commonwealth than the one that is completely in the power of the crowd. If we did not consider Syracuse to be a commonwealth, or Agrigentum, or Athens, when there were tyrants, or here at Rome when there were decemvirs, then I don't see how the name "commonwealth" is any more appropriate to the rule of the crowd. In the first place, according to your excellent definition, there is no "people" unless it is bound by agreement in law, and that mob is as much a tyrant as if it were one person. It is all the more disgusting because there is nothing more awful than the monster which pretends to the appearance and name of the people. Nor is it right – since according to law the property of madmen is under the control of their relatives, because they no longer *[58]

[four leaves missing]

[46] SCIPIO: * <the same things> can be said <about aristocracy> as were said about monarchy, to show why it is a commonwealth and a "concern of the people."

MUMMIUS: Even more so. Kings have the appearance of masters, because they are single individuals; but nothing can be more fortunate than the commonwealth in which a number of good people are in control. Even so, I prefer monarchy to a free people; that is the third form that still remains to be examined, the worst commonwealth.

56 See 2.62–63 above.

57 It is impossible to translate the phrase *res populi* (rendered throughout as "concern of the people") adequately in sects. 44–45, as C. is playing on the meaning of *res* as property, arguing in part that in an illegitimate form of government (tyranny etc.) the people are deprived of their ownership of the physical possessions of the state as well as of participation in government and civic affairs.

58 Again, C. plays on the concept of *res publica* as the property of the people, here referring to the laws concerning administration of the property of lunatics.

[47] SCIPIO: I recognize your characteristic dislike of popular government, Spurius, and even though it can be tolerated more easily than you usually tolerate it, still I agree that it is the least admirable of these three forms. But I don't agree that optimates are preferable to a just king: if it is wisdom that is wanted to rule the commonwealth, then what difference does it make whether it is found in one person or in many?[59] But in such an argument we deceive ourselves. When we hear the name "the best people,"[60] nothing can possibly seem preferable: what can be imagined that is better than "the best"? But when someone mentions a king, unjust kings come to mind automatically. But we are not talking now about unjust kings when we examine the monarchic form of commonwealth itself. So think of Romulus or Pompilius or King Tullius, and then perhaps you won't feel so unhappy about that form of commonwealth.

[48] MUMMIUS: What praise do you have left to offer for the democratic commonwealth?

SCIPIO: Well, Spurius, we were recently together in Rhodes.[61] Do you think that the Rhodians have no commonwealth?

MUMMIUS: I think that they have one, and one not at all to be condemned.

SCIPIO: You are right. But if you remember, all the people were at one time plebeians, at another, senators, and they had an alternation of the months in which they would in turn play the role of the people or the senate. In either part they received a fee, and the same people, in the theater and in the senate house, were judges of capital crimes and all other offenses. <The senate> had as much power and importance as the multitude *

Uncertain location in Book 3

[**40c**] The bravest men never . . . bravery, energy, and endurance[62] [+Nonius 125.18]

[**3 Inc. 2**] They put their spirit at risk . . . they see what they think they are going to do.[63] [+Nonius 364.7]

[**3 Inc. 3**] The Phoenicians were the first, through their trading and

[59] A variation of Laelius' question to Scipio at 1.61.

[60] Optimates; see "Text and Translation" above.

[61] During Scipio's embassy to the east, probably in 140–139. The Rhodian constitution described here is not otherwise known.

[62] The meaning is uncertain, and there is a gap in the text. It perhaps belongs in Laelius' speech.

[63] The text of this fragment is corrupt.

merchandise, to import into Greece greed and grandiosity and insatiable desire for all things. [+ Nonius 431.11]

Doubtful fragment

[2] Lactantius, *On the Workmanship of God* 3.16–19 (excerpted): Although humans are born weak and frail, still they are safe from all mute creatures, and all those things which are born with greater strength, even if they are capable of enduring the forces of nature, cannot be safe from humans. (17) Thus reason gives more to the human than nature does to mute creatures, since in their case neither great strength nor strong bodies can stop them from being destroyed by us or subjected to our power. (19) Plato (I suppose to refute these ungrateful people) thanked nature for having been born human.[64]

[64] The argument of this passage is compatible with that of the preface to Book 3, but there is no clear evidence that it is taken from C.

Book 4

[1a] Lactantius, *On the Workmanship of God* 1.11–13: *Since reference has been made to the body and the mind, I will try to explain the rationale of each within the limited understanding of my feeble intelligence. I think it particularly important to take up this task, because Marcus Cicero, a man of outstanding talent, tried to do this in the fourth book of* On the Commonwealth *but compressed a vast amount of material within a narrow compass and only touched lightly on the main points. Indeed, he removes any excuse for not having dealt with the topic thoroughly by saying himself* "that he had lacked neither the will nor the effort": *in the first book of* On the Laws, *when he was equally cursory on the same topic, he says: "As far as I am concerned, Scipio dealt adequately with this subject in the book which you have read"* [1.27]. *Even so, he tried to give a fuller treatment of the same subject in the second book of* On the Nature of the Gods.[1]

[1b] And the mind itself, which foresees the future, also remembers what is past. [+Nonius 500.9]

[1e] . . . and finally that by its regular interposition it also creates the shade of night, something that is useful not only for the reckoning of days but for rest from toil. [+Nonius 234.14]

[1f] And since in the autumn the earth has opened for the sowing of crops, in the winter has loosened for preparing them, and in the ripeness of summer has softened some and parched others . . . [2] [+Nonius 343.20]

[2] SCIPIO: * goodwill; how fitting is the orderly distribution into

[1] The introductory argument of Book 4 is close to that of *On the Nature of the Gods* 2.133–53, both on the topic of body and mind and on nature's gifts to humans.

[2] The text of this fragment is somewhat uncertain (a season is missing), but the sense is clear.

ages and classes and the cavalry.[3] This last includes the votes of the senate, although too many people now foolishly want this useful custom to be eliminated in seeking a new form of dole through a bill on returning their horses.

[**3a**] Consider furthermore how wisely all the rest has been foreseen in order to promote the citizens' shared association in a happy and honorable way of life.[4] That is, indeed, the first cause of the creation of society, and it ought to be accomplished on the authority of the commonwealth in part through institutions and in part through laws.[5] In the first place, there is the childhood education of free citizens. The Greeks have employed a great deal of futile effort in this, and our friend Polybius blames our customs for negligence in this alone, that they had no desire to ordain a definite form of childhood education, established by law, publicly defined, or uniform.[6] For *

[two or four leaves missing]

[inc. 5]: Fannius had a difficult task in giving a eulogy for a boy: one has to praise expectations rather than accomplishments. [Servius on Virgil, *Aeneid* 6.875][7]

[**3b**] Servius on Virgil, *Aeneid* 5.546: . . . *according to Cicero, who says* that it was customary to give guardians to those setting out on military service, to direct them in their first year.

[**3c**] not only as at Sparta, where boys learn to snatch and steal [+ Nonius 20.12]

[**3d**] Servius on Virgil, *Aeneid* 10.325: *It is reported that the Cretans were unbridled as far as the love of boys was concerned, and this custom spread to the Spartans and to all Greece, to such an extent that Cicero in his book* On

3 The centuriate (Servian) constitution divided voters into property classes and age groups; "cavalry" refers to the 18 centuries of the knights. The reference to the bill on returning horses (translated very literally here) must mean a measure to remove senators from the centuries of the knights; it is usually thought to be a measure of Gaius Gracchus, Tiberius' younger brother, connected with his later judicial law of 123 which replaced senators with knights in criminal courts. What Scipio says, perhaps tendentiously, is that by depriving senators of the knights' publicly supported horses, the bill would reduce the tax on widows and orphans that paid for them; see 2.36 above for this practice.

4 C. here modifies the reason for the initial organization of society (1.39 above) in an Aristotelian direction; cf. *Politics* 1.1 1252b27–30.

5 The opposition between institutions (customary behavior) and laws (statute) is significant in Book 4: the former are, in C.'s view, greatly preferable to the latter.

6 C. rejects as futile the attempts of Greek philosophers (not least Plato) to prescribe a form of education that will produce good citizens. Where Polybius said this is uncertain.

7 The location of this fragment is very uncertain; it is placed here (following Büchner) because it concerns children.

the Commonwealth *says* that it was a source of disgrace to young men if they did not have lovers.

[4] SCIPIO: * for a grown man to appear naked. The foundations of the sense of shame[8] are indeed deeply set. The athletic exercises of young men in the gymnasia are really idiotic; the military exercises of the ephebes are trivial; and their gropings and love affairs are abandoned and free. I will set aside the people of Elis and of Thebes, where the amatory passions of free men are given complete license. Even the Spartans, in permitting everything except penetration in amatory relationships with young men, use a very slender barrier to prohibit this one exception: they allow them to embrace and to sleep together provided that they are separated by a cloak.

LAELIUS: I understand very well, Scipio, that in speaking of the Greek customs of which you disapprove you prefer to strive with the greatest nations rather than with your beloved Plato, whom you do not even mention, especially since *

[nothing more of Book 4 survives in the manuscript]

[5b] And our beloved Plato goes even further than Lycurgus: he ordains that everything should be held in common so that no citizen is capable of saying of anything that it is his very own. [+Nonius 362.11][9]

[5c] I <will treat Plato> in the same way as he treats Homer: he sends him out of the city which he invented for himself, decked in garlands and covered in perfumes. [+Nonius 308.38][10]

8 The concept of *uerecundia*, "sense of shame," is central to C.'s account of the mechanisms of morality; for a definition see 5.6 below with note.

9 Compare also [5a] Lactantius, *Epitome* 33(38).1–5: *His* [sc. Socrates'] *pupil Plato, whom Cicero calls a god among philosophers, who alone of all philosophers came close to the truth – still, since he had no knowledge of God, made in many respects such mistakes that no one ever wandered further from the truth; above all, because in his* Republic *he wanted everything to be held in common by all people. That is tolerable as far as property is concerned, even if it is unjust: the fact that because of his hard work one person has more than another ought not to harm him, nor should someone be helped if by his own fault he has less. But, as I say, this is in some ways tolerable. But are wives and children also to be held in common? Is there to be no recognition of blood relationships, no definite line of descent, no families or relationships or attachments, but everything is to be mixed and disordered as in flocks of animals? Is there to be no continence among men, no chasteness among women? What marital love can there be for either, among whom there is no sure and definite relationship? Who will be dutiful towards a father if he does not know who his father is? Who will love a son who he thinks is someone else's? He has even opened the senate house to women, he has allowed them military service and public office and commands. How great will be the unhappiness of that state in which women take over the functions of men!* It is unlikely that this passage is based on C. but it is probably parallel in some respects to C.'s argument here.

10 Cf. *Republic* 3.398a. This fragment is sometimes connected to the discussion of drama, but it clearly belongs with the discussion of Plato.

[**6c**] Nor indeed should some official be put in charge of women, of the type that is regularly instituted among the Greeks.[11] There should, however, be a censor to teach men how to supervise their wives. [Nonius 499.14]

[**1g**] in providing shepherds for flocks.[12] [+Nonius 159.16]

[**6d**] So great an effect does education in the sense of shame[13] have: all women refrain from alcohol. [+Nonius 5.10]

[**6e**] And the relatives of any women of bad reputation refused to offer her a kiss. [+Nonius 306.3]

[**6f**] Therefore impudence (*petulantia*) is derived from asking (*petendo*), and lewdness (*procacitas*) was named from seeking (*procando*), that is from demanding.[14] [+Nonius 23.17, 21]

[**6a**] The censor's judgment brings no disgrace to the condemned man other than embarrassment. And therefore, since that entire procedure is entirely involved with someone's good name, the punishment is called *ignominia*.[15] [+Nonius 24.5]

[**6b**] The state is said at first to have shuddered at their[16] severity. [+Nonius 423.4]

[**7f**] Augustine, *Epist.* 91.3: Take a brief look at that book *On the Commonwealth* . . . Look at it, I ask you, and observe the great praise bestowed there on frugality and self-control, on faith in the marital bond, on chaste, honorable, and upright character.[17]

[**7c**] Good faith (*fides*) seems to me to have its name because what is said happens (*fit*). [+Nonius 24.11]

[**7d**] In a citizen of rank and nobility, flattery, display, and ambition are a sign[18] of frivolity. [+Nonius 194.26]

[**7b**] Cicero, *On Duties* 2.60: *I am sparing in my criticism of theaters, porticoes, and new temples on Pompey's account; but the most learned men do not approve of them, including Panaetius himself, whom I have followed (but not translated) to a great extent in this work, and Demetrius of Phaleron, who criticizes Pericles, the first man of Greece, because he poured so much money*

[11] The *gunaikonomos*; cf. Aristotle, *Politics* 4.15 1300a4–8. After a digression on Plato, Scipio turns from the education of children to the supervision of women.

[12] Guardianship of women is being compared to shepherds' supervision of sheep; the next fragment shows that the comparison is rejected.

[13] *Verecundia*; for its importance cf. 5.6 below. The abstemiousness of Roman women is also found in Polybius 6.11a.4.

[14] These terms are the opposite of *uerecundia*.

[15] *Ignominia* is derived from *nomen*, "name."

[16] The censors.

[17] The section omitted here is printed as Book 1, fr. 1.

[18] The text is corrupt, but the meaning is clear.

into the famous Propylaea. But there is a careful discussion of all this sort of thing in the books which I wrote on the commonwealth.

[7a] I am unwilling that the same people should be the ruler of the world and its customs collector. And I think that the best source of revenue both for private families and for the commonwealth is frugality. [+Nonius 24.15]

[9a] Augustine, *City of God* 2.14: *Cicero makes this exclamation in vain, in speaking about poets:* "When they receive the shouts and approval of the people as if of some great and wise teacher, what darkness they cover the people with, what fears they import, what desires they inflame!"[19]

[10] Augustine, *City of God* 2.13: *Just as Scipio also says in Cicero's book:* "Since they considered acting and the theater as a whole to be disgraceful, they wanted that type of person not only to lack the honors of other citizens but even to be deprived of citizenship through censorial punishment."[20]

Augustine, *Epist.* 91.4: *You should read and consider the wise argument in the same book*, that the writing and performance of comedies could not in any way have been accepted if the people accepting them were not of the same character.[21]

[11] Augustine, *City of God* 2.9: *Cicero gives evidence about the opinions of the early Romans on this subject in his book* On the Commonwealth, *where Scipio argues as follows:* "If customary behavior did not permit it, comedies could never have gained the audience's approval for their disgracefulness." *And in fact the earlier Greeks maintained a certain consistency in their views: in their country, it was legally permitted for comedy to say whatever it wanted about anyone by name. And so, just as Africanus says in the same book:*

"Whom did it not taint, or rather whom did it not ravage? Whom did it spare? Granted that it attacked evil popular politicians who caused discord in the commonwealth – Cleon, Cleophon, Hyperbolus. Let us endure that," *he says*, "even though it is better for such citizens to be rebuked by the censor rather than by a poet. But it was no more proper for Pericles, at a time when he had been in charge of his country in peace and war with the highest authority for many years, to be attacked in poetry performed on the stage, than it would be if our own Plautus or

[19] C. is almost certainly speaking of Greek dramatists (following Plato), not Roman.

[20] "They" is "our ancestors": here C. speaks of the Roman theater.

[21] Not in Ziegler. Augustine's paraphrase in this letter to Nectarius is closely related to the next quotation.

Naevius had wanted to speak ill of Publius or Gnaeus Scipio, or Caecilius to do so of Marcus Cato."[22]

[**12**] *And a little later, he says:* "Our own Twelve Tables, by contrast, although they established capital punishments for very few offenses, included among them this: if anyone should sing offensively or should compose a poem which brought disgrace or offense to someone else.[23] And they were quite right: we ought to have our lives set out for the judgments of magistrates or formal court proceedings, not for the wits of poets; nor should we hear an insult except under the condition that we can answer and defend ourselves at law."

I thought that I ought to give this verbatim selection from the fourth book of Cicero's On the Commonwealth, *abridging or slightly altering some parts for ease of understanding. It is highly relevant to the subject that I am trying to explain, if I can. He then says some more, and ends this discussion in such a way as to show that the early Romans were displeased if a living man was either praised or criticized on the stage.*

[**13b**] Augustine, *City of God* 2.11: *It is relevant to this consistency that they even thought the stage performers of these plays worthy of no small civic honor, if in fact, as is reported in the same book* On the Commonwealth, *Aeschines the Athenian, a very eloquent man, after having performed in tragedies as a young man, entered public life; and the Athenians frequently sent Aristodemus, who was also a tragic actor, as an ambassador to Philip concerning the greatest affairs of war and peace.*

[**13a**] Donatus, *Excerpts on Comedy* 22.19W: *Cicero says* that comedy is the imitation of life, the mirror of customary behavior, the image of truth.[24]

[**14**] Aristides Quintilianus *On Music* II pp. 69–71 Meibom: *Not every pleasure is blameworthy, nor is that the goal of music: its capacity to attract the soul is accidental, while its goal is assistance towards virtue. That was not seen by many people, including the man in Cicero's books on politics who speaks against music. I would not say that Cicero himself said such things: how could someone assert that he slandered music and considered it low, the branch of learning that distinguishes the virtues and vices of harmonies and rhythms – the same man who was so struck by the mime Roscius, who was*

[22] This passage is strong evidence that C. did not know the traditional story of Naevius' slander of the Metelli and subsequent imprisonment.

[23] Twelve Tables VIII, 1 Crawford. The law in question probably concerned both magical incantations and defamation.

[24] This fragment is not explicitly ascribed to *On the Commonwealth*, but its emphasis on the relationship between *consuetudo*, "customary behavior," and drama corresponds to the argument here.

renowned only for his ignoble and low rhythms, that he said that Roscius had come to mankind through the goodwill of the gods. And if anyone should say that what he said in his Commonwealth *was of his own choice, while what he said about Roscius was for the sake of his case, there is no reason not to turn the argument on its head. But anyone making such an argument would unwittingly discredit it, at least as far as the present inquiry is concerned, rather than gaining the support of the orator. Someone who is enthralled by fashionable opinion or his own tastes and is not guided by true principles does not deserve belief in the search for truth or in just judgments. Nor do I think he would blame rhetoric itself for the corruption of individual rhetoricians. So even if some musicians play ignoble music through the desire to please the crowd, that is not the fault of the art itself. Furthermore, Cicero's own country, at the time of King Numa and his successors, had citizens who were educated in music, even if they were quite rustic. According to what he himself says, it accompanied them in private festivities and in all public rituals.*[25]

[8a] I admire not only the elegance of the substance, but of the language as well.[26] "If they quarrel," it says: a quarrel is said to be the competition of men who are well disposed to one another, not a lawsuit between enemies . . . Therefore the law believes that neighbors quarrel among themselves, they do not go to law. [+ Nonius 430.29]

[8c] The limits for caring about men <are not> the same as the limits of their lives: and so the sanctity of burial is part of the pontifical law.[27] [+ Nonius 174.7]

[8d] They put innocent men to death because they had left unburied those whom they were unable to collect from the ocean because of the violence of the storm.[28] [+ Nonius 293.41]

[8e] And in that dispute I did not take the side of the people, but of the respectable citizens.[29] [+ Nonius 519.15]

[8f] It is not easy to resist a powerful populace if you give them no rights or very few.[30] [+ Priscian 3.76.14K]

[25] This wordy passage is included here because it is the only evidence that C. discussed music in Book 4; there is no reason to believe that the discussion was nearly as important in C. as in Plato's *Republic*.

[26] The citation is from the Twelve Tables (VII, 5 Crawford). Nonius here cites two sentences from the same context under a single heading.

[27] On the law of burial see *On the Laws* 2.55–67.

[28] The Athenian commanders at the battle of Arginusae in 406 BCE were subsequently condemned to death for not having recovered the bodies of the dead.

[29] A reference to Scipio's support for the Lex Cassia tabellaria of 137, which introduced the secret ballot in trials before the people. A fuller account of this debate is at *On the Laws* 3.35–38 below.

[30] On the need to give rights to the people see above, 2.56–57.

Uncertain location in Book 4

[8g] If only I could have foretold to him truly, faithfully, and fully.[31] [+Nonius 469.16]

[14b] armbands [+Priscian, *Twelve First Verses of the Aeneid* 3.462.31K]

Doubtful fragments

[7e] Whoever seeks the good opinion of men through feasts and parties and expenditures shows openly that he lacks the true glory which arises from virtue and a sense of honor. [Anonymi Paradoxa Koronne, cited by Bielowski][32]

[8b] Rufinus *De bono pacis* 2.16:[33] *Furthermore, since the peace of the household is an element of the peace of the city, if the peace of the household is to be violated by its members to avoid destroying civil peace, then the domestic peace between father and son will have to be torn apart, just as we read that those men wrote who eloquently discussed the condition of the commonwealth.*

[9b] Seneca, *Moral Letters*. 49.5: *Cicero says* that if he were to live twice as long he would not have time to read the lyric poets.

[31] The text of this fragment is uncertain, as is its significance.

[32] On the Bielowski fragments, see above, Book 2, n. 92.

[33] Rufinus of Atina wrote in the twelfth century, and it is very unlikely that he had any direct knowledge of *On the Commonwealth*.

Book 5

[1] Augustine, *City of God* 2.21: *Thus, when the Roman commonwealth was in the condition that Sallust describes,*[1] *it was no longer terrible and highly criminal, as he says, but altogether no commonwealth at all according to the argument set out in the discussion concerning the commonwealth held by the greatest leaders of the time. Cicero himself, speaking at the outset of the fifth book, not using the voice of Scipio or one of the others but in his own voice, first quoted the verse of the poet Ennius in which he said:*[2]

> The Roman state stands upon the morals and men of old.

He then said: "That verse, in its brevity and its truthfulness, he seems to me to have spoken as if from an oracle. For if the state had not had such morals, then the men would not have existed; nor, if such men had not been in charge, would there have been such morals as to be able to establish or preserve for so long a commonwealth so great and ruling so widely. And so, before our time, ancestral morality provided outstanding men, and great men preserved the morality of old and the institutions of our ancestors. [2a] But our own time, having inherited the commonwealth like a wonderful picture that had faded over time, not only has failed to renew its original colors but has not even taken the trouble to preserve at least its shape and outlines. What remains of the morals of antiquity, upon which Ennius said that the Roman state stood? We see that they are so outworn in oblivion that they are not only not cherished but are now unknown. What am I to say about the men? The morals themselves have passed away through a shortage of

[1] Sallust, *Histories* 1.16 Maurenbrecher. [2] Ennius, *Annals* 467 Warmington.

men; and we must not only render an account of such an evil, but in a sense we must defend ourselves like people being tried for a capital crime. It is because of our own vices, not because of some bad luck, that we preserve the commonwealth in name alone but have long ago lost its substance."

[**2b**] Grillius, *Commentary on Cicero's Rhetoric* p. 28.14 Martin: *In his* Politics *Cicero says that the leader of the commonwealth ought to be a very great and very learned man, so as to be wise and just and temperate and eloquent, in order to be able to express fluently and easily his inner thoughts to rule the people. He also ought to know the law and to know Greek literature. That is demonstrated by Cato's actions: by studying Greek at an advanced age he indicated how useful it was.*

[3] MANILIUS?: * <Nothing is as> regal as the explanation of equity, which involved the interpretation of the law: private citizens used to seek justice from kings, and for that reason fields and groves and pastures that were wide and fertile were marked off as royal and were cultivated without the toil and effort of the kings themselves, so that no concerns about private affairs might distract them from the affairs of the people. There were no private arbitrators of lawsuits, but everything was dealt with by royal judgments. Our king Numa seems to have held most closely to this ancient custom of the kings of Greece. All the other kings, even though they performed this function too, still spent a great deal of time in waging war and observing its laws; but the long peace of Numa was the mother of law and religion in Rome, and he also wrote laws which, as you know, still survive;[3] and that is appropriate for the citizen we are now considering. *

[two or four leaves missing]

[4] But just as for a good head of a household there is need for some experience in farming, building, and accounting. [+ Nonius 497.23]

[5] SCIPIO: * You won't mind, will you <if your overseer> has some knowledge of roots and seeds?

MANILIUS: Not at all, if there is some need.

SCIPIO: But you don't think that that is the main interest of an overseer?

MANILIUS: Certainly not, since in that case his activities would often leave the farming unsupervised.

SCIPIO: And so, just as the overseer knows the nature of the land, and

[3] See above, 2.26.

the manager knows how to read, but each of them subordinates the pleasure of learning to practical utility, so too the leader we are talking about will have been eager to learn about justice and laws and will have given close attention to their sources, but he will not distract himself by giving legal opinions and constant reading and writing, so that, in a way, he can serve as a manager and overseer for the commonwealth: he will be very learned in the fundamentals of law, without which no one can be just, and he will not be ignorant of the civil law, but in the same way that a helmsman knows the stars and a doctor physics. Each of them uses these materials for his own art, but he does not distract himself from his own function. This man will recognize *

[gap of unknown length]

[**6**] SCIPIO: * states, in which they seek the praise and respect of the best man, and flee shame and disgrace. But they are not frightened so much by the fear and penalties established by law as by a sense of shame, which nature has given men as a sort of fear of criticism that is not undeserved.[4] The leader of commonwealths strengthens this sense of shame by his opinions, and he brings it to perfection by institutions and education, so that shame does as much as fear to keep citizens from crime. These things are also relevant to praise, and they could be dilated on much more fully and elaborately.

[7] As far as private life and habits are concerned, a system has been set out involving proper marriage rites, the legitimacy of children, the sanctity of the dwellings of the Penates and the Lares of the families, in such a way that everyone makes use of the advantages of the community as well as his own, so that there is no possibility of living well in the absence of a good commonwealth, nor is anything more blessed than a well-ordered state. As a result, it is very surprising to me that so great . . . learned *

[end of the manuscript]

[**8a**] Cicero, *Letters to Atticus* 8.11.1: *I spend all my time contemplating the importance of that man whom (in your opinion at least) I portrayed quite carefully in my book. Do you have in mind that guide of the commonwealth who is the foundation of the whole system? This is what Scipio says, I think in Book 5:* "As a helmsman aims at a good voyage, a doctor at saving his patient, a general at victory, so this guide of the commonwealth aims at

[4] C.'s definition of *uerecundia* here is a translation of a Stoic definition of *aidôs* as "avoidance of justified criticism" (*Stoicorum veterum fragmenta*, ed. von Arnim, III 105.40). This perhaps reveals C.'s mechanism for linking Stoic ethics with Roman customary morality.

the blessedness of the life of his citizens, that they should be solid in their resources, rich in property, well endowed with glory, honorable in virtue. I want him to be the person to perfect this task, which is the greatest and best among mankind."

[**8b**] Augustine, *Epist.* 104.7: *And where do I find that leader of his country whom your letter praises,* "who looks out for the interest of the people more than for their desires"?[5]

[**9a**] Augustine, *City of God* 5.13: *Even Cicero could not conceal this in his book* On the Commonwealth, *where he speaks of the education of the first citizen of the state, who he says* must be nourished on glory *and then states* that his ancestors did many great and wonderful deeds out of desire for glory.

[**9c**] Then the character of a great man would be sought in virtue, labor, and industry if his fierce nature did not with too much spirit somehow . . . him . . . [+ Nonius 233.33][6]

[**9d**] This virtue is called courage, and it includes greatness of spirit and great scorn for death and pain. [+ Nonius 201.29]

[**10a**] Marcellus in his fierceness and pugnacity, Maximus in his caution and deliberation. [+ Nonius 337.34]

[**11b**] Ammianus Marcellinus 30.4.10: *Because of their stubbornness, rashness imitates liberty, headlong boldness imitates steadfastness, and an empty flow of speech imitates eloquence; but as Cicero states, it is immoral for a judge under oath to be deceived through the deceit of such arts. What he says is:* "And since nothing ought to be so uncorrupted in the commonwealth as a vote or as a formal opinion, I do not undertand why someone who corrupts them by money deserves punishment while someone who does so by eloquence gets praised. In my opinion, the person who corrupts a judge through his oratory rather than through bribery does all the more harm, because no one can corrupt a decent person with money, but he can with speech."[7]

Ammianus Marcellinus 30.4.7: *After them* [sc. the early orators], *Cicero is the greatest of all; and in rescuing people trapped in the conflagration of the courtroom through the torrents of his commanding eloquence, he affirmed* that

5 An almost identical phrase is found in Cicero's speech *On Behalf of Sulla* 25, but it may well also have been used in *On the Commonwealth*, the text Augustine is discussing here.

6 The sentence is incomplete and the text is corrupt; this translation accepts Leopardi's emendation (*indoles* for *indolem*), but the sense is still unclear.

7 Scipio is presumably the speaker; the location of this fragment is determined by its connection with the next one.

it might not be blameworthy for men not to be defended, but that it could not fail to be criminal for them to be defended badly.[8]

[11a] Aulus Gellius, *Attic Nights* 12.2.6–7: *And after this he* [Seneca] *adds most crudely: "You will find even in Cicero's prose writings some things that will show you that his reading of Ennius was not a waste of time." Then he quotes things that he finds objectionable in Cicero because of their Ennian origin, such as what he wrote in his book* On the Commonwealth: "just as the Laconian Menelaus had a certain sweet-speaking charm"; *and elsewhere:* "he should cultivate brief-speaking in oratory."

[11c] When Scipio had said this, Mummius approved completely – he was in fact steeped in hatred of the rhetoricians. [+Nonius 521.12]

[10b] bounded by the circuit of the globe [+Charisius 1.139.17K][9]

[10c] because he could present your families with a share of the burdens of his old age . . . [+Nonius 37.23][10]

[11d] Then excellent seeds were sown for the best crop. [+*Brevis Expositio* on Virgil, *Georgics* 1.1]

[8] Not in Ziegler. Heck plausibly assigns this otherwise unlocated fragment to Book 5 because of its close connection to Ammianus' other citation from what appears to be a similar context. A discussion of the proper use of rhetoric was clearly a part of the description of the statesman.

[9] Cited for the use of *orbi* as ablative; there is no context.

[10] The reference and point of this fragment are unclear.

Book 6

[1a] Cicero, *Letters to Atticus* 7.3.2: *If I had not had that idea about a triumph, which you also approve of, then you would not find me much short of that man who is described in the sixth book. Why should I be silent with you, who gobbled up those books? As it is, I will have no doubts about abandoning so grand a thing, if it is better to do so; it is impossible for both to proceed together, to campaign for a triumph and to speak freely on public affairs.*[1]

[1b] You are awaiting the complete foresight of this leader, which derives its name from seeing ahead.[2] [+Nonius 42.3]

[1c] Therefore this citizen must so prepare himself as always to be armed against things which disturb the stability of the state. [+Nonius 256.27]

[1d] That discord of the citizens which is called sedition because people go apart in following different leaders.[3] [+Nonius 25.3]

[1e] And in fact in a civil discord, when the respectable citizens are more important than the majority, I believe that citizens should be weighed rather than counted. [+Nonius 519.17]

[1f] The passions exercise powerful control over thoughts; they compel and command innumerable things, and since they can in no way be fulfilled and satiated, they drive to every sort of crime those whom they

[1] C. was torn between his desire to be awarded a triumph for his military actions as governor of Cilicia in 51–50 – to be eligible for which he could not reenter Rome and formally relinquish his proconsulate – and his hope of being able to mediate between the senate and Caesar. The letter was written only three weeks before the outbreak of war.

[2] For the derivation of *prudentia*, "wisdom," from *prouideo*, "to foresee," see "Text and Translation" above and 2.67 n. 81.

[3] Sedition is derived from *se-*, "apart," and *ire*, "to go."

have inflamed with their enticements. [+ Nonius 424.31]
[1g] Who has beaten down its force and unbridled ferocity. [+ Nonius 492.1]
[2a] Which was all the greater, since, although the two colleagues were in the same position, they were not only not hated equally, but affection for Gracchus dispelled the hatred for Claudius.[4] [+ Aulus Gellius, *Attic Nights* 7.16.11 and Nonius 290.15]
[2b] Whoever among the number of the best men and leading citizens has offered <aid to sedition?> abandons the solemn and dignified sound of his voice and respectability.[5] [+ Nonius 409.31]
[2c] so that, as he writes, a thousand men should go down to the forum daily with cloaks dyed in purple[6] [+ Nonius 501.27]
[2d] In their case, as you remember, the funeral was suddenly adorned by a crowd of the most insignificant people, collected with cash.[7] [+ Nonius 517.35]
[2e] Our ancestors wanted marriages to be solidly established. [+ Nonius 512.27 and Priscian 3.70.11K]
[2f] The speech of Laelius, which we have all read, <shows> how pleasing to the immortal gods are the earthenware vessels of the priests and the sacrificial vessels (as he writes) of Samian pottery.[8] [+ Nonius 398.28]
[8] Macrobius, *Commentary* 1.4.2–3: *It was this occasion that provoked Scipio to tell of the dream about which he said that he had kept silence for a long time. For when Laelius complained that there were no public statues of Scipio Nasica in gratitude for his having killed a tyrant,*[9] *Scipio replied, after other comments, in the following words:*

"SCIPIO: But although for wise men the consciousness of noble deeds is itself the greatest reward for virtue, it is also true that virtue, which is divine, has no desire for statues anchored in lead or for tri-

[4] Tiberius Sempronius Gracchus (father of the tribune) and Gaius Claudius Pulcher were censors in 169. Both were accused of treason (*perduellio*); Gracchus' support kept Claudius from being convicted.

[5] The text is corrupt and the translation and supplement are uncertain.

[6] "As he writes" introduces a quotation from the archaic Greek elegist Xenophanes of Colophon (fr. 3.3–4 West) describing the decadence resulting from Colophon's alliance with Lydia. [7] The subject of this fragment (possibly demagogues) is uncertain.

[8] A verb is supplied for the incomplete quotation. The fragment refers to Laelius' speech "On the priestly colleges" delivered in 145 against proposals to have members of the colleges elected rather than coopted.

[9] Publius Cornelius Scipio Nasica Serapio, the pontifex maximus, led the mob that murdered Tiberius Gracchus.

umphs with fading laurel leaves, but seeks some more lasting and fresh kinds of reward.

"LAELIUS: And what are those?

"SCIPIO: Permit me, since this is now the third day of our holiday" *and the rest which leads to the narration of the dream, in which he teaches that those are the more lasting and fresh kinds of reward which he himself saw in heaven set aside for good leaders of commonwealths.*

[3] Favonius Eulogius, *On the Dream of Scipio* 1.5H: *Cicero, writing about the commonwealth in imitation of Plato, made use also of the passage concerning the return to life of Er the Pamphylian*[10] *who, as he says,* "came to life again after being placed on the pyre and reported many secrets about the underworld"; *but he did not contrive it with a storyteller's fiction, as Plato had done, but composed it using the reasonable vision of an intelligent dream, thus cleverly pointing out that* "the things which are reported about the immortality of the soul and about heaven are neither the fictions of dreaming philosophers nor the incredible tales that the Epicureans laugh at, but are the speculations of men of judgment."[11]

[4] Augustine, *City of God* 22.28: *There are quite a few Christians who love Plato because of his superb style and because of a number of his opinions which are truthful, and therefore say that he had an opinion similar to ours concerning the resurrection of the dead. Cicero refers to this in his book* On the Commonwealth *in such a way as to assert* that he was playing a game rather than wanting to speak the truth.

[6] Macrobius, *Commentary* 1.1.8–2.5: *In keeping this order, Cicero shows equal judgment and genius. After having given in his argument the prize to justice in all private and public actions of the commonwealth, he placed the sacred home of the immortal souls and the mysteries of the heavenly realms at the very summit of his finished work, showing where those people must go – or rather where they must return – who have served the commonwealth with wisdom, justice, courage, and moderation. But in Plato, the man who reports these secrets was a Pamphylian soldier named Er; after seeming to have given up his life from wounds received in battle, on the twelfth day, as he was about to be honored on the funeral pyre along with the others who had died with him, he suddenly recovered or received back his soul and reported all that he had done and seen in the days between his two lives, as if bearing public witness to the human race. Even though Cicero, who knew the*

[10] Plato, *Republic* 10.614b.

[11] The Epicurean philosopher Colotes had criticized the Myth of Er for its implausibility, and Scipio rebuts any similar objections to his own dream.

truth, was sorry that this story had been laughed at by the ignorant, he wanted to avoid this precedent of foolish criticism and chose to have his narrator be awakened rather than brought back to life.

[Scipio's Dream]

[9] SCIPIO: After I had come to Africa, as you know, as military tribune to the fourth legion when Manilius here was consul, my first desire was to meet King Masinissa, a close friend of my family for the best of reasons.[12] When I came to him, the old man embraced me and wept; and after a little he looked up to the sky and said: "I offer thanks to you, great Sun, and to you the other heavenly gods, because before I depart from this life I see in my kingdom and in my own home Publius Cornelius Scipio, whose very name revives me: the memory of that best and most unconquerable of men never departs from my mind." Then I asked him about his kingdom, and he asked me about our commonwealth; the day passed with much conversation between us.

[10] Later, after dining royally, we stretched our conversation late into the night; the old man spoke of nothing but Africanus and called to mind not only all his actions but also his words. Then we went to bed; and as I was exhausted from the trip and from staying awake so late, I was gripped by a deeper sleep than usual. At this point – and I believe that it was the result of what we had said: our thoughts and words often bring forth in sleep something like Ennius' report of Homer, about whom he obviously used to think and speak a great deal when he was awake[13] – Africanus showed himself to me in the appearance which I knew better from his portrait than from having seen him.[14] When I recognized him, I shuddered; but he said, "Stay calm and don't be afraid, Scipio, and remember what I tell you."

[11] "Do you see that city, which I forced to obey the Roman people but which now renews its earlier wars and is incapable of remaining

[12] Scipio's dream was in 149 BCE, 20 years before the dramatic date of the dialogue, at the beginning of the Third Punic War. Masinissa died at the age of 90 or so shortly after the scene narrated here; he had switched sides from Carthage to Rome in 206, at an opportune moment in the Second Punic War, and had remained loyal to Rome for the rest of his long life. The visit is probably as fictional as the dream: Scipio's only known meeting with Masinissa was more than a year earlier.

[13] At the opening of his *Annals* (frr. 4–13 Warmington), Ennius had reported a dream in which a vision of Homer had appeared to him and announced that Ennius, through the process of transmigration of souls, possessed (or was) the same soul as Homer himself.

[14] Scipio was only 2 years old when the elder Africanus died.

peaceful?" (He was pointing at Carthage from a spot high up and filled with stars, that was bright and glorious.) "You are coming to besiege it now as little more than a simple soldier, but within two years you will destroy it as consul, and you will receive on your own account the name which you have already inherited from me.[15] But after you have destroyed Carthage, have celebrated a triumph, and have been censor, and after you have as an ambassador visited Egypt, Syria, Asia, and Greece, you will be elected consul for the second time in your absence and you will bring to a conclusion a major war by destroying Numantia. But after you ride up the Capitol in your triumphal chariot, you will encounter the commonwealth in a state of disorder because of the plans of my grandson.[16] [12] At this point, Africanus, you will have to display to your country the brilliance of your mind and talent and judgment. But I see at this point a double path of fate: when your span of years has traversed seven times eight turns and returns of the sun, and these two numbers, each of which is considered perfect for various reasons, have made up the sum of your fate by their natural circling, the whole state will turn to you alone and to your name: the senate, all upstanding citizens, the allies, and the Latins will look to you; you will be the one person on whom the safety of the state rests. To be brief: you will have to restore the commonwealth as dictator – if you escape the impious hands of those close to you."[17]

At this point Laelius shouted out, and all the others groaned deeply, but SCIPIO smiled gently and said: Hush, please! or you will wake me up. Listen for a short time to the rest.

[13] "But so that you may be all the more eager, Africanus, to protect the commonwealth, know this: for all those who have saved, aided, or increased the fatherland there is a specific place set aside in the sky where they may enjoy eternity in blessedness. There is nothing that can happen on earth that is more pleasing to that leading god who rules the whole world than those councils and assemblages of men associated through law which are called states; the guides and preservers of these have set out from here, and here they return."

[14] At this point, even though I was terrified not so much by the fear of death as of treachery on the part of my own people, I still asked him

[15] Africanus exaggerates: Scipio was not a simple soldier in 149, and he destroyed Carthage 3 years later, receiving the same honorific cognomen, Africanus, that his grandfather had been given. [16] Tiberius Gracchus, the son of Africanus' daughter Cornelia.

[17] The dictatorship never happened (because of Scipio's death), and it is probably C.'s invention that it was even contemplated in 129: there had been no dictatorship for many years and was to be none again until Sulla seized power more than 40 years later.

whether he was alive, along with my father Paullus and the others whom we think of as dead. "Yes indeed," he said, "these people are alive; they have escaped from the chains of the body as if from a prison, and what is called life among you is in fact death.[18] Don't you see your father Paullus approaching you?" And when I saw him, I wept heavily, but he embraced me and kissed me and told me not to weep.

[**15**] As soon as I could quell my tears and began to be able to speak, I said: "I ask you, best and most sacred of fathers, since this is life, as Africanus tells me, why am I delaying on earth? Why don't I hurry to come here to you?"

"That isn't the way things are," he said. "Unless the god, whose precinct is all that you behold, frees you from the guardianship of your body, you have no access to this place.[19] Men are created under these terms, that they are to look after that globe which you see in the middle of this precinct, which is called earth; and they are given a soul from those eternal fires which you call constellations and stars, which are spherical globes endowed with divine minds and accomplish their rotations and revolutions with amazing speed. And so, Publius, both you and all pious people must keep your soul in the guardianship of the body, and you must not depart from human life without the order of him who gave you your soul: you must not seem to run away from the human duty assigned by the god. [**16**] But, Scipio, you should be like your grandfather here and like me your father in cultivating justice and piety; it is important in relation to your parents and family, but most important in relation to your fatherland. That way of life is the way to the heavens and to this gathering of those who have ceased to live and after having been released from the body now inhabit the place you see" (it was a bright circle shining among the stars with a most radiant whiteness), "which you have learned from the Greeks to name the Milky Way." And from that point, as I studied everything, it all seemed to me glorious and marvelous. There were stars which we never see from this place, and their size was such as we have never suspected; the smallest one was the one furthest from the heavens and closest to earth and shone with borrowed light.[20]

[18] The ideas of the body as a prison and life as death are taken from Plato (e.g. *Phaedo* 67d, *Phaedrus* 250c, *Gorgias* 492e–493a), who attributes them to "Pythagorean" sources. C. gives similar discussions of the soul and afterlife at *Tusculan Disputations* 1.71–75 and *On Old Age* 77–84.

[19] The discussion of suicide is based on Plato, *Phaedo* 61d–62c. "Guardianship of your body" means both that you are in charge of looking after your body and that your body is your prison guard.

[20] The moon.

The globes of the stars easily surpassed the size of the earth, and earth itself now seemed so small to me that I was ashamed of our empire, which touches only a little speck of it.[21]

[17] And as I kept looking, Africanus asked me: "I wonder how long your mind will be fixed on the ground? Don't you see the precinct into which you have come? Everything is linked, you see, in nine circles or rather spheres. One of them, the outer one, is the sphere of the heavens which embraces all the rest; it is the highest god himself protecting and limiting the rest, and in it are fixed the eternal revolving courses of the stars. Within that are seven which revolve in the opposite direction from the heavens.[22] The first sphere belongs to the planet which humans call Saturn's;[23] then the light giving favor and safety to men called Jupiter's; then the red one hateful to earth which you call Mars'; then the one below, roughly in the center, belongs to the Sun, the ruler, leader, and guide of the remaining celestial bodies, the mind and balance of the universe, so large that it traverses and fills all with its light. The orbits of Venus and of Mercury follow it like attendants,[24] and in the lowest sphere the Moon revolves, lit by the rays of the Sun. Below that there is nothing that is not mortal and perishable except the souls given to the human race by the gift of the gods; above the Moon everything is eternal.[25] The sphere that is ninth, in the middle, is Earth; it is stationary and the lowest one, and all weights are borne towards it of their own accord."

[18] I was staring dumbfounded at all this, but when I recovered

[21] The topic of Rome's smallness within the universe is taken up below at 6.20ff.

[22] The cosmos described here (which is based as much on poetic cosmographies as on philosophical texts) consists of an outer sphere incorporating the fixed stars which turns from east to west, seven inner concentric spheres (in descending order: Saturn, Jupiter, Mars, Sun, Venus, Mercury, Moon) turning from west to east, and in the center the unmoving globe of the earth. C. here follows the order of Archimedes and a few others who place the Sun in the middle – essential for C.'s analogy between the sun and the statesman – rather than that used by Plato in which the sun is between Venus and the moon.

[23] C.'s terminology ("Saturn's star," not "Saturn") is maintained here, although it is awkward: in his day divinities were associated with the planets but were not yet identified with them.

[24] The relative position of Mercury and Venus is a problem in geocentric astronomy, in which it is impossible to determine which is closer to the earth. C. is deliberately vague in his language.

[25] The idea of the moon as the boundary between mortal and immortal probably goes back to the Pre-Socratics but is more fully developed in later Platonism.

myself I said: "Tell me: what is the sound which fills my ears, so great and so sweet?"

"This is the sound that is caused by the action and motion of the spheres themselves. Its harmony is based on uneven intervals, but the inequality of the intervals is proportional and based on reason, and by blending high notes with low itself causes balanced music.[26] Such vast motions cannot proceed without sound, and the furthest in one direction naturally makes a deep note, and the furthest in the other a high one. For that reason the highest sphere of the heavens with the stars in it, which turns very rapidly, moves with a high and agitated sound, and the lowest sphere of the Moon with a very deep one – the ninth, the Earth, is unmoving and always stays in the same place, embracing the center of the universe. But those eight orbits, of which two have the same pitch, create seven sounds distinguished by their intervals; and that number is really at the heart of the matter.[27] Learned men who have imitated it with stringed instruments and song have opened for themselves their return to this place, just like others who have used outstanding intelligence to cultivate divine studies in their human lives. [**19**] Men's ears have been filled with this sound and consequently grown deaf to it. You have no duller sense than hearing, just as at the point where the Nile plunges from high mountains at the place called Cataract, the race of men that lives there is completely deaf because of the magnitude of the sound. The sound made by the rapid revolution of the universe is so great that human ears cannot grasp it, just as you are unable to look directly into the Sun, because your sight and sense are overcome by its rays."[28]

[**20**] Although I marveled at all this, I still kept bringing my eyes back to earth. Then Africanus said: "I realize that you are still looking at the home and dwelling of men; but if it seems to you as small as in fact it is, you must always look at these heavenly bodies and scorn what is human. What fame can you achieve in what men say, or what glory can you achieve that is worth seeking? You see that humans inhabit small and scattered portions of the earth, and that huge emptiness separates the blotches of human habitation.[29] The people who inhabit the earth are not

[26] C.'s account of the music of the spheres is not Platonic, and although the idea itself was said to be Pythagorean, the mathematics of it belong to the fourth century or later. C.'s account is deliberately nontechnical and carefully leaves various problems unresolved.

[27] The numbers 7 and 8 are also crucial in the prophecy of Scipio's death above, 6.12.

[28] C. is presumably alluding to Plato's use of the Sun as the image of the Good; cf. *Republic* 7.515e–516b.

[29] The picture of the earth which Africanus uses (and explains more fully in the next

only so broken up that nothing can pass from one group of them to another, but some of them live across from you, others below you, and some directly opposite you on the earth; and it is clear that you can expect no glory among them.

[21] "But you see also that the earth is bound and girdled by belts of a sort, of which the two that are most distant from one another and rest on the opposing poles of the sky are stiff with cold, while the central and largest one is parched by the heat of the Sun. There are only two that can be inhabited, and of those the southern one, the inhabitants of which have their feet opposite yours, has no connection with your nation; while you see that of the other one to the north, which you inhabit, only a tiny portion belongs to you. The whole territory that you possess is narrow at the ends and wider in the middle, but it is a little island surrounded by the sea which you on earth call 'Atlantic' or 'great' or 'Ocean' – but despite its grand name you see that it is really quite small. [22] And you surely don't believe that from the lands which you know and cultivate, your name or the name of any of us can cross the Caucasus which you see there, or swim the Ganges over there? Who is there in the rest of the earth, at the extremes of east, west, north, or south, who will hear your name? And if you remove those, you of course see the narrow bounds set on the expansion of your glory. And even the people who talk about us – how long will they do that?

[23] "In fact, even if the offspring of the men to come should wish to pass on to their descendants the praise of each one of us that they have received from their parents, it is still true that because of the floods and fires that necessarily destroy the earth at appointed times we cannot achieve long-lasting glory, far less eternal.[30] And what difference does it make if future generations speak of you if none of those in previous generations did so? They outnumber us, and they were clearly better men. [24] And even among those who are able to hear of us, not one will

paragraph) is Pre-Socratic in origin, but again C. is drawing primarily on poetic descriptions. The globe is divided into five zones: icecaps at either pole, and two temperate zones isolated from one another by a torrid one. The temperate zones themselves seem to be divided into two separate halves, such that there are only four habitable regions of the earth, of which the Roman world occupies a part of one. The description of the European quadrant in sect. 21 seems to superimpose a flat world (the known region surrounded by the Ocean) on the spherical globe required by the cosmography.

[30] This is not the Stoic theory of cosmic conflagration at fixed intervals (*ekpurosis*), but the periodic fires and floods mentioned by Plato, *Timaeus* 22c, and known also from a fragment of Aristotle. The same combination of forms of destruction in C. is found at *On Divination* 1.111.

be able to remember for a single year. Men use the popular reckoning and measure the year by the cycle of only one star, the Sun; but in fact the true passage of a year can be so named only when all the stars have returned to the place where they started and brought back the same arrangement of the entire heavens after a very long interval – and I scarcely dare to say how many human generations that contains.[31] For just as the Sun once seemed to men to fail and be extinguished at the time that the soul of Romulus entered this precinct, and when the Sun again fails at the same point at the same time, then you can consider that a year has been completed and all the constellations and stars have been recalled to the same beginning; and of that year you must know that the twentieth part has not yet been traversed.

[25] "Thus, even if you lose hope of returning to this place, where all things exist for great and outstanding men, still – what is that human glory really worth which can last scarcely a fraction of a single year? Therefore look on high if you wish; contemplate this dwelling and eternal home; and do not give yourself to the words of the mob, and do not place your hopes in human rewards: virtue itself by its own allurements should draw you towards true honor. Let others worry about what they say about you – and they will say things in any case. But everything they say is bounded by the narrow limits of the area, as you see, and it is never eternal about anyone, and it is overwhelmed by the deaths of men and extinguished by the forgetfulness of future generations."

[26] After he had said this, I replied: "For my part, Africanus, if in fact there is a kind of path to the heavens for those who have deserved well of their fatherland, even if through following your footsteps and those of my father from my childhood I have not fallen short of your glory, still now, when I see such a prize set before me, I will struggle all the more vigorously."

And he answered me: "Keep at it; and know this: it is not you that is mortal but your body. You are not what your physical shape reveals, but each person is his mind, not the body that a finger can point at. Know then that you are a god,[32] as surely as a god is someone who is alert, who

[31] According to a fragment of C.'s lost *Hortensius* (35 Mueller), the "great year" is equivalent to 12,954 solar years. Both here and in *Hortensius* (fr. 54), C. used the apotheosis of Romulus as the marker for the start of the great year, equating Roman and cosmic time.

[32] The identification of the person with the soul (or mind) alone was elaborated in the Platonic tradition; cf. Ps.-Plato, *Alcibiades* I 128e–133c; the soul is called a god (rather than divine) by Plato at *Laws* 10.899b.

feels, who remembers, who looks ahead, who rules and guides and moves the body of which he is in command just as that leading god does for the universe. And just as the eternal god moves the universe, which is partly mortal, so too does the eternal soul move the fragile body.[33] [**27**] What is always in motion is eternal; but whatever brings motion to something else and is itself stirred up from elsewhere, when that motion ceases must necessarily cease its life. Therefore only what moves itself, because it never deserts itself, also never ceases to move; and it is in fact the source and beginning of motion for everything else that moves. There is no origin of beginning, but everything arises from a beginning, and the beginning itself can be born from nothing else – if it arose from elsewhere, it would not be a beginning. But if it never starts, it also never stops: for if the beginning is extinguished it will not be reborn from something else, nor will it create something else from itself, since it is necessary that everything start from a beginning. Thus the beginning of motion comes from that which is moved by itself; and it can neither be born nor die; otherwise the whole heaven and all nature would collapse and come to a stop and there would be no force that it could find to move it from the start. [**28**] And since it is clear that what is moved by itself is eternal, who could deny that the soul has such a nature? Whatever is moved by an external force is inanimate; but whatever is animate is stirred by its own internal motion. That is the special nature and force of the soul. And if it is the one thing of all which moves itself, then it is certainly not born and is therefore eternal. [**29**] Use your soul in the best activities! And the best concerns are those that involve the safety of the fatherland; the soul which is aroused and exercised by them will fly more swiftly to this, its dwelling and home. It will do so all the more swiftly if even when it is enclosed in the body it projects outward and by contemplating those things that are outside it draws itself as much as possible from the body. The souls of men who have surrendered themselves to the pleasures of the body and have made themselves into the servants of those pleasures, and at the urging of desires that are directed by pleasure have broken the laws of gods and men – those souls, when they have departed from the body, circle around the earth and only after having been harried for many generations do they return to this place."

He departed, and I awoke.[34]

[33] Sects. 27–28 translate Plato's proof of the immortality of the soul at *Phaedrus* 245c–246a.

[34] Although the *Dream* was the last major episode of *On the Commonwealth*, there was almost certainly at least one more paragraph which brought the conversation to its conclusion.

Unplaced fragments of *On the Commonwealth*

[2] strive [Diomedes 1.339.31K][35]
[3] they excel [Diomedes 1.374.17K]
[4] Marius Victorinus, *Commentary on Cicero's Rhetoric* p. 156.4H: *This virtue is identified by Cicero in his rhetorical works with wisdom* [sapientia], *but elsewhere, in* On the Commonwealth, *it is said to be the same as judgment* [prudentia].
[6] Lactantius, *Inst.* 1.18.11–13: *In Ennius, Africanus says:*[36]

> If it is right for anyone to ascend into the tracts of the gods
> For me alone the greatest gate of heaven stands open.

. . . *Cicero agrees with this vanity, saying:* "True enough, Africanus; that same gate stood open for Hercules."
[7] Seneca, *Moral Letters* 108.32: *When a grammarian explains the same text, he first reports that Cicero used the words* reapse *for* re ipsa *and* sepse *for* se ipse *and then passes on to things that the custom of the times has altered, as when Cicero says:* "since we have been called back by his summons from the very end of the race." *The ancients used the word* calx *[finish line] for what we now call* creta *in the circus.*
Anonymous Byzantine *Dialogue on Politics*, p. 27.26–30 Mazzucchi: *In saying this, Menodorus, you agree with Cicero, who says* that it is proper for a king's entire thought to concern the selection of ten of the best men, *who will be adequate and sufficient to make a selection of others whom they can use for the administration of the government.*[37]

[35] This and the following fragment are quoted for their grammatical forms.
[36] Ennius, *Epigrams* 3–4 Warmington.
[37] *Menae patricii cum Thoma referendario De scientia politica dialogus*, ed. C. Mazzucchi (Milan, 1982). This citation from an anonymous sixth-century Byzantine dialogue on politics was first identified in 1974. It is unclear whether the quotation ends at ". . . ten of the best men" or ". . . government." It is also extremely unclear to what it refers, and whether the mention of a king is C.'s or the Byzantine author's. It has generally been placed in Book 5, but in fact it need not even come from *On the Commonwealth*.

On the Laws

Book 1

[1] ATTICUS: I recognize that grove and the oak tree of the people of Arpinum: I have read about them often in the *Marius*.[1] If that oak tree survives, this is surely it; it's certainly old enough.

QUINTUS: It survives, Atticus, and it will always survive: its roots are in the imagination. No farmer's cultivation can preserve a tree as long as one sown in a poet's verse.

ATTICUS: How so, Quintus? What sort of thing do poets sow? In praising your brother, I suspect that you are looking for praise for yourself.[2]

[2] QUINTUS: Be that as it may, as long as Latin literature has a voice, there will always be an oak at this spot called "Marius's," and as Scaevola says about my brother's *Marius*, "it will grow old for countless generations."[3] But perhaps you think that your beloved Athens has been able to keep the olive tree on the Acropolis alive forever, or that the palm that they show today on Delos is the same as the tall and slender tree that Homer's Ulysses says that he saw there:[4] many other things in many places last longer in recollection than they could in nature. And so let us assume that this "acorn-bearing" oak is the same as the one from which once flew off "the tawny messenger of Jove, seen in

[1] Both C. and Marius came from the Volscian town of Arpinum, about 115 km SE of Rome. C. had written an epic poem on the life of his fellow townsman (perhaps only on his exile and return) at an uncertain date, but probably in the 50s.

[2] Quintus Cicero was himself a poet and tragedian; only one fragment of his verse survives.

[3] Fr. 1 Courtney. The Scaevola in question was probably the grandson of C.'s teacher Scaevola the augur.

[4] The Delian palm is mentioned at *Odyssey* 6.162; Athena supposedly gave the olive tree on the Acropolis to the Athenians in her contest with Poseidon over the patronage of the city.

wondrous shape."[5] But whenever a storm or old age destroys it, there will still be in this spot an oak which they will call "Marius' oak."

[3] ATTICUS: Of that I have no doubt. But my question is not for you, Quintus, but for the poet himself: was it your verses that planted this oak, or was your account of what happened to Marius based on something you had learned?

MARCUS: I will give you an answer, Atticus, but not before you give me one: is it true that it was not far from your house that Romulus took a stroll after his death and told Proculus Iulius that he was a god and was named Quirinus, and ordered a temple to be dedicated to himself on that spot?[6] And is it true that in Athens, not far from your former home, the North Wind picked up Orithyia?[7] – that is what they say.

[4] ATTICUS: What is your point? Why do you ask?

MARCUS: Only that you should not be too particular in your researches into things that are handed down in stories of this kind.

ATTICUS: But people are curious about the truth or falsehood of many things in the *Marius*, and since you are dealing with recent events and a man from Arpinum, they expect the truth from you.

MARCUS: I certainly don't want to be considered a liar, but those people, Titus, behave ignorantly in such circumstances, in looking for the truth of a witness when examining a poet. No doubt these same people think that Numa had conversations with Egeria and that an eagle placed the priest's cap on Tarquin's head.[8]

[5] QUINTUS: I gather, brother, that you think that there are different rules to be observed in a poem from those that apply to history.

MARCUS: In the one case, Quintus, everything aims at truth; in the other, much aims at pleasure; although there are countless fables both in Herodotus the father of history and in Theopompus.

ATTICUS: Now I have the chance that I wanted, and I will not miss it.

MARCUS: What chance, Titus?

ATTICUS: For a long time, people have been asking – demanding – a history from you. They think that if you undertake it, then in this type of writing too we may rival the Greeks. My own opinion is that you owe this task not only to the interest of those who take pleasure in your

[5] Cicero, *Marius* frr. 15–16 Courtney. [6] The same tale is in *On the Commonwealth* 2.20.
[7] Near the river Ilissus; cf. Plato, *Phaedrus* 229b.
[8] Cf. Livy 1.19.5, 1.34.8. C. leaves these legends out of his account in *On the Commonwealth* Book 2.

writing, but to your country: the nation that has been preserved by you should be glorified by you as well. History is missing from our literature, as I know myself and as I have often heard from you. And you are the one who can fill the gap, since history is, as you yourself believe, a kind of writing particularly suited to an orator.[9] [6] Therefore we ask you to undertake it and to find the time for something which up to now has been ignored or abandoned by the Romans. Nothing could be drier than the annals of the pontifex maximus;[10] and if you turn to what follows them, to Fabius or to Cato – to whom you refer constantly – or to Piso or Fannius or Vennonius, even if each of them occasionally writes forcefully, still, what is as flat as the whole bunch? Fannius' contemporary Coelius Antipater was a little more vigorous, but the strength he had was rustic and rough, with no polish or skill; still, he could serve as a reminder to the others to write with more care. But look at his successors: Gellius,[11] Clodius, and Asellio are nothing like Coelius, although they stand comparison with the sloth and ignorance of the early writers. [7] I won't even consider Macer: he has some wit in his verbosity, but it derives from Latin hacks, not from the learned eloquence of the Greeks; his speeches are filled with awkwardness, and when he writes in a high style, he is completely over his head. His friend Sisenna easily surpassed all our writers up to now – unless there are some who have not yet made their work public, about whom we can't form a judgment.[12] But he was never considered an orator in your class, and he strives for childish effects in his history writing: the only Greek he seems to have read is Clitarchus, whom he simply tries to imitate; and even if he were able to achieve that, he would still be well below the ideal. And so the task is yours, and people await it from you. Unless, of course, Quintus has a different opinion.

[8] QUINTUS: Not at all, and we have often talked about it. But we do have a slight disagreement.

ATTICUS: What is that?

QUINTUS: What period he should take as his starting point. I think

[9] C.'s friend Cornelius Nepos agreed and imitated this passage in his work *On Latin Historians* (fr. 58 Marshall). For history as a form related to oratory cf. *On the Orator* 2.51–64.

[10] The earliest form of historical writing in Rome; cf. *On the Commonwealth* 1.25. "Drier" (*ieiunius*) is an emendation of the manuscripts' "more pleasing" (*iucundius*).

[11] Gellius' name is an emendation; the text is corrupt.

[12] In all probability C. is referring to his friend Lucceius, whom he had asked (unsuccessfully) to write a monograph on his (C.'s) consulate; cf. *Letters to His Friends* 5.12.

that he should begin from the beginning, since what has been written about those events is unreadable. He demands a contemporary subject, to include events in which he took part.

ATTICUS: I agree with him. Great things have happened in our memory and our lifetime. He will be able to bestow praise on our good friend Gnaeus Pompeius, and he will include his own glorious and memorable consular year. I would rather have him speak of these things than (as they say) of Remus and Romulus.[13]

MARCUS: I realize there have been demands for some time that I undertake this task, Atticus, and I wouldn't refuse if I had any free and unencumbered time. It is impossible to undertake something so large when you are busy or when your mind is on other things: you need to be free of both cares and business.

[9] ATTICUS: What do you mean? You have written more than any of us, and what free time did you have?

MARCUS: Snatches of time turn up, and I don't let them go to waste. If there are a few days free to spend in the country, I match what I write to the time that I have. But a history can't be undertaken unless free time is arranged in advance, and it can't be finished quickly. When once I begin something and am forced to change directions I am always left in a state of suspense; and I find it harder to pick up the threads when I am interrupted than to work through a project in a single push.

[10] ATTICUS: What you say seems to demand an ambassadorial appointment[14] or some similar respite giving you freedom and leisure.

MARCUS: I have been counting on the free time that comes with old age, especially since I would not refuse to follow ancestral custom and sit in a counselor's seat and give advice to clients, performing the useful and honorable function that belongs to a productive old age.[15] Then I would be able to give as much effort as I wanted to the subject that you desire, and to many larger and richer subjects as well.

[11] ATTICUS: But I'm afraid that no one would accept that excuse and that you would always have to make speeches: all the more, as you have changed yourself and taken up a different style of speaking. Just as your friend Roscius, when he grew old, softened the rhythms of his

[13] Presumably a proverb, although not otherwise attested.

[14] A so-called free embassy (*legatio libera*), an official appointment with no official duties (C. himself objected to such appointments; see 3.8 below).

[15] The giving of legal advice was a traditional function of senior senators; see below, 1.17 and *On the Orator* 1.199.

songs and made the flutes play more slowly, so too you, day by day, reduce somewhat the high intensity that you used to display; the result is that your oratory is now not very different from the relaxed style of philosophers. And since even a very old man can manage this style, I foresee that you will be given no vacation from the courts.

[12] QUINTUS: I certainly think that the people might approve of your giving legal advice; so when you like, I think that you should try it.

MARCUS: I would, Quintus, if there were no risk in such an experiment. But I'm afraid that the desire to lessen my work would actually increase it, and that the interpretation of law would simply be added to my work on cases, which I never approach without preparation and practice. Giving legal advice would not be a burden to me so much because of the work as because it would take away time from planning my speeches, without which I have never dared approach any major case.

[13] ATTICUS: Since this is one of those "snatches of time," as you call them, why don't you explain this very subject to us, and write about civil law more subtly than the others? I know that you have studied the law from the time you were very young, when I too used to study with Scaevola.[16] You have never seemed to me to be devoted to oratory to the exclusion of civil law.

MARCUS: You summon me to a long discussion, Atticus; but unless Quintus has something else in mind I will undertake it, and – since we have free time – I will speak.

QUINTUS: I would be happy to listen. What better is there for me to do, or how better should I occupy the day?

[14] MARCUS: Then let us move on to our walks and benches; when we have walked enough we will rest, and there will be no lack of pleasure in inquiring into one topic after another.

ATTICUS: That's fine with us, and if you like we will go this way to the Liris along the shady bank. But now, please, begin to explain your ideas about the civil law.

MARCUS: My ideas? I think that there have been very eminent men in our state who have made it their business to interpret the law to the people and to give opinions, but although they have made great claims they have been occupied in small matters. What is as grand as the law of a state? What is so trivial as the function of the jurists, necessary

[16] Quintus Mucius Scaevola the augur, to be distinguished from his cousin the pontifex, whose legal opinions are discussed below at 2.47ff.

though it be to the people? I don't believe that the men who were in charge of this function were ignorant of universal law, but they have only explored what they call the civil law to the extent that they wanted to provide it to the people; that, however, is as slight intellectually as it is necessary in practical matters. So where do you want me to go, and what are you urging me to do? that I write pamphlets on the law about water running off roofs or about shared walls? that I write the formulas for contracts or civil judgments? Many people have done that diligently, and it is more humble than I think is expected of me.[17]

[15] ATTICUS: If you ask what I expect, it is this: since you have written about the best form of the commonwealth, it seems logical that you should also write about the laws. I know that your beloved Plato did just that, a man you admire, exalt above all others, and cherish greatly.[18]

MARCUS: Then is this your wish? Just as with the Cretan Clinias and the Lacedaemonian Megillus, as he describes it, he spent a summer day in the cypress groves and forest paths of Cnossos, frequently stopping and occasionally resting, discoursing on public institutions and the best laws, in the same way let us walk and rest among these tall poplars on this green and shady bank and inquire into these same subjects more deeply than is required by the practical uses of the courts.

[16] ATTICUS: That is exactly what I want to hear.

MARCUS: What about Quintus?

QUINTUS: Nothing better.

MARCUS: And quite right too: you must understand that there is no subject for discussion in which it can be made so clear[19] what nature has given to humans; what a quantity of wonderful things the human mind embraces; for the sake of performing and fulfilling what function we are born and brought into the world; what serves to unite people; and what natural bond there is among them. Once we have explained these things, we can find the source of laws and of justice.

[17] ATTICUS: So you don't think that the discipline of law should be drawn from the praetor's edict (as is the current custom) or from the

[17] C. makes similarly disparaging comments about the jurists at *On Behalf of Murena* 23–29 and at *On the Orator* 1.236.

[18] Just as Plato's *Laws* was meant as the sequel to the *Republic*, so *On the Laws* is the sequel to *On the Commonwealth*; see 1.20 below. The difference is that the *Laws* provides legislation not for the ideal state of the *Republic* but for a second-best state; C. does not recognize this.

[19] Accepting Vahlen's conjecture *posse ita* for the transmitted *honesta*.

Twelve Tables (as our predecessors did),[20] but from the deepest core of philosophy?

MARCUS: The object of inquiry in this conversation, Atticus, is not how to write legal documents or how to answer legal questions. Granted, that is a great task, which used to be performed by many famous men and is now done by one man of the greatest authority and wisdom[21] – but in this discussion we must embrace the whole subject of universal justice and law, so that what we call "civil law"[22] will be limited to a small and narrow area. We must explain the nature of law, and that needs to be looked for in human nature; we must consider the legislation through which states ought to be governed; and then we must deal with the laws and decrees of peoples as they are composed and written, in which the so-called civil laws of our people will not be left out.

[18] QUINTUS: You are looking deep, and (as is right) to the source of what we seek; people who teach civil law differently are teaching not so much the way of justice as of the courtroom.

MARCUS: That isn't true, Quintus, and in fact ignorance of law leads to more lawsuits than knowledge of it. But that comes later; now we should consider the origins of law.

Philosophers have taken their starting point from law; and they are probably right to do so if, as these same people define it, law is the highest reason, rooted in nature, which commands things that must be done and prohibits the opposite.[23] When this same reason is secured and established in the human mind, it is law. [19] And therefore they think that law is judgment, the effect of which is such as to order people to behave rightly and forbid them to do wrong; they think that its name in Greek is derived from giving to each his own, while I think that in Latin it is de-

[20] Although the Twelve Tables (traditionally dated to the mid fifth century BCE) provided the main statutory basis for Roman law, most civil law in the late republic was based on the annual edict of the urban praetor, which announced the actions and remedies that he would permit.

[21] C. refers to his contemporary Servius Sulpicius Rufus (consul in 51), the last great jurist of the republican period.

[22] The phrase *ius civile* is used here to mean Roman law as opposed to the broader ideas of equity referred to in Latin as *ius gentium*, "the law of nations," or as opposed to justice itself; it is also commonly used to mean praetorian law (also called *ius honorarium*, "magistrates' law"), as opposed to statute law. It is not used in Latin (as it is in English) as the complementary term to "criminal law."

[23] The definition of law as command and prohibition is drawn from the opening of the treatise *On Law* of the Stoic Chrysippus (Long and Sedley, 67R). C.'s account of natural law is Stoic and develops the brief description given by Laelius at *On the Commonwealth* 3.33.

rived from choosing.[24] They put the essence of law in equity, and we place it in choice; both are attributes of law. I think that these ideas are generally right; and if so, then the beginning of justice is to be sought in law: law is a power of nature, it is the mind and reason of the prudent man, it distinguishes justice and injustice. But since all our speech is based on popular conceptions, we must sometimes speak in popular terms and call that a law (in the language of the common people) which prescribes in writing what it wants by ordering or forbidding. But in establishing the nature of justice, let us begin from that highest law, which was born aeons before any law was written or indeed before any state was established.

[**20**] QUINTUS: That is certainly more convenient and appropriate to the manner of the conversation we have begun.

MARCUS: Then shall we go back to the beginning, to the source of justice itself? Once we have found it, there will be no doubt about how to judge what we are seeking.

QUINTUS: In my opinion that is what we should do.

ATTICUS: I subscribe to your brother's opinion.

MARCUS: Then since we want to preserve and protect that form of commonwealth which Scipio showed was the best in the six books of *On the Commonwealth*, and since all the laws must be fitted to that type of state, and since morals must be planted and we should not rely on the sanctions of written laws, I will seek the roots of justice in nature, under whose leadership our entire discussion must unfold.

ATTICUS: Absolutely, and with nature's leadership there will be no possibility of getting lost.

[**21**] MARCUS: Then, Atticus, will you grant me this (I know Quintus' opinion), that all nature is ruled by the force or nature or reason or power or mind or will – or whatever other word there is that will indicate more plainly what I mean – of the immortal gods? If you don't accept this, then I will have to make it the starting point of my case.

ATTICUS: Of course I will grant it, if you wish; the singing of the birds and the noise of the river give me reason not to fear that any of my fellow students will hear me.[25]

[24] The Greek word for law (*nomos*) was derived from *nemô*, to divide; Latin *lex* from *lego*, to select. The explanation of the Greek word is basically Stoic.

[25] As an Epicurean, Atticus believed that the gods did not intervene in human affairs and that the world was not guided by any supernatural intelligence.

MARCUS: But you need to be careful: they can become very angry, as good men do, and they will not take it lightly if they hear that you have betrayed the opening sentence of the best of men, in which he wrote that god is not troubled by his own affairs or those of others.[26]

[22] ATTICUS: Go on, please. I am waiting to hear the relevance of what I have conceded to you.

MARCUS: You don't have long to wait. This is its relevance: this animal – provident, perceptive, versatile, sharp, capable of memory, and filled with reason and judgment – which we call a human being, was endowed by the supreme god with a grand status at the time of its creation. It alone of all types and varieties of animate creatures has a share in reason and thought, which all the others lack.[27] What is there, not just in humans, but in all heaven and earth, more divine than reason?[28] When it has matured and come to perfection, it is properly named wisdom. [23] And therefore, since there is nothing better than reason, and it is found both in humans and in god, reason forms the first bond between human and god. And those who share reason also share right reason; and since that is law, we humans must be considered to be closely allied to gods by law. Furthermore, those who share law also share the procedures of justice;[29] and those who have these things in common must be considered members of the same state, all the more so if they obey the same commands and authorities. Moreover, they do obey this celestial order, the divine mind and the all-powerful god, so that this whole cosmos must be considered to be the common state of gods and humans.[30] And as in states distinctions in the legal condition of individuals are made in accordance with family relationships (according to a kind of system with which I will

[26] Epicurus, *Principal Sayings* 1 (tr. Inwood and Gerson): "What is blessed and indestructible has no troubles itself, nor does it give trouble to anyone else, so that it is not affected by feelings of anger or gratitude. For all such things are signs of weakness." C. is perhaps being ironic about the inability of the Epicureans to live up to their principles: Epicurus himself was renowned for his vitriolic attacks on other philosophers.

[27] The emphasis on reason as the guiding principle of the universe is Stoic, as is the sharing of reason between humans and gods. See *On the Commonwealth* 3.3–4, 33; 4.1; also *On the Nature of the Gods* 2.16 = Long and Sedley 54E.

[28] A Stoic maxim (Chrysippus); cf. *On the Nature of the Gods* 2.16.

[29] *Ius*, here translated as "procedures of justice," can mean either the workings of a legal system (as opposed to the law itself) or the broader principles of justice (in the modern sense) that extend beyond positive law, including e.g. the pontifical law, which is *ius* rather than *lex*, as it is not a matter of statute. See "Text and Translation" above.

[30] The connection between right reason, law, and the cosmic city is Stoic; cf. *On the Commonwealth* 1.19; also *On the Nature of the Gods* 2.154 and Long and Sedley 67L.

deal at the proper time), it is all the more grand and glorious in nature at large that men should be a part of the family and race of gods.[31]

[24] For when people consider the nature of human beings, it is usual to argue (and I think that the argument is right) that in the constant motions and revolutions of the heavens a proper season came for planting the seeds of the human race; when it was scattered and sown over the earth, it was enhanced by the divine gift of souls. And although all the other things of which humans are composed came from mortal stock and were fragile and bound to perish, the soul was implanted in us by god. Hence there is in truth a family relationship between us and the gods, what can be called a common stock or origin. And thus out of so many species there is no animal besides the human being that has any knowledge of god, and among humans themselves there is no tribe, either civilized or savage, which does not know that it must recognize a god, even though it may not know what kind of god it should recognize.[32] [25] The result is that they acknowledge god as a sort of recollection and acknowledgment of their origin.[33] Furthermore, virtue is the same in human and god, and it is found in no other species besides; and virtue is nothing else than nature perfected and taken to its highest level. There is, therefore, a similarity between human and god. And since that is so, what closer or more certain relationship can there possibly be? That is why nature has bestowed such an abundance of things for human convenience and use, such that those things which exist seem to have been deliberately given to us, not randomly created – and this applies not only to the earth's profusion in bringing forth crops and fruits, but even to animals, some of which were created for human use, some for enjoyment, and some for food.[34] [26] Countless branches of knowledge have been discovered under the tutelage of nature, which reason imitated in order skillfully to achieve things necessary for life.

Nature also not only adorned the human being with swiftness of mind, but also gave him the senses as servants and messengers; she supplied the

[31] C. makes an analogy between the Roman agnatic family (shared descent through males from a common ancestor), with its emphasis on the power of the father over his descendants (*patria potestas*), and the structure of the cosmic family under divine authority. The later passage to which C. alludes here is lost.

[32] For universal acknowledgment of the existence of gods cf. *On the Nature of the Gods* 2.12 = Long and Sedley 54C.

[33] C. here combines Stoic belief with the Platonic concept of "recollection" of prior lives (*anamnêsis*).

[34] The teleological argument is again Stoic; cf. *On the Nature of the Gods* 2.37 = Long and Sedley 54H.

latent and not completely formed conceptions of many things as the basis of knowledge, and she gave a bodily shape that is both adaptable and suited to the nature of man. For although she made all other animate creatures face the earth for grazing, she made the human alone upright and roused him to look on the sky, as if on his family and former home; and she shaped the appearance of his face so as to mold in it the character hidden within.[35] [27] For the eyes most expressively say how we feel in our minds, and what is called the expression, which cannot exist in any other creature besides the human, indicates character (the Greeks know the idea, but they have no equivalent word).[36] I leave out the capacities and abilities of the rest of the body, the modulation of the voice and the power of speech, which is the greatest force in promoting bonds among humans. Not everything is appropriate to this discussion and this moment, and it seems to me that Scipio dealt sufficiently with this subject in the book that you have read.[37] Now, since god produced and equipped the human being in this way, desiring humans to have the first place among all other things, it is clear (to be selective in my discussion) that human nature itself has gone further: with no instruction, and taking as a starting point the knowledge of those things whose characteristics she knew from the first inchoate conceptions, she herself has strengthened reason and perfected it.

[28] ATTICUS: Good lord! What a distant starting point you take for the origins of justice! But you do it in such a way that I am not only not in a hurry to hear what I was waiting for from you on the civil law, but I could happily spend the whole day in this conversation. What you are discussing now, perhaps for the sake of other subjects, is more important than the things to which it serves as a preface.

MARCUS: Important they are, however briefly I am mentioning them now. But of all the things which are a subject of philosophical debate there is nothing more worthwhile than clearly to understand that we are born for justice and that justice is established not by opinion but by nature. That will be clear if you examine the common bonds among human beings. [29] There is no similarity, no likeness of one thing to another, so

35 The upright stature of the human is a commonplace of popular philosophy; cf. e.g. Xenophon, *Memorabilia* 1.4.11; Sallust, *Conspiracy of Catiline* 1.1. For the senses as servants cf. *On the Nature of the Gods* 2.140. For "conception" (*intellegentia* = Gk. *ennoia*, cf. *On the Supreme Good and Evil* 3.21), "preconception," and "impression" as technical terms of Stoic epistemology cf. e.g. Long and Sedley 39E–F with their commentary.

36 Greek uses *prosôpon* to mean both "face" and "expression."

37 See above, *On the Commonwealth* 4.1.

great as the likeness we all share. If distorted habits and false opinions did not twist weak minds and bend them in any direction,[38] no one would be so like himself as all people would be like all others. Thus, whatever definition of a human being one adopts is equally valid for all humans. [**30**] That, in turn, is a sufficient proof that there is no dissimilarity within the species; if there were, then no one definition would apply to all. In particular, reason, the one thing by which we stand above the beasts, through which we are capable of drawing inferences, making arguments, refuting others, conducting discussions and demonstrations – reason is shared by all, and though it differs in the particulars of knowledge, it is the same in the capacity to learn. All the same things are grasped by the senses; and the things that are impressed upon the mind, the rudiments of understanding which I mentioned before, are impressed similarly on all humans, and language, the interpreter of the mind, may differ in words but is identical in ideas. There is no person of any nation who cannot reach virtue with the aid of a guide.

[**31**] The similarity of the human race is as remarkable in perversities as it is in proper behavior. All people are ensnared by pleasure; and even if it is an enticement to bad conduct it still has some similarity to natural goodness: it gives delight through its fickle sweetness. Thus through a mental error it is adopted as something salutary; by a similar sort of ignorance death is avoided as a dissolution of nature, life is sought because it keeps us in the state in which we were born, and pain is considered one of the greatest evils both because of its own harshness and because the destruction of our nature seems to follow from it. [**32**] Because of the similarity between honor and glory, people who have been honored seem blessed, and those who have no glory seem wretched. Trouble, happiness, desires, and fears pass equally through the minds of all, and if different peoples have different beliefs, that does not mean that the superstition that affects people who worship dogs and cats is not the same as that which besets other races. What nation is there that does not cherish affability, generosity, a grateful mind and one that remembers good deeds? What nation does not scorn and hate people who are proud, or evildoers, or cruel, or ungrateful? From all these things it may be understood that the whole human race is bound together; and the final result is that the understanding of the right way of life makes all people better. If you

[38] The text here is uncertain, but the sense is clear.

agree with all this, then we can go on to the rest; if you think anything is left out, then we should discuss that first.

ATTICUS: We are quite satisfied, if I may answer for both of us.

[33] MARCUS: It follows, then, that we have been made by nature to receive the knowledge of justice one from another and share it among all people.[39] And I want it to be understood in this whole discussion that the justice of which I speak is natural,[40] but that such is the corruption of bad habits that it extinguishes what I may call the sparks given by nature, and that contrary vices arise and become established. But if human judgment corresponded to what is true by nature and men thought nothing human alien to them (to use the poet's phrase),[41] then justice would be cultivated equally by all. Those who have been given reason by nature have also been given right reason, and therefore law too, which is right reason in commands and prohibitions; and if they have been given law, then they have been given justice too. All people have reason, and therefore justice has been given to all; so that Socrates rightly used to curse the person who was first to separate utility from justice, and to complain that that was the source of all ills.[42] Where did Pythagoras get his famous statement about friendship? A place . . .[43]

[34] From this it is clear that, when a wise man offers this goodwill, which is spread so far and wide, towards another who is endowed with equal virtue, then what some people think is unbelievable (but which is actually necessary) comes to pass, that he loves himself no more than the other: what difference can there be when everything is equal? If the slightest distinction could be made in friendship, moreover, the name of

[39] Goerler's interpretation of the text is followed here.

[40] The text here is uncertain, and Goerler is followed here. Keyes translates "what I call nature is [that which is implanted in us by Nature]," following Vahlen.

[41] Terence, *Hautontimoroumenos* 77.

[42] So also *On Duties* 3.11; the report comes from a Stoic source.

[43] There is a lacuna in the text, and the meaning of the last few words is unclear; they may contain a heading ("commonplace on friendship") indicating the contents of a passage omitted at some point in the transmission. The gap clearly contained an argument on the natural basis of friendship in goodwill (*benevolentia*); cf. *On Friendship* 50. Ziegler includes here the following passage from Lactantius, *Inst.* 5.8.10, which Schmidt assigns to Book 4:

> Now, however, men are evil through ignorance of what is right and good. Cicero saw that, and in his discourse on laws he says:
>
> > Just as by one and the same nature the universe holds and presses together with all its parts similar to one another, so all men are held together by nature, but they disagree, confused by evil, and they do not understand that they are blood relatives and all subject to one and the same guardian. If this were maintained, then men would really live the life of the gods.

friendship would cease to be: its significance is such that as soon as someone wants something for himself more than for the other, it no longer exists.

All this is preparatory to the rest of our discussion, so that the natural basis of justice can more easily be recognized. And after I have said a little about this, I will come to the civil law, which was the starting point of this whole discourse.

QUINTUS: You need to say very little indeed. From what you have said, Atticus believes, and I certainly do too, that justice arises from nature.[44]

[35] ATTICUS: Could I think otherwise, since this has already been proven: first, that we have been equipped and adorned as if by gifts of the gods; secondly, that there is one equal manner of life, shared by all people; and finally, that all people are bound by a sort of natural goodwill and benevolence as well as by the bond of justice? Since we have agreed (rightly, I think) that these things are true, how could we separate laws and justice from nature?

[36] MARCUS: You are right, and that is how things are. But in the manner of philosophers – not the old style[45] but that of those who have set up philosophical workshops of a sort – what used to be discussed on a broad scale is now analyzed bit by bit. They don't think that this topic that is now in hand is dealt with adequately unless they argue separately that justice exists by nature.

ATTICUS: I suppose that you have lost your own freedom of speech, or that you are the sort of person to follow someone else's authority rather than your own judgment in speaking!

[37] MARCUS: Not always, Titus, but you see the direction of this discussion. My whole discourse aims at making commonwealths sound, establishing justice, and making all peoples healthy. For that reason I am afraid of making the mistake of starting from first principles that are not well considered and carefully examined; not that everyone should agree with them – that is impossible – but so that they will have the approval of those who believe that all right and honorable things are desirable on their own account, and that either nothing at all should be considered good unless it is praiseworthy in itself or at least that nothing should be

[44] The text here is probably corrupt; Büchner and Kenter read "even if Atticus is not convinced that justice arises from nature, I certainly am."

[45] I.e. philosophers up to Plato's time.

considered a great good except what can truly be praised on its own account.[46] [38] All these people, whether they have stayed in the Old Academy with Speusippus, Xenocrates, and Polemo, or have followed Aristotle and Theophrastus, who agree with them in substance but use a slightly different type of argument, or those who, like Zeno, have changed the terminology without changing the substance, or even have followed the difficult and demanding system of Aristo, which has now been overcome and refuted, namely that with the exception of virtues and vices all things should be considered entirely equal[47] – all these people agree with what I have said. [39] Those, however, who indulge themselves and are enslaved to their bodies, who judge everything that is to be sought or avoided in life by pleasures and pains – even if what they say is true (and there is no need for arguments about it here), we tell them to talk in their gardens, and we ask them to stand away for a little while from all bonds of civic society, of which they know nothing and have never wanted to know anything.[48] As for the Academy, the new one of Arcesilaus and Carneades that confuses all these questions, we request it to remain silent.[49] For if it attacks these things that seem to us neatly arranged and composed, it will cause excessive damage. I would like to conciliate it, and I don't dare push it aside.[50]

[40] . . . for even in these things we have been purified without his fumigations.[51] But there is no purification for crimes against humans and for acts of impiety,[52] and so they pay the penalty, not so much in courts – which used not to exist anywhere and now do not exist in many places, and where they do, they are often corrupt – as through being chased and hounded by the Furies, not with burning torches as in the myths, but with the pains of conscience and the tortures of deceit.[53] If it were the penalty rather than nature that was supposed to keep men from doing in-

[46] The first definition belongs to the Stoics and Aristo, the second to the Old Academy and Peripatos. C.'s account of the development of ethics after Plato is closely based on the ideas of Antiochus of Ascalon (cf. 1.54), who tried to demonstrate the similarity in all but terminology of Stoic, Peripatetic, and early Academic ethics. For a valuable assessment of his importance see now J. Barnes, "Antiochus of Ascalon," in *Philosophia Togata*, ed. Griffin and Barnes (Oxford, 1989), 51–96.

[47] For Aristo's system cf. Long and Sedley 58F.

[48] The Epicureans.

[49] The skeptical Academy denied the possibility of true knowledge and made a point of arguing against all dogmatic arguments; for Carneades' balanced speeches on justice see *On the Commonwealth* Book 3.

[50] There is a lacuna following this sentence.

[51] Possibly a reference to Pythagoras and to the use of purifications for ritual purposes.

[52] Reading *inpietatum*.

[53] C. (following Aeschines, *Against Timarchus* 190–91) contrasts the Furies of tragedy with the pangs of conscience also at *On Behalf of Roscius of Ameria* 67.

justice, what worry would trouble the wicked if the fear of punishment were removed?[54] In fact, however, no criminal has ever been so bold that he did not either deny the commission of a crime or invent some reason for just resentment and seek the defense of his deed in some natural right. And if the wicked dare to make this claim, then how eagerly should it be embraced by the good! If penalties and the fear of punishment rather than the criminal behavior itself are the deterrent from an unjust and criminal existence, then no one is unjust, and the wicked should rather be considered incautious.[55] **[41]** Furthermore, those of us who are not moved by the idea of honor itself to be good men, but rather by some sort of utility or profit, are not good men, but crafty. What will a person do in the dark if he is afraid only of witnesses and judges? What will he do in some deserted place if he encounters someone from whom he can steal a lot of gold, someone weak and alone? Our naturally just and good man will talk to him, help him, and lead him on his way; the man who does nothing for someone else's sake and measures everything by his own interest – I think you know what he will do! And if he denies that he will kill him and take his gold, he will never deny it on the ground that he considers it to be wrong by nature, but because he is afraid that word will get out and therefore that it will cause trouble to him. That is something to cause peasants as well as philosophers to blush.

[42] The most stupid thing of all, moreover, is to consider all things just which have been ratified by a people's institutions or laws. What about the laws of tyrants? If the famous thirty tyrants at Athens had wanted to impose laws, or if all the Athenians were pleased with tyrannical laws, is that a reason for calling those laws just? No more than the one carried by our interrex, that the dictator could put to death with impunity whatever citizens he wished, even without a trial.[56] There is only one justice, which constitutes the bond among humans, and which was established by the one law, which is right reason in commands and prohibitions. The person who does not know it is unjust, whether the law has been written anywhere or not. And if justice is obedience to the written laws and institutions of a people, and if (as these same people say)[57] everything is to be measured by utility, then whoever thinks that it will

[54] In what follows C. argues against Epicurean utilitarian interpretations of justice.

[55] For the arguments of this and the following section see *On the Commonwealth* 3.26–31.

[56] The interrex is Lucius Valerius Flaccus, who in 82 BCE proposed the law making Sulla dictator.

[57] Still the Epicureans.

be advantageous to him will neglect the laws and will break them if he can. The result is that there is no justice at all if it is not by nature, and the justice set up on the basis of utility is uprooted by that same utility:[58] [43] if nature will not confirm justice, all the virtues will be eliminated. Where will there be a place for liberality, for love of country, for piety, for the desire to do well by others or return kindness? These all arise because we are inclined by nature to love other humans, and that is the foundation of justice.[59] Not only deference to humans but religious observances towards the gods will be destroyed, which I believe need to be preserved not because of fear but because of the bond which exists between human and god. If justice were determined by popular vote or by the decrees of princes or the decisions of judges, then it would be just to commit highway robbery or adultery or to forge wills if such things were approved by popular vote. [44] If the opinions and the decrees of stupid people are powerful enough to overturn nature by their votes, why don't they ordain that what is evil and destructive should be considered good and helpful? If law can make justice out of injustice, why can't it make good from evil? But in fact we can divide good laws from bad by no other standard than that of nature. And it is not only justice and injustice that are distinguished naturally, but in general all honorable and disgraceful acts. For nature has given us shared conceptions and has so established them in our minds that honorable things are classed with virtue, disgraceful ones with vice.[60] [45] To think that these things are a matter of opinion, not fixed in nature, is the mark of a madman. What we call (and it is a misuse of the word) the virtue of a tree or of a horse is not a matter of opinion; it is natural. And if that is true, honorable and disgraceful can also be distinguished by nature. For if virtue as a whole is determined by opinion, then the same is true of its parts. And therefore who would judge a man to be prudent or, to use another word, shrewd from some external circumstance rather than from his own bearing? Virtue is reason brought to completion, which certainly exists in nature; and therefore the same is true of all honorable behavior. For just as true and false, logical and illogical are judged in themselves and not by external considerations, so too a constant and consistent manner of life, which is virtue, and similarly inconstancy, which is vice, will be judged by their own nature. Will we test the character of a tree or a horse by the standard of nature and not judge the characters of young men in the same way? [46] Or are charac-

[58] For Epicurus' own statement of the utilitarian basis of law cf. *Principal Sayings* 31–37.

[59] Cf. *On the Commonwealth* 3.39a.

[60] The text here is very uncertain.

ters to be judged by nature, but virtues and vices – which derive from character – to be judged differently? Or will we judge virtue and vice in the same way as character but not find it necessary to refer honorable and dishonorable to the standard of nature? Whatever good thing deserves praise must necessarily have in itself something that is to be praised; the good itself is not a matter of opinion but of nature. If that were not the case, then men would be happy by opinion – and nothing dumber than that could possibly be said. Therefore, since good and bad are judged by nature, and they are fundamental concepts of nature, then certainly honorable and dishonorable things must be judged in a similar way and referred to nature.

[47] But the variety of opinions and the discord of humans disturb us; and because we do not have the same problems with our senses, we consider them to be certain by nature, but we say that because moral qualities seem different to different people and not even the same person always sees them the same way, they must be false.[61] That is completely untrue: our senses are not distorted by a parent, a nurse, a teacher, a poet, or the stage; the agreement of the multitude does not lead them from the truth.[62] All sorts of traps are directed against our minds, either by those whom I just listed, who take them when they are tender and inexperienced and corrupt and bend them as they wish, or by that which lurks entwined deep in all our senses, namely pleasure, which imitates the good but is the mother of all evils. Those who are corrupted by her blandishments do not perceive sufficiently well what things are good by nature, because these things lack the sweet itch of pleasure.

[48] The result (to bring my whole argument to a close) is what is obvious from what has already been said, that justice, like every honorable thing, is desirable on its own account. In fact all good men love equity and just behavior for themselves, and it is not the part of a good man to go wrong and to love something that is not lovable for itself; and therefore what is just is to be sought and loved for itself. And if that is true of what is just, then it is true of justice; and if justice, then all the other virtues are to be cultivated for themselves. What of liberality? is it gratuitous or for a reward? If someone is benevolent without a price, then it is gratuitous; if for a reward, then it is bought.[63] Nor is there any doubt that the person who is said to be liberal or benevolent is following duty, not profit.

[61] Cf. *On the Commonwealth* 3.13.

[62] A very similar argument is at *Tusculan Disputations* 3.2–3.

[63] Cf. *Academica* 2.140 for the argument that virtuous acts are necessarily gratuitous.

Therefore justice too seeks no reward and no prize, and thus it is sought for itself, and the same is the case for all virtues. [**49**] And furthermore, if virtue is sought for its rewards, not for its own intrinsic merits, then the only virtue will be the one most rightly called wicked conduct. The more a man judges his actions by his interest, the less good he will be, and those who measure virtue by its reward think nothing to be a virtue except wickedness. Where is the benevolent man if no one behaves benevolently on another's behalf? Where is the grateful man if people are not genuinely grateful to the person to whom they owe gratitude?[64] Where is holy friendship if the friend is not loved, as they say, with whole heart? He will have to be deserted and abandoned if there is no hope of profit and reward; and what more terrible thing could possibly be said? And if friendship is to be cultivated for itself, then the fellowship of men, equality, and justice are desirable in themselves. And if that is not so, then there is no such thing as justice at all. For that is the most unjust thing of all, to seek a reward for justice.

[**50**] What about moderation, temperateness, and self-restraint? What about modesty, shame, and chastity? Are people to refrain from aggression through fear of disgrace, or of laws and courts? Are people innocent and modest in order to have a good reputation, and do they blush in order to gain good opinion? I am ashamed to talk about chastity, and I am ashamed of those philosophers who think the avoidance of a bad reputation more important than the avoidance of vice. [**51**] What then? Can we call those people decent who are kept from adultery by the fear of disgrace, although the disgrace is the necessary consequence of the baseness of the act? What can properly be praised or criticized if you ignore the nature of what you think should be praised or criticized? Do great physical deformities cause offense, but not a misshapen mind? The dishonorableness of that can be seen most easily from the vices themselves. What is uglier than greed, what is more horrible than lust, what is more contemptible than cowardice, what is lower than sloth and stupidity? What then? Those who are remarkable for single vices or even for several – do we call them wretched because of material losses or torture, or because of the nature and the dishonor of the vices themselves? And the same is true, in the opposite direction, of virtue. [**52**] Finally, if virtue is desirable for other reasons, it is necessary that there be something better than virtue; is it money, or office, or beauty, or health? When these are present,

64 The text here is very uncertain.

they are trivial, and it is impossible to have certain knowledge of how long they will last. Or is it (the vilest thing to mention) pleasure?[65] But it is in spurning and repudiating pleasure that virtue is most clearly recognized.

Do you see what a long chain of subjects and ideas this is, and how one thing is bound to another? I would go on even further unless I stopped myself.

QUINTUS: In what direction? I would be happy to go further with you in this discussion.

MARCUS: To the supreme good, by which all things should be judged and for the sake of gaining which all things should be done; that is a matter of controversy, filled with disagreement among philosophers, but a judgment must be made about it eventually.[66]

[53] ATTICUS: How can that be, now that Lucius Gellius is dead?

MARCUS: How is that relevant?

ATTICUS: Because I remember hearing in Athens from my friend Phaedrus that your friend Gellius, when he came to Greece as proconsul after his praetorship,[67] summoned all the philosophers who were then in Athens to one place and vigorously urged them to bring their controversies to an end. And if they did not want to waste the rest of their lives in disputes, some accommodation could be made, and he promised them his assistance in reaching some agreement.

MARCUS: That was very funny, Atticus, and has been a source of amusement to many people. But I would like to have been assigned as arbitrator between the Old Academy and Zeno.[68]

ATTICUS: How so?

MARCUS: Because they disagree on only one thing, and they are in remarkable accord about everything else.

ATTICUS: Do you think so? Is there only one disagreement?

[54] MARCUS: Only one essential thing: the Old Academy decided that everything in accordance with nature was good if it helped us in life, while Zeno thought nothing good that was not also honorable.

ATTICUS: I suppose that's a small matter, not the sort to make such a great division.

[65] The Epicurean position.

[66] C. devoted his dialogue *On the Supreme Good and Evil* to the question of ends; he gives a brief doxography at *Tusculan Disputations* 5.84–85. For Hellenistic debates on the subject cf. Long and Sedley 63–64.

[67] In 93 BCE.

[68] In what follows, C. again accepts the views of Antiochus of Ascalon, who grouped Aristotle and the early Peripatetics with the successors of Plato.

MARCUS: I would agree with you if they differed in substance and not just in words.

ATTICUS: So you share the opinion of my friend Antiochus (I don't dare call him my teacher), with whom I lived and who nearly plucked me out of the Garden[69] and brought me almost into the Academy.

MARCUS: He was a wise and clever man, perfect of his own sort, and a friend of mine, as you know; but we will see soon whether or not I agree with him in everything. I will say this, that the whole dispute can be settled.

[55] ATTICUS: How do you see that?

MARCUS: If, like Aristo of Chios, Zeno had said that the only good is what is honorable, and that only what is dishonorable is bad, and that all other things are quite equal, and that it made no difference at all whether they are present or absent, then he would have a serious difference from Xenocrates and Aristotle and the disciples of Plato, and there would be a disagreement among them about the most important thing and about the whole basis of life. But since Zeno said that virtue was the sole good, while the Old Academy said it was the highest good; and he said that vice was the only evil, and they said it was the greatest evil; he calls wealth, health, and beauty convenient rather than good, and poverty, weakness, and pain inconvenient rather than evil, he has the same idea as Xenocrates and Aristotle but uses different language. From this difference in words rather than substance arose the controversy about ends, and since the Twelve Tables forbade ownership to be obtained by possession within five feet of a boundary line, we will not allow the ancient possession of the Academy to be displaced by this clever man; and we will serve as a board of three arbitrators to settle the boundary according to the Twelve Tables rather than assigning a single arbitrator by the Mamilian law.[70]

[56] ATTICUS: What, then, will be our verdict?

MARCUS: That the boundary markers set out by Socrates should be found and that they should hold good.

QUINTUS: You are making fine use, brother, of the language of civil law, the subject of the discussion that I am still waiting for. The arbitration that you describe is a significant one, as I have often heard from you.

[69] A reference to Epicureanism.

[70] C. makes an extended play on the two meanings of *finis* as "end" in the philosophical sense and as "boundary" in the terminology of Roman property law. The Lex Mamilia Roscia Peducaea Aliena Fabia (probably of 59 BCE) substituted a single arbiter for the three permitted under the Twelve Tables (fr. VII, 5 Crawford).

But certainly it is the case that it is the highest good either to live in accordance with nature, that is, to enjoy a moderate life equipped with virtue, or to follow nature and to live in accordance with what can be called its law, that is insofar as possible to do everything to accomplish the demands of nature, who wishes us to live in accordance with virtue as if it were a law.[71] So I don't know whether this dispute can ever be settled; we certainly can't solve it in this discussion, at least if we are to accomplish what we set out to do.

[57] MARCUS: This digression was my responsibility, and I enjoyed it.

QUINTUS: Leave it for another time. Now let us do what we began, especially since this disagreement about the greatest good and evil has nothing to do with it.

MARCUS: Very wise, Quintus. What I have already said . . .[72]

QUINTUS: . . . I am not asking you [to discuss] the laws of Lycurgus or Solon or Charondas or Zaleucus or our own Twelve Tables or legislation passed by the people, but I expect you to give in today's discussion the laws and the discipline of life both for peoples and for individuals.

[58] MARCUS: What you expect certainly belongs to this discussion, Quintus; I only wish I had the capacity for it. But as things are, since law ought to correct vices and encourage virtues, then the knowledge of how to live should be drawn from it. Thus it is the case that wisdom is the mother of all good things, from the love of which philosophy took its name in Greek.[73] The gods have given to human existence nothing richer, nothing more outstanding, nothing more noble. Philosophy alone has taught us, in addition to everything else, the most difficult of all things, that we should know ourselves; and the force and significance of this maxim are such that it was attributed not to some human but to the god of Delphi. **[59]** The person who knows himself will first recognize that he has something divine and will think that his own reason within himself is a sort of consecrated image of the divine. He will always do and think things worthy of this great gift of the gods; and when he has studied and made a complete examination of himself, he will understand how he came into life fitted out by nature, and what tools he has for getting and possessing wisdom, since in the beginning he formed the first sketchy conceptions of all things in his mind; and when light has been cast on them under the guidance of wisdom he recognizes that he is a good man

[71] The two alternatives represent the Academic/Peripatetic and Stoic positions respectively. The text is uncertain.

[72] There is a lacuna in the text.

[73] Greek *sophia*, "wisdom," is the root of *philosophia*, "love of wisdom."

and for that reason he perceives that he will be blessed. [60] For when the mind, through the knowledge and perception of virtue, has departed from obedience to and indulgence of the body, and has conquered pleasure like some blot of disgrace, and has escaped all fear of death and pain, and has entered the bond of affection with his own – and has recognized as his own all those who are linked with him by nature – and has taken up the worship of the gods and pure religion, and has sharpened the gaze of his mind, like that of the eyes, for the selection of good things and the rejection of the opposite, the virtue which is called "prudence" from the capacity to see ahead,[74] – what can be said or thought to be more blessed than he? [61] And when he has studied the heaven, lands, seas, and the nature of all things, and has seen where they come from and where they are going and when and how they will perish, what in them is mortal and bound to die, what is divine and eternal; and when he has (so to speak) got a grip on the god who guides and rules these things and has recognized that he is not bound by human walls as the citizen of one particular spot but a citizen of the whole world as if it were a single city[75] – then in this perception and understanding of nature, by the immortal gods, how he will know himself, as Pythian Apollo commands, how he will scorn and despise and think as nothing all those things which are commonly called magnificent! [62] And he will fortify all these things as if by a fence through the method of argument, the knowledge of judging true and false, the science of understanding logical consequences and contradictions. And when he realizes that he is born for civil society, he will realize that he must use not just that refined type of argument but also a more expansive style of speaking, through which to guide peoples, to establish laws, to chastise the wicked and protect the good, to praise famous men and to issue instructions for safety and glory suited to persuading his fellow citizens, to exhort people to honor, to call them back from crime, to be able to comfort the afflicted, to enshrine in eternal memorials the deeds and opinions of brave and wise men together with the disgrace of the wicked. And of all these great and numerous things which are recognized as present in man by those who wish to know themselves, the parent and the teacher of them all is philosophy.

[63] ATTICUS: Your praise of philosophy is both profound and true. But where does it lead?

MARCUS: First to those things, Atticus, with which we will be con-

[74] See *On the Commonwealth* 2.67 n 81.

[75] The Stoic idea of the *cosmopolis*, the universal city; see above, 1.23.

cerned, which we want to be so grand, and they won't be unless their sources are also perceived to be magnificent. Secondly, I have spoken willingly and I hope truly, because I cannot pass over in silence the subject to which I am devoted and which has made me what I am.

ATTICUS: You are right to do so: it is both deserved and respectful on your part, and as you say it was necessary to do so in this discussion.

Book 2

[1] ATTICUS: Since we have already walked enough and you have to make a start on a new topic, why don't we move and sit down for the rest of the conversation on the island in the Fibrenus – I think that that is the name of the other river?

MARCUS: Certainly. I use that spot regularly with great pleasure, whether I am thinking something over or reading or writing something.

[2] ATTICUS: For my part, since I have just now come here, there are no bounds to my pleasure, and I have only contempt for grand villas and marble pavements and paneled ceilings. Those water channels that some people call "Nile" or "Euripus" can only arouse laughter when you have seen this spot.[1] And just as you, in speaking of law and justice a little while ago, made nature the standard for everything, so too in seeking aids for mental relaxation and pleasure nature is best. I used to wonder – I thought that there was nothing here but rocks and mountains, basing my opinion on your own speeches and poetry – I wondered, as I said, why you took such pleasure in this place. Now I wonder why when you are away from Rome you ever go anywhere else.

[3] MARCUS: When I have enough free time, particularly at this season, I seek out the beauty and the healthfulness of this place – though that is not very often. But in fact I have another cause of pleasure here, which is not so relevant to you.

ATTICUS: What is that?

MARCUS: Because, in truth, this is my own and my brother's real

[1] It was fashionable to name landscaped features of great estates after famous natural sites, as to name (as C. himself did) buildings after the Academy or Lyceum at Athens. The Euripus is the strait between Euboea and the mainland of Greece.

fatherland. Here is the most ancient origin of our stock; here are our family rituals[2] and our family; here there are many traces of our ancestors. In brief: you see this house? It was made larger and fancier by our father, who spent most of his life here in study, because of his poor health; but on this very spot, while my grandfather was still alive and it was a small house of the old style, like the house of Curius in the Sabine country, I was born. And so something abides deep in my mind and feelings which makes me take all the more pleasure in this place, just as that wisest of men is said to have refused immortality so that he could see Ithaca again.[3]

[4] ATTICUS: I think that you have an excellent reason to enjoy coming here and for loving this place. To tell the truth, I too am made more fond of that house and this whole land in which you were born and raised. We are somehow moved by the places in which the signs of those we love or admire are present. My beloved Athens pleases me not so much because of the grand buildings and refined arts of the ancients as because of the recollection of great men – where each one lived, where he sat, where he used to teach – and I make a point of visiting their tombs as well. And so I will love even more in the future the place where you were born.

MARCUS: Then I am delighted to have shown you my cradle, so to speak.

[5] ATTICUS: And I too am delighted to have seen it. But what you said a few moments ago, that this place – by which I take it you mean Arpinum – is your real fatherland: what did you mean? Do you have two fatherlands, or is the one we share the only one? Unless, perhaps, the fatherland of wise old Cato[4] was not Rome but Tusculum.

MARCUS: Indeed, I believe that both Cato and all those who come from the towns[5] have two fatherlands, one by nature, the other by citizenship. Cato was born at Tusculum but was given Roman citizenship, and so he was Tusculan by origin, Roman by citizenship, and had one fatherland by place of birth, the other by law. In the same way the people of your Attica, before Theseus ordered them to move in from

[2] *Sacra*: the graves of ancestors and the rituals associated with the dead, particularly the rite of the Parentalia, observed in February. These religious observances are the subject of an extended discussion below, at 2.46–53.

[3] *Odyssey* 5.135–36.

[4] The elder Cato; see biographical notes.

[5] In essence *municipia* were previously independent towns which were given Roman citizenship, as opposed to colonies, which were settlements sent out from Rome. After 89 BCE all towns that were not colonies became *municipia*.

the countryside to the city (the *astu*, they call it), were citizens both of their own places and of Attica, so we consider that too to be a fatherland where we were born. But of necessity that one takes precedence in our affections whose name "commonwealth" belongs to the entire citizen body, on behalf of which we have an obligation to die, to which we should give ourselves entirely and in which we should place and almost consecrate everything we have. But in our affections the one that bore us stands almost as high as the one that received us; and so I will never deny that this is my fatherland, while recognizing that the other one is greater and that this one is contained within it . . .[6] has two citizenships but thinks of them as one citizenship.

[6] ATTICUS: Then our friend Pompey was right to say in my hearing, when he was defending Ampius in court together with you, that our commonwealth had very just cause to thank this town, because two of its saviors had come from here;[7] as a result, I am inclined to agree that this place that gave you birth is your fatherland.

But we have reached the island. Really, nothing could be more charming. The Fibrenus is split by this prow, so to speak: it divides into two equal channels flowing along the sides and then swiftly comes together into one, including just enough for a palaestra of moderate size. And after doing that, as if that was its function – to create a place for us to sit and converse – it immediately plunges into the Liris, and, like someone entering a patrician family, it loses its unfamiliar name;[8] it also makes the Liris much colder. I've never touched a river colder that this, although I've seen many. I can scarcely put my foot in it, as Socrates does in Plato's *Phaedrus*.[9]

[7] MARCUS: True enough. But to judge from what Quintus has often said, your own Thyamis in Epirus is the equal of this in charm.[10]

QUINTUS: Quite true. You shouldn't think that anything surpasses the Amaltheum and the plane trees of our friend Atticus. But if you agree, let us sit here in the shade and return to that part of the discussion from which we digressed.

MARCUS: You're a careful creditor, Quintus – I thought that I had escaped – and nothing of this debt to you can be left unpaid.

6 There is a gap in the text.

7 Marius was the other famous citizen of Arpinum; see 1.4 above.

8 The image is of someone of undistinguished family being adopted into a noble family and taking the famous name.

9 *Phaedrus* 230b.

10 Atticus' villa; in 61 C. asked for details about the Amaltheum to use in his own construction at Arpinum (*Letters to Atticus* 1.16.15).

QUINTUS: Then begin; we give the whole day over to you.

MARCUS: "From Jupiter the beginnings of song," as I began in my *Aratea*.[11]

QUINTUS: What is your point?

MARCUS: That now too we must take the starting point of the discussion from Jupiter and the other immortal gods.

QUINTUS: Fine, brother; it's right to do so.

[8] MARCUS: Then before we get to particular laws, let us consider again the meaning and nature of law, so that – since everything else in our discussion rests on this – we don't slip from time to time in the misuse of language and make mistakes about the meaning of the [word][12] by which our laws are to be defined.

QUINTUS: Fair enough; that's the right course of instruction.

MARCUS: This has, I know, been the opinion of the wisest men: that law was not thought up by human minds; that it is not some piece of legislation by popular assemblies; but it is something eternal which rules the entire universe through the wisdom of its commands and prohibitions.[13] Therefore, they said, that first and final law is the mind of the god who compels or forbids all things by reason. From that cause, the law which the gods have given to the human race has rightly been praised: it is the reason and mind of a wise being, suited to command and prohibition.

[9] QUINTUS: You have dealt with that subject several times already. But before you come to legislation enacted by popular vote, please explain the meaning of that heavenly law, so that we may not be sucked in by the tide of habit and drawn to the customs of everyday language.

MARCUS: From the time we were small, Quintus, we were taught to call "if there is a summons to court" and other things of that sort "laws."[14] But in fact it should be understood that both this and other commands and prohibitions of peoples have a force for summoning to proper behavior and deterring from crime, a force which is not only older than the age of peoples and states but coeval with the god who protects and steers heaven and earth. [10] It is not possible for there to be a divine mind without reason, nor does divine reason lack this force in sanctioning right and wrong. The fact that it was not written down anywhere that one man should stand on the bridge against all the forces of the enemy and order the bridge to be cut down behind him does not

[11] See *On the Commonwealth* 1.56. [12] The text is corrupt. [13] See above, 1.18.

[14] The opening clause of the Twelve Tables (fr. 1, 1 Crawford).

mean that we should not believe that the famous Horatius Cocles performed his great deed in accordance with the law and command of bravery; nor does the absence of a written law on sexual assault during the reign of Lucius Tarquinius mean that the violence which Sextus Tarquinius brought against Lucretia the daughter of Tricipitinus was not contrary to the eternal law. Reason existed, derived from nature, directing people to good conduct and away from crime; it did not begin to be a law only at that moment when it was written down, but when it came into being; and it came into being at the same time as the divine mind. And therefore that true and original law, suitable for commands and prohibitions, is the right reason of Jupiter, the supreme god.

[11] QUINTUS: I agree, brother, that what is right and true is also eternal and neither rises nor falls with the texts in which legislation is written.

MARCUS: Therefore, just as that divine mind is the highest law, so too when in a human being it is brought to maturity, <it resides>[15] in the mind of wise men. The legislation that has been written down for nations in different ways and for particular occasions has the name of law more as a matter of courtesy than as a fact; for they[16] teach that every law that deserves that name is praiseworthy, using arguments such as these: it is generally agreed that laws were invented for the well-being of citizens, the safety of states, and the calm and happy life of humans; and that those who first ordained legislation of this sort demonstrated to their peoples that they would write and carry such legislation the adoption of which would make their lives honorable and happy; and that what was so composed and ordained they would call laws. From this it should be understood that those who wrote decrees that were destructive and unjust to their peoples, since they did the opposite of what they had promised and claimed, produced something utterly different from laws; so that it should be clear that in the interpretation of the word "law" itself there is the significance and intention of choosing something just and right. [12] So I ask you, Quintus, as they generally do: if the lack of something causes a state to be worthless, is that something to be considered a good thing?

QUINTUS: Among the very best.

MARCUS: Then should not a state lacking law be considered as nothing for that very reason?

[15] Conjectural supplement; there is a gap in the text. [16] I.e. philosophers.

QUINTUS: No other conclusion is possible.

MARCUS: Then it is necessary that law be considered one of the best things.

QUINTUS: I agree completely.

[13] MARCUS: What of the fact that many things are approved by peoples that are damaging and destructive, which no more approach the name of law than whatever bandits have agreed upon among themselves? The instructions of doctors cannot truly be so called if in ignorance and inexperience they prescribe poisons in place of medicine; nor, even if the people approve of it, will something harmful in a nation be a law of any kind. Law, therefore, is the distinction between just and unjust things, produced in accordance with nature, the most ancient and first of all things, in accordance with which human laws are constructed which punish the wicked while defending and protecting the good.

QUINTUS: I understand entirely, and I now think that any other law should not only not be accepted, but should not even be given the name of law.

[14] MARCUS: So you think that the laws of Titius and Appuleius are no laws at all?[17]

QUINTUS: And not even the laws of Livius.[18]

MARCUS: Rightly, since in a single moment they were removed by a single word from the senate. The law whose force I have explained, however, can be neither removed nor abrogated.[19]

QUINTUS: So the laws that you will pass, I imagine, are never to be abrogated.

MARCUS: Certainly, so long as you two accept them. But I think that I must do as Plato did, the most learned of men and also the most serious of philosophers, who first wrote about the commonwealth and also wrote a separate work about its laws,[20] namely to speak in praise of the law before I recite it. And I see that Zaleucus and Charondas did the same thing, not as a matter of intellectual enjoyment but in writing laws for their states for the sake of the commonwealth. In imitating them Plato appears to have thought that it was a function of law to persuade rather than to compel all things through force and threats.[21]

[17] Laws passed through violence by the radical tribunes of 100 and 99 BCE.

[18] The tribune of 91 BCE.

[19] Compare the definition of the natural law at *On the Commonwealth* 3.31.

[20] Accepting *eius*, which Ziegler deleted. For C.'s error about the relationship between Plato's two dialogues see 1.15 n. 18.

[21] Cf. *Laws* 4.723a.

[15] QUINTUS: What of the fact that Timaeus denies that Zaleucus ever existed?

MARCUS: But Theophrastus, a no worse authority in my opinion (and many people think him a better one), says that he did, and his own fellow citizens, our clients the Locrians, refer to him. But it makes no difference whether he existed or not: what I say is what has been reported.

Therefore let the citizens be persuaded of this at the outset, that the gods are lords and managers of all things, and whatever happens happens by their judgment and will; that they have treated the human race very well; that they observe what sort of person each man is, what he does, what he permits himself, in what state of mind and with what sort of piety he observes religious customs; and that they keep account of the good and the wicked. [16] Minds that are steeped in these beliefs will not be averse to useful and true opinions. What is more true than that no one ought to be so stupid and arrogant as to think that he has reason and a mind but not to believe the same of the heavens and the universe? Or to think that things which are barely understood by the greatest intelligence and reason are moved without reason? Anyone who is not compelled to be grateful by the order of the stars, the alternations of day and night, the balance of the seasons, the crops which grow for our enjoyment – why is it proper for someone like that to be counted human at all?[22] And since all things endowed with reason are superior to those which lack reason, and since it is wrong to say that anything is superior to the natural universe, it must be admitted that the universe has reason. Who could deny that such opinions are useful when he understands how many things are secured by oaths, how conducive to safety are the religious guarantees of treaties, how many people have been kept from crime by the fear of punishment, how holy the bond of citizens one with another is, with the presence of the immortal gods as judges or as witnesses? This is the proem to the law, to use Plato's term.[23]

[17] QUINTUS: Yes indeed, brother, and I am particularly pleased that you concentrate on subjects and ideas different from his. There is nothing so unlike Plato as what you said earlier, or as this preface concerning the gods. The only thing that you seem to me to imitate is the style.

[22] Compare *On the Commonwealth* 1.26–29, 4.1. [23] *Laws* 4.722d.

MARCUS: Perhaps I wish to; but who can or ever will be able to imitate him? It's easy enough to translate his ideas, and I would do that if I didn't prefer to be myself. What is the difficulty in translating the same things in virtually the same words?

QUINTUS: I quite agree. But as you yourself just said, I prefer you to be yourself. But please give us your laws concerning religion.

[18] MARCUS: I will give them as well as I can; and since both this place and our conversation are private, I will set forth the laws in the language of laws.

QUINTUS: What is that?

MARCUS: There are words that belong to laws, Quintus: not as archaic as in the ancient Twelve Tables or the Sacred Laws, but still, to have more authority, a little more antique than our conversation.[24] To the best of my ability I will imitate that custom and its terseness. The laws which I will propose are not complete – that would be endless – but only the leading ideas of these subjects.

QUINTUS: That is certainly necessary; so let us hear them.

[19] MARCUS: Let them approach the gods in purity, let them display piety, let them remove luxury.[25] If anyone behave otherwise, the god himself will enforce the law.

Let no one have gods separately, neither new nor foreign, unless they have been recognized publicly; let them worship in private those whose worship has been duly handed down by their ancestors.

Let them have sanctuaries in the cities; let them have groves in the country and homes for their Lares.

Let them preserve the rituals of their family and ancestors.

Let them worship both those who have always been considered gods of heaven and those whose deeds have placed them in heaven: Hercules, Liber, Aesculapius, Castor, Pollux, Quirinus. Furthermore, as to those praiseworthy qualities on account of which ascent into heaven is granted to humans – Intelligence, Virtue, Piety, Faith – let there be sanctuaries for them, but none for vices.[26]

Let them take part in customary rites.

Let disputes be absent from holidays, and let them observe holidays

[24] The translation that follows makes no attempt to imitate the pseudo-archaic language that C. employs in his laws.

[25] "Let them . . .": C. uses archaic imperative forms, imitating the language of old laws; it should be noted that early legal language (like C.'s here) is vague about the subjects of verbs, which change from clause to clause without warning. The notes on C.'s code (here and in Book 3) are brief: C.'s own commentary, which follows, should be consulted.

[26] A longer list of allegorical gods is at *On the Nature of the Gods* 2.61.

among their slaves when work has been finished; and let it be ordained that they correspond to the changing seasons of the year. Let priests make public offerings of specific crops and fruits on days prescribed for specific sacrifices; [20] and let them reserve other days for the offerings of milk and offspring. And so that offense against this may not be possible, let the priests set out the plan and annual pattern for these rites, and let them prescribe what sacrificial victims are seemly and pleasing to each divinity.

Let there be different priests for the different divinities; let there be pontifices for all, and let there be flamines for individual gods.[27] Let the Vestal Virgins in the city guard the eternal fire of the public hearth.

That these things may take place duly and with the proper ritual both privately and publicly, let those who are ignorant learn from the public priests. Let there be three types of these:[28] one to preside over ceremonies and rituals; a second to interpret the mysterious utterances of prophets and soothsayers summoned by the senate and people. And also let the interpreters of Jupiter Optimus Maximus, the public augurs, see to the future by signs and auspices; [21] let them maintain the discipline;[29] let them instruct the priests;[30] let them employ augury for vineyard and orchard and for the safety of the people; let them advise by augury the leaders of military and civic affairs; and let these leaders obey them. Let them foresee the anger of the gods and take heed of it; let them observe lightning in the sky in the customary regions; let them keep free and well-defined the city, the fields, and the temples.[31] Whatever an augur has declared to be unjust, wrong, criminal or ill-omened, let those things be void; and let anyone who does not obey be put to death.

Of treaties of peace, of war, of injuries to ambassadors let the fetials be judges and messengers; let them make decisions in regard to wars.[32]

If the senate so order, let them refer prodigies and omens to the Etruscan soothsayers, and let Etruria teach its leaders the discipline. Let them perform expiatory rites to whatever divinities they decree, and let them also expiate lightning and things struck by lightning.

Let there be no nocturnal rites of women other than those which are duly performed on behalf of the people.[33] Let them initiate no one except

[27] For the flaminate cf. *On the Commonwealth* 2.26 n. 27.

[28] The three varieties are the pontifices, the board of 15 for performing rituals (*quindecimuiri sacris faciundis*) who were in fact in charge of the oracular Sibylline books, and the augurs.

[29] I.e. the "Etruscan discipline" of interpreting various forms of omens.

[30] Accepting de Plinval's <*docento*>.

[31] The text of this sentence and its meaning are very unclear.

[32] The meaning here is uncertain and the text corrupt; this translation accepts Rawson's emendation of *indotiarum* to *iniuriarum*, retains the manuscript reading *oratorum*, and accepts Vahlen's *nontii* for the manuscripts' *non*.

[33] In particular, the ritual of the Bona Dea celebrated in the home of the urban praetor (the occasion for Clodius' sacrilege: below, 2.36).

to Ceres in the customary Greek rite.[34]

[22] Whatever offense against religion is committed that cannot be expiated shall be judged to have been committed impiously; let the public priests expiate what can be expiated.

At public games which take place without chariots and physical combat[35] let them supervise public joy in song with lyre and flute, and let them join it with honors to the gods.

Let them observe the best of the ancestral rites.

Other than the slaves of the Idaean Mother – and they on the permitted days only – let no one beg for alms.[36]

Whoever steals or snatches something consecrated or entrusted to a consecrated place, let him be as a murderer.

For perjury the divine penalty is destruction; the human one, disgrace.

Let the pontiffs punish incest by the ultimate penalty.

Let no impious person dare to appease the anger of the gods with gifts.

Let vows be carried out scrupulously. Let there be a penalty for the violation of this law.

Let no one consecrate a field. Let there be moderation in dedications of gold, silver, and ivory.

Let private rituals remain in perpetuity.

Let the rights of the spirits of the dead be holy. Let them hold good men who have died to be gods. Let them limit expense and mourning for them.

[23] ATTICUS: How succinctly you have constructed this great law! But it seems to me that your establishment of religion is not very different from the laws of Numa and our own customs.[37]

MARCUS: Given that Africanus, in the work *On the Commonwealth*, seems persuasive in claiming that our early state was the best of all commonwealths, don't you think that it is necessary to give laws corresponding to the best commonwealth?

ATTICUS: Indeed I do.

MARCUS: Then you should expect laws which maintain that best type of commonwealth; and if I happen to propose some today that neither are nor have been part of our government, they were in any case part of ancestral custom, which then had the force of law.

34 A Greek priestess from southern Italy was in charge of the ritual of Ceres, parallel to the Eleusinian Mysteries in Athens.

35 There may be something missing in the text describing the athletic contests.

36 The Idaean Mother is Cybele (*Magna Mater*), whose worship was introduced in Rome from Phrygia in 204 BCE; her slaves were the castrated Galli.

37 For the laws of Numa see *On the Commonwealth* 2.26.

[24] ATTICUS: Then please argue in favor of your law, so that I may vote for it.

MARCUS: Really, Atticus? You won't disagree?

ATTICUS: Certainly I would suggest nothing major, and in minor matters I will defer to you, if you wish.

QUINTUS: My opinion is the same.

MARCUS: Be careful; it may take a long time.

ATTICUS: I hope so. What else would we rather do?

MARCUS: The law orders people to approach the gods in purity – purity of mind, of course, in which everything else resides.[38] It doesn't exclude physical purity, but it should be understood how much the mind is superior to the body: purity of body should be respected in approaching the gods, but it is all the more important to preserve that of the mind. Physical impurity can be removed by a splash of water or the lapse of a fixed number of days, but a stain on the mind does not fade with time, nor can it be washed out by any river. [25] As for the commands to display piety and remove luxury, they signify that integrity is pleasing to god, and expense should be rejected. Surely that is so: if we wish poverty and wealth to be treated equally among men, then why should we bar poverty from approaching the gods by adding expense to rituals?[39] Especially as nothing will be less appealing to the god himself than not to permit all people equal access to pleasing and cultivating him. The establishment of the god himself rather than a judge as the enforcer of the law seems to reinforce religion by the fear of imminent punishment.

For people to worship their own gods, either new or foreign, makes for confusion of religions and for ceremonies unknown to our priests. [26] It is right for the gods handed down by our ancestors to be worshiped if our ancestors themselves obeyed this law.

I believe that there should be sanctuaries in cities, and I do not follow the view of the Persian magi under whose persuasion Xerxes is said to have burned the temples of Greece because they enclosed within walls gods for whom everything ought to be open and free and whose temple and home is this entire universe.[40] The view of the Greeks and of our own people is better, who wanted the gods to dwell in the same cities as we do in order to increase piety towards the gods. This view

[38] So also *On the Nature of the Gods* 2.71.

[39] Compare *On the Commonwealth* 2.26–27 on Numa's religious laws.

[40] See *On the Commonwealth* 3.14.

supplies a religion useful to states, inasmuch as the statement of Pythagoras, a most learned man, is true, that piety and religion occupy people's minds most particularly when we are attending to divine worship; Thales, the wisest of the Seven Sages, also said that humans ought to think that all which they see is full of the gods, and that all people would then be more pure, just as when they were in the most sacred shrines. People think that there is a way in which the gods appear to our sight as well as to our minds. [27] Groves in the country have the same rationale, nor should we reject the worship of the Lares, handed down by our ancestors for both masters and slaves, placed in sight of the farm and farmhouse.

As for preserving the rituals of family and ancestors, that is – since antiquity comes as close as possible to the gods – to preserve a religion that is almost handed down by the gods.

That the law orders the worship of those of the human race who have been consecrated, like Hercules and the rest, indicates that the souls of all people are immortal but that those of the brave and good are divine. [28] It is also good that Intelligence, Piety, Virtue, and human Faith be consecrated, to all of whom temples at Rome have been publicly dedicated, so that people who have those qualities – and all good people have them – should think that they have actual gods located in their minds. For what the Athenians did after the expiation of the crime of Cylon under the advice of Epimenides the Cretan was wrong: they made a shrine to Insult and Impudence. It is proper to consecrate virtues, not vices. The ancient altar to Fever on the Palatine, and the other on the Esquiline to Bad Luck are execrable, and all such are to be rejected. If names are to be invented for gods, then that of Vicapota (named for conquest and control) is preferable, or Stata for standing firm; so also the titles Stayer and Unconquerable for Jupiter, and the names of desirable things, such as Safety, Honor, Resource, and Victory. And since the mind is aroused by the expectation of good things, it was right for Calatinus to consecrate Hope. Let there be a Luck of This Day – which is good for all days – or Luck Paying Notice for bringing aid, or Chance Luck, signifying uncertain events particularly, or Luck First Born, from birth . . .[41]

[29] The reason for holidays and festivals is to provide respite from lawsuits and quarrels for free men, and rest from work and toil for

[41] There is a gap in the text, and the last word of the paragraph is corrupt.

slaves; and the organization of the year ought to match these to the completion of agricultural work. In order that the sacrificial offerings and the young animals referred to in the law may be kept for this occasion, it is important to keep close account of intercalation; that practice was skillfully instituted by Numa but has collapsed through the negligence of later pontifices.[42] Furthermore, the traditional instructions of the pontifices and haruspices concerning sacrifices should not be altered: what victims should be offered to which god, and to which god there should be sacrifices of full-grown animals, to which of suckling, to which male, to which female.

That there should be a number of priests for all the gods, and single ones for individual gods, provides ease in interpreting the law and performing religious observances. And since Vesta almost contains the hearth of the city (so she is named using the Greek name, to which ours is amost identical, not a translation),[43] six virgins should preside over her worship, so that they may more easily be alert in guarding the fire and so that women may recognize that the nature of woman permits complete purity.

[30] The clause that follows, however, is relevant not only to religion but also to the condition of the state: that proper private worship should not be possible without the people who are in charge of public rites. For it sustains the commonwealth to have the people always be in need of the judgment and authority of the nobility, and the organization of the priesthoods omits no type of legitimate religion. Some are established to please the gods, and they are in charge of recurring rituals; others, for interpreting the prophecies of soothsayers – not so many soothsayers that their task should be unending, nor in such a way that anyone outside the college should know even those that are the object of public attention. [31] The greatest and most important right in the commonwealth, which has great authority as well, is that of the augurs. I think this not because I am an augur myself, but because we are obligated to hold this opinion.[44] If we are considering law, what is more important than to be able to dismiss electoral or legislative assemblies summoned by the highest magistrates and officials or to rescind their ac-

[42] Until Caesar's reform of the calendar in 46 BCE, regular intercalation of months was necessary to keep the civil calendar in line with the solar year. In the late republic, the practice was not adequately maintained, and to correct the calendar the year 46 had 445 days. [43] Greek *hestia* is both the hearth and the goddess.

[44] C. was coopted into the augural college in 53.

tions even after they have been taken? What is more solemn than for business once begun to be broken off if a single augur says "on another day"? What is more grand than to be able to decree that the consuls should resign their office? What is more deeply involved in religion than to give or refuse the right of conducting assemblies of the people or the plebs?[45] Or to annul a law if it was not legally passed, as Titius' law was annulled by the decree of his colleague, as Livius' laws were by the judgment of Philippus who was both consul and augur?[46] Or that nothing done by a magistrate in civil or military matters can be approved without their authority?

[32] ATTICUS: All right; I see and agree that all that is very important. But there is a great dispute in your college between Marcellus and Appius, both excellent augurs – I happen to have been reading their books. One says that the auspices were established for utility to the commonwealth; the other, that your discipline is capable of divination. I would like to know what you think.

MARCUS: Me? I believe that there is such a thing as divination, which the Greeks call *mantikê*, and that the portion of it which concerns birds and other omens belongs to our discipline. If we admit that gods exist and that the universe is ruled by their mind, and that they also pay attention to the human race and are capable of showing us signs of future events, then I don't see why I should deny the existence of divination.[47] [33] And since my assumptions are true, then we must necessarily reach the desired conclusion. Our own commonwealth is replete with numerous instances, and so too are all kingdoms, nations, and tribes, that many things beyond belief have turned out to be true in accordance with the predictions of augurs. Polyidus would not have such a great reputation, nor would Melampus or Mopsus or Amphiaraus or Calchas or Helenus,[48] nor would so many nations retain augury up to this time, such as the Phrygians, Lycaonians, Cilicians, and particularly the Pisidians, if antiquity had not shown them to be true. Our own Romulus would not have taken the auspices before founding

[45] "The people" includes both patricians and plebeians, and met in the regular voting assemblies (*comitia tributa* and *comitia centuriata*); the plebs did not include the patricians, and met as the *concilium plebis*. Measures that it passed were technically *plebiscita*, not laws, but from the third century BCE they had the force of laws.

[46] On Titius and Livius see above, 2.14. Philippus was consul in 91.

[47] On this topic see *On Divination* 1.82–83. The grounds for belief in divination given here are Stoic.

[48] Mythical seers whose prophetic activities were reported in early Greek epic.

the city, nor would the name of Attus Navius have been remembered for so long, if all these men had not said many things remarkable for their truthfulness.[49] On the other hand, there can be no doubt that the scientific discipline of augury has faded away through negligence and the passage of time. And so I agree neither with the one in his denial that this knowledge ever existed in our college, nor with the other in his assertion that it still exists. It seems to me that it had two uses for our ancestors: occasionally for crises in the commonwealth, very frequently in deliberations on policy.

[34] ATTICUS: I certainly believe that is true, and I agree with your explanation. But explain the rest.

MARCUS: I will explain it as briefly as I can. What follows concerns the law of war; we have ordained that in undertaking, waging, and ending wars both justice and good faith should be as strong as possible, and that there should be official interpreters of them.[50]

Concerning the religious role of the haruspices and about expiations and purifications, I think that the law itself is clear enough.

ATTICUS: I agree, since this whole section concerns religious actions.

MARCUS: But as to what follows, I am very curious to know, Titus, how you might agree or how I might refute you.

ATTICUS: What is that?

[35] MARCUS: About women's nighttime rituals.

ATTICUS: In fact I agree with you, and particularly with the exception made in the law for regular public sacrifices.

MARCUS: Then what will become of Iacchus and our Eumolpids, and those revered mysteries, if we remove nocturnal rites? We are not making laws for the Roman people, but for all good and established nations.

[36] ATTICUS: You make an exception, I believe, for those rites in which we have been initiated ourselves.[51]

MARCUS: I will make an exception. Your beloved Athens seems to me to have brought forth many superb and divine things and given them to human life, but nothing is better than the Mysteries through which we have been developed and civilized from a rustic and crude existence into humanity. We recognize the initiations, as they are called, as the true beginning of life, and we have accepted with joy not only this plan for living in happiness, but also a better expectation in

[49] For Romulus and the auspices see *On the Commonwealth* 2.16; for Attus Navius, 2.36.

[50] On the law of war (fetial law) see *On the Commonwealth* 2.31.

[51] The Eleusinian mysteries, into which many Roman visitors to Greece were initiated.

death. What displeases me about nocturnal rites is shown by the comic poets. If such license were given at Rome, what would that man have done who brought his lewd plans into a sacrificial rite on which it was a sin to gaze even unintentionally?[52]

ATTICUS: You can pass that law for Rome, but leave our own laws to us.

[37] MARCUS: Then I will go back to my own laws. There is certainly need for very careful regulation, so that broad daylight may guard the reputation of women by having many witnesses, and they should be initiated to Ceres by the ritual in use at Rome. The sternness of our ancestors in matters of this sort is shown by the old senatorial decision concerning Bacchanals, along with the inquiry and punishments by the consuls using military force.[53] This should not make us seem too harsh: consider Diagondas of Thebes in the heart of Greece, who eliminated all nocturnal rites by a permanent law.[54] Aristophanes, the cleverest poet of the old comedy, attacks new gods and the all-night rituals that are a part of their worship so vigorously that in his works Sabazius and several other foreign gods are tried and expelled from the state.[55]

The public priest should liberate from fear imprudent actions that have been carefully atoned for; but he should condemn and judge as impious the boldness [that causes the deliberate violation of religious law].[56]

[38] Since public festivals are divided between the theater and the circus, in the latter there should be athletic contests – footrace, boxing, wrestling, and chariot racing towards a specified goal. The theater should resound with singing to the lyre and flute, so long as it be moderate in accordance with the law. I agree with Plato that nothing so easily flows into tender and unformed minds as the various sounds of song; and it is hard to express the magnitude of their influence in one direction or the other.[57] Music can stir up the lazy and soothe people who

52 Publius Clodius Pulcher dressed as a woman and violated the rite of the Good Goddess, open only to women, in 62. C. testified against him (disproving his alibi) at his trial, but Clodius was acquitted through bribery; his resulting enmity towards C. was at least one reason for C.'s exile in 58, and C.'s loathing for Clodius is apparent in much of his writing in the 50s.

53 The decree of the senate in question (of 186 BCE) survives on a bronze tablet from southern Italy; there is a long account of the episode in Livy 39.8–19.

54 Neither Diagondas (often emended to Pagondas) nor the episode is otherwise known.

55 In a lost play.

56 The bracketed words supply the probable sense of a corrupt passage.

57 Cf. Plato, *Republic* 3.401–2; *Laws* 7.800.

are stirred up; it can let minds run or rein them in. It was in the interest of many Greek states to preserve the ancient style of music, and their morals slid to decadence along with the alteration of songs: either (as some people think) they were depraved by the sweetness and corruption of music, or when their toughness collapsed because of other vices, then there was room in their altered ears and minds for this change as well.[58] [**39**] For that reason the wisest man of Greece, and by far the most learned, was particularly afraid of this failing. He denied that the rules of music can be altered without alteration of public laws.[59] However, I think that we don't need to fear this so greatly, but I don't think that we should make light of it either. Certainly the people who used to be filled with a stern pleasure by the music of Livius and Naevius now toss their heads and roll their eyes in time with the twists and turns of the music.[60] In the old days, the Greeks used to punish such things harshly, having recognized in advance how gradually the destruction might slide into the minds of citizens and suddenly overturn whole states through evil studies and evil ideas: at least, there is a story that stern Sparta ordered the strings beyond the number of seven to be cut off the lyre of Timotheus.

[**40**] What follows in the law is that the best of ancestral rites should be cultivated. When the Athenians consulted Pythian Apollo to ask what religions they should particularly preserve, the oracle came back: those which are part of ancestral custom. When they came back and said that ancestral custom had changed frequently, and asked which of the various customs they should follow, he answered: the best. And in fact it is true that whatever is best should be considered oldest and closest to the god.

I removed alms-gathering except for that peculiar to the Great Mother during a few days. It fills minds with superstition, and it drains houses.

The penalty for sacrilege applies not only to someone who steals a sacred object but also to someone who steals an object deposited in a sacred place. [**41**] That custom is observed in many temples: Alexander is said to have deposited money in a shrine at Soli in Cilicia, and Clisthenes the great Athenian is said to have entrusted his daughters' dowries to Juno at Samos when he was worried about his own security.

There is no need to say more here about perjury and incest.

[58] Cf. Plato, *Laws* 3.700a–701b. [59] Plato, *Republic* 4.424c.

[60] The text of this sentence is corrupt, but the general sense is clear.

For the prohibition against impious people daring to placate the gods with gifts, people should listen to Plato, who forbids any doubts about the god's attitude, since no good man wishes to receive gifts from a bad one.[61]

Concerning care in performing vows, enough has been said in the law . . .[62] and in vows the promise by which we are bound to the god. There can be no reasonable cause to reject the establishment of a penalty for violating religious obligations. Why should I use here the examples of criminals that abound in tragedy? I will rather mention those that are familiar to us all. And even though what I recall here may seem to be beyond human good fortune, still, since I am talking to you, I will keep nothing back, and I will hope that what I say will seem to express gratitude to the immortal gods rather than severity towards humans. [42] When, at the time of my exile, the laws of religion were polluted by the crime of abandoned citizens, our family Lares were attacked, and in their place was built a temple to License, and the man who had guarded our sanctuaries was driven from them.[63] Contemplate briefly – there is no point in naming anyone – what happened as a result: I, who did not permit the goddess who guards the city to be violated by impious people, even though all my own property was stolen and destroyed, took her from my home to that of her father[64] – I was declared by the verdicts of the senate, of Italy, and of all nations to have saved my country. What more glorious could happen to a man? The people by whose crime religion was laid low and attacked – some of them are scattered and destroyed, and those who were the leaders in these crimes and beyond the rest impious towards all religion not only received every punishment and disgrace in their lives, but were deprived of burial and the rites of a funeral.[65]

[43] QUINTUS: I know that, brother, and I give the gods the thanks they are owed. But things often seem to work out rather differently.

MARCUS: We do not judge rightly, Quintus, what divine punishment

[61] Cf. Plato, *Laws* 4.716c–717a. [62] There is a gap in the text.

[63] While C. was in exile, his house was burned down and Clodius had a temple to Liberty built on the site; the restoration of C.'s house after his return was the occasion of considerable violence and several orations.

[64] When he left Rome in 58, C. took his own statue of Minerva and placed it in the temple of Jupiter on the Capitoline Hill.

[65] C. is gloating over the murder of Clodius in 52 in a brawl on the Appian Way with the equally violent supporters of C.'s ally Milo. Many of the participants on both sides (including Milo) were condemned. Clodius' body was burned in the Forum by his supporters, incidentally incinerating the senate house as well.

is, but we are drawn into error by the opinions of the mob, and we do not see the truth. We weigh human misery in terms of death or physical pain or mental anguish or the verdict of the court: and I admit that these things are part of human life and happen to many good men. The punishment of crime is dire, and even aside from its consequences is itself immense: we have seen men, who would never have been our enemies if they had not hated their fatherland, on fire with greed or fear, or through a guilty conscience for their actions in turn fearing and scorning religion: it was human justice, not divine, that they overturned and corrupted. [44] I will limit myself and pursue the subject no further, particularly since I have received more vengeance than I sought. I will say this only briefly, that there is a twofold punishment from the gods, which comprises both the ravaging of their minds when alive and, when they are dead, a reputation that causes their destruction to be greeted by the approval and pleasure of the living.

[45] In forbidding the consecration of land, I agree entirely with Plato, who uses the following words (if I can translate him correctly):[66] "Like the household hearth, the earth is sacred to all the gods. And therefore let no one consecrate it again. Moreover, gold and silver in cities, either held privately or in temples, breeds envy, while ivory, drawn from a corpse, is an insufficiently pure gift for a god. Furthermore, bronze and iron are tools of war, not of religion. However, anyone who wishes may dedicate in the common shrines a wooden object made from a single piece of wood, or something made of stone, or something woven, provided it has not required more work than a woman can perform in a month. The color most seemly for a god is white, in all things but particularly in woven items; only military insignia should be dyed. The most divine gifts are birds and paintings completed by a single painter in a single day; and other offerings should be similar to this." That is Plato's view; my own is not quite so restrictive in other respects, and I yield to human vice or to modern wealth; but I fear that agriculture will be less vigorous if an element of superstition is added to the use and ploughing of the earth.

ATTICUS: I accept that. What is left concerns the perpetuity of rites and the laws concerning the spirits of the dead.

MARCUS: What an amazing memory you have, Atticus! I had forgotten those things completely.

[66] *Laws* 12.955e–956b.

[46] ATTICUS: So I believe. But I have remembered – and await – these things particularly because they concern both pontifical and civil law.

MARCUS: True enough, and there have been many legal opinions and books written on these subjects by experts. For my own part, in this entire conversation, to whatever area of law our discussion leads me, I will deal to the best of my ability with our civil law on the subject; but I will do so in such a way that the source of each part of the law may be known, so that it should not be difficult for someone using his intelligence to grasp the legal basis of whatever new case or issue arises when you know the source from which it derives. [47] But the jurisconsults, either for the sake of obfuscation, to make themselves seem to know a greater amount of difficult material, or (what is in fact more likely) from their incompetence as teachers – for skill is needed not only to know something but to teach it as well – often make infinite divisions of what is in fact a single issue. The issue that you raise is one of those: what a huge thing the Scaevolae have made of it, both pontifices and both great experts in the law![67] "I have often heard from my father," says Publius' son, "that there is no good pontifex who is not knowledgeable in the civil law." The whole thing? To what end? Why should a pontifex know the laws concerning walls or water or anything at all that has nothing to do with religion? And that, in fact, is a tiny area – on rituals, vows, festivals and graves, and other things of that kind. Why do we make so much of these things? All of them are of very little account except for rituals, which is a matter of greater significance but can be dealt with by one statement, namely that they be preserved forever and be handed down continuously in families, and, as I laid down in my law, that rituals should be maintained in perpetuity? [48] By the authority of the pontifices, these laws have been established: that (so that the memory of rituals should not disappear at the death of the head of the family) those to whom money comes at a person's death should also have responsibility for the rituals. From this one principle, which is adequate for understanding the rule, have sprung up countless regulations which fill the books of the jurisconsults. There is a question about who is obligated by the rituals. The case of the heirs is most just: there is no one who is closer to taking the place of the person who has

[67] Publius Mucius Scaevola (consul in 133) and his son Quintus Mucius Scaevola the pontifex (consul in 95; to be distinguished from Quintus Mucius Scaevola the augur, his cousin), under whom C. studied as a boy.

passed away. Then the person who by the death or the will of the decedent receives as much as all the heirs together:[68] that is reasonable too, and consistent with the original principle. In the third place, if there should be no heir, comes the person who acquires ownership by possession of the greater part of the property of the decedent. Fourth, if no one has received any property, is the creditor of the decedent who receives the greatest portion of the estate. [**49**] Finally comes the person who owed money to the decedent and has not repaid it to anyone; he should be held to have received that debt as money.

This is what we learned from Scaevola, although it was not written in this way by the ancients. Their teaching was in the following language: that there are three ways of being obligated by rituals: by inheritance, or by taking the greater portion of the property, or if the greater part of the property was in the form of legacies, through receiving any portion of it. But let us follow Scaevola the pontifex. [**50**] You see that everything derives from the one fact that the pontifices want the rituals to be joined to the estate and think that these same people should be responsible for the rites and ceremonies.

The Scaevolas add this too, that when there is a division, as in the case that a reserved portion is not written in the will and the legatees on their own accept less than is left to all the heirs, that the legatees should not be obligated by the rituals. In the case of a gift, they interpret the same circumstance differently: whatever the head of a family approved in gifts made by someone under his control should be valid; if he did not approve, it is invalid.[69] [**51**] From these principles arise many minute questions; and anyone of intelligence can easily resolve them for himself if he pays attention to their origin. For instance: if someone had accepted less in order to avoid being obligated by the rituals, and then later one of his heirs had demanded for himself what had been refused by the original legatee, and if, taken together with the original bequest,

[68] A valid Roman will had to begin with the institution of an heir or heirs to the whole or proportions of the entire estate; the heir(s) could then be required to pay legacies from the estate, which might in total amount to the bulk of the estate itself (certain limits affected large estates only). In intestate succession the estate would pass to the closest relatives, who would acquire ownership by possession.

[69] C.'s description of the law of succession as it related to family ritual is as opaque as he says the pontifical law was. He is here describing various ways of evading ritual obligations (or the rules governing inheritance) through gifts, third-party transactions, and collusive sales. His general point (in sects. 52–53) is that there is an inherent contradiction between the role of the pontifices in ensuring religious continuity and their role as civil lawyers in helping people evade their religious obligations through legal technicalities.

the sum were no less than had been left to all the heirs, then the person who had demanded that money would alone (without his co-heirs) be obligated by the rituals. They also offer the opinion that the person to whom a larger legacy is given than it is permissible to take without religious obligation may release the heirs from the payment of the legacy through an act of sale: if the inheritance is thus disencumbered of the legacy, it is as if the money had not been given as a legacy at all.

[52] In this instance and in many others, I ask you Scaevolae, chief pontifices both and men whom I consider to be extremely intelligent, why you seek to add civil law to pontifical law? Through the knowledge of the civil law, in fact you destroy in a sense the pontifical law: the link between ritual obligation and money comes from the authority of the pontifices, not from the law; and thus if you were purely pontifices, the authority of the pontifices would survive; but because you are also the most learned in the civil law, you make mockery of one branch of learning through the other. It was the opinion of Publius Scaevola and Tiberius Coruncanius, both chief pontifices, and of others as well, that those who received as much as all the heirs combined were obligated by the rituals. That is the statement of pontifical law. [53] What is added to this from the civil law? The clause dividing the property is written with cautious precision, that 100 sestertii should be deducted: a reason has been found to free the cash from the burden of ritual. But if the person who made the will had not wanted to take this precaution, Mucius himself the pontifex – acting as a jurisconsult – advises him to take less than is left to all the heirs. But previously[70] they said that he was obligated whatever he had accepted: now they are freed from ritual obligation. This really has nothing to do with pontifical law but comes from the heart of the civil law – to release the heir through an act of sale to restore the situation, as if the money had not been a legacy, even if the person who is given the legacy makes the stipulation that the money that had been owed through the legacy is now owed through the stipulation, and that it is not *[71]

[70] Reading *supra* with Goerler rather than *superiores*.

[71] There is a gap in the text at this point; it is likely that C. here referred to the practice of Decimus Brutus of offering sacrifice to the dead in December rather than in February, as was customary; cf. Plutarch, *Roman Questions* 34. Lambinus in the sixteenth century offered the following supplement for what is missing: ". . . and that it is not bound by the rituals. I turn now to the law regarding the spirits of the dead (*Manes*), which our ancestors established with great wisdom and observed most devoutly. They wanted ritual sacrifice to the dead to be offered in February, which was then the last month of the year;

[54] * certainly a learned man, and a close friend of Accius – but I believe that just as the ancients regarded February as the last month of the year, so he regarded December. He thought it to be a matter of piety to use a large animal for sacrifice to his ancestors.

[55] The religious quality of graves is so great that they declare it to be a religious violation for someone who is not a participant in the rituals and the family to be brought in, and in ancestral times that was the judgment of Aulus Torquatus in the case of the Popillian family. Nor would the days of purification [*denicales*] (which are named from death [*a nece*], because they are celebrated for the dead)[72] be called holy days of rest like those of the other divinities if our ancestors had not wanted those who have departed from this life to be numbered among the gods. It is right for such days to be offered to them as are neither public nor private holidays. The whole organization of this branch of pontifical law indicates the importance of the religion and ceremony. Nor do we need to explain the limits of family mourning, the kind of sacrifice made to the family god (*Lar*) with rams, the method of covering a severed bone with earth, the ritual obligations involving the sacrifice of a sow, or the moment at which a burial site begins to be under religious protection. [56] My own view is that the oldest variety of burial is that which Cyrus uses in Xenophon's book:[73] the body is returned to earth and so placed and laid out as if enveloped by its mother's covering. We have been told that our king Numa was buried in the same manner in the tomb which is not far from the altar of Fons, and we know that the Cornelian clan used that type of burial into our own times: the victorious Sulla, spurred on by a hatred more bitter than he would have experienced if he had been as wise as he was passionate, ordered the buried remains of Gaius Marius to be scattered in the river Anio; [57] perhaps as a result of fear that the same thing could happen to his own body, he was the first of the patrician Cornelii to want to be cremated. Ennius says of Africanus: "Here lies . . .";[74] he speaks the truth, since those who are buried are said to "lie." But we cannot speak of it as a tomb until the rituals are performed and a pig is sacrificed. Nowadays it is common usage to speak of all entombed people as "buried," but that

but as Sisenna reports, Decimus Brutus used to do so in December. When I investigated the reason for this, I found that Brutus had departed from ancestral custom for this reason – I see that Sisenna did not know the reason why he departed from ancestral custom, but it seems unlikely to me that Brutus carelessly rejected ancestral customs . . ."

[72] An unlikely etymology. *Nex* normally means violent death.

[73] *Cyropaedia* 8.7.25.

[74] Ennius, *Epigrams* 5–6 Warmington; quoted more fully in *On the Commonwealth* 3.66.

used to be correct only of those who were covered by earth, and pontifical law confirms that custom. For before sod has been placed over the bones, the place where a body has been cremated is not sanctified; once it has been placed, then the dead man is said to be buried, and it is called a tomb.[75] Only at that point does it come under the jurisdiction of the many religious laws. So too in the case of a man who had been killed on a ship and then thrown into the sea, Publius Mucius declared that the family was free of pollution because his bones were not above the earth; the sacrifice of a sow was obligatory to the heir, together with the observation of a three-day festival and purification through the sacrifice of a female pig. If he had died in the ocean, the same would obtain except for the purification and the festival.

[58] ATTICUS: I see what the pontifical regulations contain, but I wonder whether there is anything in the laws themselves.

MARCUS: Very little, Titus, and I believe that it's familiar to you. But the provisions have less to do with religion than with the law of tombs. A law of the Twelve Tables says, "Do not bury or burn a dead body in the city."[76] That, I think, is because of the danger of fire. And the addition of "or burn" indicates that only the person who is inhumed is buried, not the one who is burned.

ATTICUS: What do we make of the fact that after the Twelve Tables there were famous men buried within the city?

MARCUS: I believe, Titus, that it involved either those to whom this had been awarded prior to the law on account of their virtue, as to Publicola or Tubertus, and that their descendants maintained this right, or those who, like Gaius Fabricius, were exempted from the law and achieved this on account of their virtue. And just as the law forbids burial within the city, so too the pontifical college decreed that it was not proper for a tomb to be made on public property. You know the shrine of Honor outside the Colline gate: the story is that there was formerly an altar on that spot, but when a metal plate was found there with the inscription "This belongs to Honor," that was the reason for the dedication of this shrine. But since there were many tombs there, they were dug up: the pontifical college decided that a public place could not be under the constraints of private religious observance.

[59] There are other provisions in the Twelve Tables for reduction of expense and of funeral lamentation; almost all are taken from Solon's

[75] The text of the last clause is corrupt, but the meaning is clear.

[76] The quotations from the Twelve Tables in sects. 58–61 are frr. X, 1–10 Crawford.

laws. "Do no more than this," they say; "do not smooth the pyre with a trowel." You know the rest: we used to learn the Twelve Tables as boys as if it were a required chant, but nobody learns it nowadays. The expense was limited: three veils, one small purple tunic, and ten flute players. They eliminated lamentations: "Women are not to scratch their cheeks or make wailing [*lessum*] on account of a death." The older interpreters, Sextus Aelius and Lucius Acilius, said that they were not certain of the meaning of this, but they suspected that it was some kind of funeral clothing; Lucius Aelius said that *lessum* was lugubrious howling, as the word itself implies. I think that he is right, particularly because the law of Solon forbids the same thing.[77] These provisions are admirable and are common to both the rich and the common people; and that is completely in accord with nature, since differences of wealth are removed by death. [**60**] The Twelve Tables also removed other funeral customs which increase grief. "Let no one gather the bones of a dead man to conduct a funeral later"; an exception is made for deaths in war or while abroad. The laws also contain this: "Let there be no anointing of slaves or rounds of drinking."[78] It is right to eliminate these customs, but they would not have been eliminated if they had not been practiced. "No expensive perfumes, no long garlands, no thuribles" – we can pass over that. But there is a clear indication that the ornaments of praise are relevant to the dead, in that the law orders that there should be no offense involved in placing a garland won by courage both on the person who gained it and on his parent.[79] I suppose that it was because it was not uncommon for more than one funeral to be performed and more than one ritual dinner for a single death that the law ordained that this should not be done. And since the law stated "and do not add gold," you should note the humanity of the sequel: "But there should be no offense involved in burying or cremating someone whose teeth are bound with gold." And again you should note that a distinction is made between burial and cremation.

[**61**] There are two further laws about tombs, one concerning private buildings, the other concerning the tombs themselves. The prohibition against "a pyre or new cremation being performed within sixty feet of another person's home against the will of the owner" reflects a fear of fire.[80] As for the clause that prohibits the *forum* – that is, the entry to

77 Cf. Plutarch, *Solon* 21. 78 The text is corrupt and the meaning obscure.

79 Various types of garland (*corona*) were awarded for various acts of military valor.

80 The text of the last few words is corrupt, and the translation is conjectural.

the tomb – "or the burial place to be subject to ownership by possession," that is a protection of the rights of tombs. All this is in the Twelve Tables, clearly in accord with nature, which is the measure of law. The remainder is customary: that there should be an announcement at the funeral of any games; that the person in charge of the funeral should use an attendant and lictors, **[62]** that the praise of men of distinction should be spoken in a public assembly, and that they should be accompanied with dirges to the sound of the flute. The name of this is *neniae*, which is given to dirges by the Greeks as well.

ATTICUS: I am glad to know that our laws are in accordance with nature; the wisdom of our ancestors pleases me greatly. But I look for limitations on tombs themselves as of other expenses.

MARCUS: Quite right. I believe that you have seen in the case of the tomb of Gaius Figulus the extent to which such expenditure has gone.[81] There are many examples among our ancestors to show that in the past there was little desire for such things. The interpreters of our law, in connection with the rubric which orders them to remove expense and grief from behavior concerning the spirits of the dead, should understand above all that the grandiosity of tombs should be reduced. **[63]** Nor have the wisest legislators neglected this subject. At Athens, as they say, the rule concerning burial has descended from Cecrops: after the closest relatives had performed the burial and earth was drawn over the grave, it was sown with grain, so that the inner recess, as if of one's mother, was given to the dead man, but the soil was purified with grain to give it back to the living. A banquet followed, which the relatives attended wearing garlands; and when they had said something truthful in praise of the dead man – they consider it wrong to lie – the rites were complete. **[64]** Later, however, as Demetrius of Phalerum writes, when funerals began to be costly and filled with lamentations, they were eliminated by a law of Solon, a law which our own decemvirs inserted into Table X in almost identical words; all that about the three veils and much of the rest are Solon's, and the passage about lamentation is in these words: "Women are not to scratch their cheeks or make wailings on account of a death."

Concerning tombs, on the other hand, there is nothing more in Solon than "let no one destroy them or bring in an unrelated body,"

[81] Presumably Gaius Marcius Figulus; nothing is known of his tomb, but some extraordinarily elaborate burial monuments survive from this period.

with a penalty "if anyone violates, casts down, or breaks a tomb (the Greek word is *tumbon*) or a column." Slightly later on, because of the size of the tombs which we can see in the Ceramicus, the law ordained "that no one should make a tomb more elaborate than what ten men can build in three days" [**65**] and that it should not be ornamented with decoration. Nor was it permitted to place what they call herms on them; nor to speak in praise of the dead except at public burials, nor by anyone other than the person publicly appointed to do so. Large gatherings of men and women were eliminated in order to reduce the lamentation; crowds increase grief. [**66**] For that reason Pittacus forbids anyone to attend a burial of someone not in his family. But Demetrius says that once again the grandiosity of funerals and tombs became common, just as it is now at Rome, and he himself made a law to diminish the custom. Demetrius was, as you know, not only very learned but also a very public-spirited citizen and very ready to look out for his country. He reduced the cost of burials not only through penalties but by the use of timing: he ordered burials to take place before dawn. He also established a limit for new tombs: he did not want anything on top of the mound except a small column no higher than three cubits, or a table or a small basin; and he appointed a specific magistrate to take charge of this.

[**67**] That is what your Athenians did. But we should look to Plato, who hands the funeral rituals over to the interpreters of religious customs, as we do too. What he says about tombs is this:[82] he forbids any cultivated or arable land to be used for a tomb, but instructs that such land should be used as can hold the bodies of the dead without loss to the living; whatever land is capable of bearing crops and providing food like a mother should be reduced by neither the living nor the dead. [**68**] He forbids any tomb to be built up higher than five men can complete in five days, nor should any stone be raised up or placed on it larger than is needed to hold such praise of the dead as can be included in no more than four hexameter verses, the ones that Ennius calls "long verses."[83] So we have the authority of this great man about burials; and he also limits the expense of funerals – based on the wealth of the family – to between 1 and 5 minae. And after that he gives the well-known passage about the immortality of the soul and the peace of the good after death and the punishments of the wicked.

[82] *Laws* 12.958de. [83] Ennius p. 562 Warmington.

[**69**] That, I believe, concludes the explanation of the laws on religion.

QUINTUS: And very amply done too, brother; but now go on to the rest.

MARCUS: I will, and since it pleases you to push me onward, I will complete it in one day's conversation, I hope – particularly on this day. I see that Plato did the same thing, and that his whole speech about the laws was concluded on a single summer day. I will do the same, and I will speak about magistracies. Once religion has been established, that is what is most important in creating a commonwealth.

ATTICUS: Then go on, and stick to the plan which you have begun.

Book 3

[1] MARCUS: Then I will continue to follow that divine man whom I perhaps praise more frequently than I need to because of the admiration for him which moves me.

ATTICUS: You mean Plato, I suppose.

MARCUS: Precisely, Atticus.

ATTICUS: You could never praise him too much or too often. Even my own people, who never want anyone except their own founder to be praised,[1] permit me to esteem him at my own discretion.

MARCUS: A good decision on their part. What could be more worthy of your own refinement? Your life and language appear to me to have achieved that most difficult combination of seriousness and humaneness.

ATTICUS: I'm very glad to have interrupted you, since you have given me such a grand statement of your opinion. But go on.

MARCUS: Then shall we start by praising the law in accordance with the true praise appropriate to its kind?

ATTICUS: Yes, just as you did with the religious law.

[2] MARCUS: You see, then, that this is the power of the magistrate, that he be in charge and ordain behavior that is right and useful and in accordance with the laws. Just as the laws are in charge of the magistrates, so the magistrates are in charge of the people; it can truly be said that a magistrate is a law that speaks, and a law is a silent magistrate. [3] There is nothing so consonant with the justice and structure of nature – and when I say that, I want you to understand that I am speaking of the

[1] Epicureans; for their narrowness see 1.21.

law – as the power of command, without which no home or state or nation or the whole race of mankind can survive, nor can nature or the world itself. The world obeys god, and land and sea obey the world, and human life follows the commands of the supreme law. [4] And to come to things closer and more familiar to us: all early peoples once obeyed kings.[2] This type of power was first offered to the most just and wise men (and that was true of our own commonwealth, so long as monarchic power was in charge), and then it was handed on in turn to their descendants, a custom which remains true among contemporary monarchies. Even people who were not in favor of monarchic power did not want to have no one to obey, but wanted not always to obey the same person. But since we are giving laws for free peoples and have given our ideas about the best commonwealth in our six previous books on that subject, we will at this point suit the laws to the form of state of which we approve. [5] So there is need for magistrates, without whose judgment and effort the state cannot exist; the allocation of their powers defines the organization of the commonwealth. Nor must we instruct them only in the manner of ruling, but also in the manner of obeying the citizens. For the good commander must necessarily at some time be obedient, and the person who is properly obedient seems like someone worthy at some time of commanding. The person who obeys should expect that he will sometime give commands, and the person who is in command should think that he will soon have to obey.[3] We ordain not only that people should follow and obey the magistrates but that they should cherish and love them as well, as Charondas instructs in his laws. Plato himself decided that people who oppose magistrates belong to the race of the Titans, who similarly disobeyed the gods.[4] That being the case, let us (if you approve) turn to the laws themselves.

ATTICUS: What you have said and your plan of action both appeal to me.

[6] MARCUS: Let the powers be just, and let the citizens obey them decently and without refusal. Let the magistrate check the disobedient and harmful citizen by fine, chains, or whipping if no equal or greater authority or the people forbid it; let there be the right of appeal to the people.[5]

[2] The arguments about *imperium* (translated as "the power of command") are similar to those advanced in favor of monarchy by Scipio at *On the Commonwealth* 1.58–61.

[3] Cf. Aristotle, *Politics* 3.4 1277b7–32 on ruling and being ruled as part of the virtue of a citizen.

[4] *Laws* 3.701bc.

[5] Roman magistracies were characterized by collegiality: 2 consuls and 8 (in C.'s time) praetors. The order of any one could be countermanded by a colleague or (in the case of the

When the magistrate has judged or proposed a penalty, let there be a public contention over the fine or penalty. Let there be no right of appeal on military service from the commander, and let whatever the person waging war has commanded be right and ratified.

Let there be several minor magistrates over the several areas of divided jurisdiction. On military service let there be tribunes in command of those whom they are ordered to command.[6] In civilian affairs let them guard the public funds, let them supervise the chains of the guilty, let them inflict capital punishments, let them publicly coin bronze, silver, or gold, let them judge lawsuits that have been joined,[7] and let them perform whatever the senate shall decree.

[7] Let there also be aediles as caretakers of the city, of the grain supply, and of the recognized festivals. Let this be their first stage towards higher office.

Let censors review the ages, children, families, and property of the people; let them watch over the temples, roads, watercourses, treasury, and taxes of the city; let them divide the groups of the people into tribes, then distribute them in terms of property, age, and rank; let them assign the members of the cavalry and infantry; let them prohibit celibacy; let them regulate the morals of the people; let them leave no disgraceful person in the senate. Let there be two of them, and let them hold office for five years;[8] let the remaining magistrates serve for one year, and let the offices exist in perpetuity.

[8] Let the praetor be the legal arbiter to judge private cases or assign them for judgment. Let him be the guardian of civil law. Let there be so many of them with equal power as the senate shall have decided or the people ordered.

Let there be two men with royal power of command, and from leading, judging, and advising let them be called praetors, judges, or consuls.[9] On military service let them have the highest authority, and let them obey no other. For them let the safety of the people be the highest law.

[9] Unless ten years shall have intervened, let no man hold the same

praetors) by one of the consuls. The ability of the people to forbid punishment is the right of *provocatio* (appeal); cf. *On the Commonwealth* 2.53–54.

[6] Military tribunes were junior officers in command of one legion (for Scipio Aemilianus as military tribune cf. *On the Commonwealth* 6.9).

[7] The four offices in question are the quaestors, the board of 3 in charge of punishments (*tresuiri capitales*), the board of 3 in charge of coinage (*tresuiri aere argento auro flando feriundo*), the board of 10 in charge of deciding lawsuits (*decemuiri stlitibus iudicandis*).

[8] The most significant change in C.'s laws from the actual practice in Rome: the Roman censors were (in theory) elected every 5 years but were in office for only 18 months.

[9] From *praeeo, iudico*, and *consulo* respectively. The original magistrates were the praetors; the title was changed to consul when the lesser magistracy (the praetorship) was introduced in the third century.

magistracy. Let them preserve the times of holding office according to the law of years.[10]

Whenever a serious war or civil discord shall arise, should the senate so decide, let one man hold power equal to that of the two consuls for no longer than six months. Having been declared by a favorable omen, let him be the master of the people. Let him have someone to command the cavalry with equal power to that of whoever shall be the legal arbiter.[11]

Whenever there shall be no consuls or master of the people, and when there shall be no other magistrates, let the auspices belong to the Fathers, and let them produce from among themselves someone duly to create consuls through the assembly.[12]

When the senate shall so have decreed or the people so ordered, let commanders, men in authority, or embassies depart from the city. Let them wage just wars justly; let them be sparing of the allies; let them contain themselves and their men; let them augment the glory of their people; let them return home with honor.

Let no one be an ambassador for the sake of his own affairs.

Let those ten men whom the people have created on their own behalf as aid against violence be their tribunes, and let whatever they have forbidden or had approved by the plebs be duly ratified; let them be sacred, and let them not abandon the plebs to be bereft of tribunes.

[10] Let all magistrates have the right to take the auspices and give judgment, and let the senate be composed of them. Let its decrees be duly ratified, and let them preserve in writing decrees that an equal or greater authority has prohibited.

Let the senatorial order be free from fault; let it be a model to others.

Let the creation of magistrates, the judicial decisions of the people, and their orders and prohibitions be ascertained by ballot known to the best citizens but free to the plebs.

Should there be anything outside the scope of the normal magistrates for which it may be useful to provide, let the people create someone to provide for it and let him have the right so to act.

Let the consul, the praetor, the master of the people and of the cavalry, and the one whom the Fathers have produced for the sake of selecting consuls have the right to conduct business with the people and the senate; let the tribunes whom the plebs has created for itself have the right to con-

[10] The *lex annalis* regulated the minimum age for holding various offices and the intervals between them.

[11] Master of the people (*magister populi*) is the archaic title for the dictator (see also *On the Commonwealth* 1.63); his subordinate was master of the horse (*magister equitum*). Their relationship is here made equivalent to that of consul and praetor.

[12] The *interrex*; cf. *On the Commonwealth* 2.23.

duct business with the senate; and let them bring to the plebs whatever shall be useful.

Let those things which are brought before the people or the senate be moderate.

[11] Let any senator who is not present have a reason or be held culpable. Let him speak in his place and with moderation. Let him understand the concerns of the people.

Let there be no violence in public. Let equal or greater power have more authority.[13] Let any disturbance in the conduct of public business be the fault of the person conducting it. Let the citizen who intervenes in evil affairs be regarded as a savior of the community.

Let those who conduct public business observe the auspices; let them heed the public augur; let them conduct business after proposals have been made public, and let them preserve them in the treasury;[14] let them not bring forward proposals on specific matters more than once; let them instruct the people about the matter, and let them permit them to be instructed by the magistrates and by private citizens.

Let them not bring forward proposals affecting single individuals. Let them not decide measures concerning the status of a citizen except in the greatest assembly and before those whom the censors have placed in the divisions of the people.[15]

Let them neither receive nor give gifts in seeking or conducting office or after the conclusion of a term of office. Whatever of these someone has violated, let the penalty be equivalent to the crime.

Let the censors protect the fidelity of the laws. Let private citizens bring their actions to them for approval, but let them not thereby be freed from the law.

Here ends the law: I will order you to depart and be given ballots.

[12] QUINTUS: What a brief survey you have given of the distribution of all the magistracies! They are almost those of our own state, although you have added a little new material.

MARCUS: Your observation, Quintus, is quite right. This is the blended commonwealth which Scipio praises in that other book and which he most approves of, and it could not be brought to pass without such a distribution of offices. You must know that the commonwealth is bound up with the magistrates and those in charge, and from their organization can be understood what sort of commonwealth each is. And

[13] On the ability of magistrates of equal or greater authority to countermand the decrees of their colleagues or of lesser magistrates see above, n. 5.

[14] The text is corrupt and the translation conjectural.

[15] The centuriate assembly; for its organization see *On the Commonwealth* 2.39–40.

since this was established with great wisdom and moderation by our ancestors, I had little or nothing which I thought needed to be reformed in the laws.

[13] ATTICUS: As you did in the case of the religious laws at my urging and request, now you should give us an account of the magistrates, to explain why you approve of this organization in particular.

MARCUS: I will do as you wish, Atticus, and I will explain this whole topic as it has been investigated and explained by the most learned men of Greece; and, as I undertook, I will touch on our own laws.

ATTICUS: Just the kind of exposition I look for.

MARCUS: In fact, I said a great deal in my previous book, as was necessary in investigating the best form of commonwealth. But in connection with the subject of magistrates, there are particular issues discussed first by Theophrastus, then in fairly narrow terms by Diogenes the Stoic.

[14] ATTICUS: Is that so? Have even the Stoics dealt with this subject?

MARCUS: Only by the one I just named, and then later by Panaetius, who was a great man and singularly learned. The earlier Stoics discussed the commonwealth, but while they were very sharp in their linguistic analysis, it had little to do with the practice of real peoples and states.[16] This subject primarily derives from the group descending from Plato;[17] and later Aristotle illuminated the whole subject of civic affairs, and Heraclides of Pontus, who likewise took his start from Plato. As you know, Theophrastus (who was educated by Aristotle) virtually lived in this region of studies, and Dicaearchus, who was also instructed by Aristotle, did his part in this area of research. Later Demetrius of Phalerum, whom I have already mentioned, a pupil of Theophrastus, did a wonderful job of bringing the subject out from the shaded retreats of scholars not only into sunlight and the dust of the real world but

[16] On Stoic political theory see the passages collected in Long and Sedley 67; for recent discussion see particularly M. Schofield, *The Stoic Idea of the City* (Cambridge, 1991). The criticism of impracticality is the same that C. regularly levels at Plato.

[17] The obvious meaning of this clause (that Plato and Aristotle employed early Stoic writings) is impossible, and any translation (including this one) involves some contortion of the Latin and the word order. Haupt's emendation of *ab hac familia* to *ab Academia* is probably not right but at least makes sense: "This subject spread from the Academy under the leadership of Plato . . ." C. here mentions the principal writers on politics whose work he studied; compare also his statement about *On the Commonwealth* at *On Divination* 2.3, "an important subject that belongs to philosophy, examined extensively by Plato, Aristotle, Theophrastus, and the whole group of Peripatetics."

right into the front lines of battle. It's possible to think of many men of only moderate learning who were important in public life, and great scholars who were not active in public life; but aside from this one man, who is there who excelled in both areas, to be a leader both in scholarship and in government?[18]

ATTICUS: I can think of someone, and in fact it's one of us three. But go on.

[15] MARCUS: The subject of their inquiry was whether or not there should be one magistrate in the state whom the rest should obey. I know that that was the view of our ancestors, once the kings were driven out; but since the monarchic form of state, although it once met with approval, was rejected not so much because of the faults of monarchy as because of the faults of the monarch, the title alone of king will seem to have been rejected, but the substance will remain if there is a single person who commands all the other magistrates. [16] That is why there was good reason for Theopompus to set up ephors at Sparta to oppose the kings, and for us to have tribunes against the consuls.[19] For the consul has this legal authority, that all the other magistrates should obey him except for the tribune, who was brought into being later to avoid the state of affairs that had existed. This was the first thing that reduced the power of the consul, in that someone was created who was not subordinate to him, and also because he brought assistance not only to the other magistrates but even to private citizens who disobeyed the consul.

[17] QUINTUS: You are speaking of a great evil. Once that power was created, the importance of the optimates was reduced and the force of the mob was strengthened.

MARCUS: You're wrong, Quintus. It was unnecessary for that single power to seem too haughty and violent to the people. And after a moderate and wise blending was added to it *[20]

How will he be able to look out for the allies, if he cannot choose between useful and useless things? (+ Macrobius, *On Differences and Similarities of Greek and Latin Verbs* 17.6)

* apply; the law governs everyone.

[18] As in *On the Commonwealth*, C. views Demetrius as similar to himself (and to the earlier Seven Sages) in blending practical knowledge and theoretical analysis.

[19] On the similarity of the ephorate and the tribunate see *On the Commonwealth* 2.58.

[20] The large gap included C.'s commentary on chaps. 6–9; the first word after the gap is corrupt, and the meaning is uncertain. The quotation in Macrobius clearly comes from the commentary on the phrase "be sparing to the allies" in sect. 9.

[18] "Let them return home with glory": good and innocent men should not bring back anything but praise either from enemies or from allies.

Now it is also fairly obvious that there is nothing more disgraceful than for someone to be made an ambassador except on public business. I will say nothing about how the people who use ambassadorial appointments to pursue inheritances or contracts conduct themselves and have conducted themselves; that may simply be a fault of human nature. But I do ask what can in fact be more disgraceful than for a senator to be an ambassador without a function, without instructions, without any public duty? When I was consul, I would have eliminated that kind of embassy, with the approval of the full senate even though these appointments are useful for senators, if a frivolous tribune had not interposed his veto. But I did reduce the length of these appointments and put the limit of a year on what had been indefinite. The disgrace remains, but at least it's not long-term.

But with your approval we should leave the provinces and come back to the city.

ATTICUS: We approve, but the Romans in the provinces don't at all.

[19] MARCUS: But if they obey these laws, Titus, they will find nothing sweeter than the city and their homes, and nothing more full of toil and trouble than a province.

The law that follows is the one that ordains the tribunician power which exists in our own commonwealth. There is no need for me to say anything about that.

QUINTUS: But, brother, I must ask your opinion of that power. It seems to me truly pestilent, as you might expect from something born in sedition and for sedition. If we want to look back to its first origin, we see that it was created during civil strife when parts of the city were seized and besieged. Then, although it was put to death quickly (like a very deformed child, in accordance with the Twelve Tables), in a short time it somehow came to life again, and its second birth was even more disgraceful and disgusting.[21] What has it not produced? First, as is worthy of something with no sense of duty, it took every office away from senators;[22] it made the basest things equal to the best – it stirred

[21] The "second birth" is the restoration of the tribunate (along with the regular magistracies) after the fall of the decemvirate in 450–449. For the law on infanticide cf. Twelve Tables, fr. IV, 1 Crawford.

[22] "With no sense of duty" translates *inpio*: Quintus argues that tribunes are like sons who

them up and mixed them. And once it had ravaged the dignity of the leaders, it has never come to rest. [**20**] Even setting aside as ancient history the case of Flaminius and other things that now seem long ago, what rights did the tribunate of Tiberius Gracchus leave to respectable men? And five years earlier, Gaius Curiatius the tribune – the lowest and vilest of men – threw into chains the consuls Decimus Brutus and Publius Scipio – and what great men they were! – something that had never happened before. And the tribunate of Gaius Gracchus: didn't it overturn the entire structure of the commonwealth with disasters and with the daggers which he himself said that he had thrown into the forum for citizens to butcher one another with?[23] What is there to say about Saturninus and Sulpicius and the rest? The commonwealth could not even defend itself from them without violence. [**21**] And why should I talk about the past and other people rather than the recent things that happened to us? Who would ever have been so bold or so hostile to us as to think of undermining our position if he hadn't sharpened the sword of some tribune against us? And when these degenerate criminals couldn't find such a man in any house or family, they thought they had to confound the system of families in that dark night of the commonwealth. It is truly extraordinary and glorious for the immortality of our fame that no tribune could be found to attack us at any price, except for one who had no right to be tribune at all.[24] [**22**] But what a carnage he created! the kind that the madness of a filthy animal could create with no reason and with no honorable expectations, inflamed by the madness of the mob. And therefore I strongly approve of Sulla in this at any rate, that he took away by his law the power of the tribunes to do harm and left them the right of bearing aid; and while in everything else I have always praised our friend Pompeius in the highest terms, I keep silent concerning the tribunate. I don't want to criticize him, but I can't praise him.[25]

[**23**] MARCUS: You have a brilliant understanding of the faults of the

violate the obligations of children to fathers, playing on the two meanings of *patres*. What he means is that tribunician action compelled the opening of offices that had been limited to patricians (then the only senators) to plebeians.

23 Cf. Gracchus, fr. 45 Malcovati.

24 Clodius. As a patrician he was ineligible to be tribune of the plebs and had himself adopted (in a transaction that C. found fraudulent and farcical) by the plebeian Fonteius in order to stand for the tribunate.

25 Sulla in his dictatorship had removed the legislative capacities of the tribunes and made them ineligible to stand for higher office; Pompey in his consulate in 70 restored the traditional powers and status of the tribunes.

tribunate, Quintus, but in making any accusations it isn't fair to pass over the good things and select and enumerate only the bad and the faulty. You could use that technique to criticize the consulate if you collected the faults of consuls whom I am unwilling to list. I admit that there is something bad in the tribunician power, but without the bad we would not have the good that was sought in creating it. "The power of the tribunes of the people is excessive." Everyone agrees. But the violence of the people is much more savage and uncontrolled, and having a leader sometimes makes it more calm than if there were none. The leader realizes that he acts at his own risk, while when the people attack they don't reckon with their own danger. [**24**] "But at times they are inflamed." And they are often calmed. What college of tribunes is so desperate as not to have one out of the ten be sane? In fact, Tiberius Gracchus himself was overturned by not only neglecting but removing the one who vetoed his actions. What else was there that brought him down, if not the abrogation of the power of a colleague who intervened?[26] But you should recognize in this the wisdom of our ancestors: when the senate yielded this power to the plebeians, the weapons were put down, the sedition was calmed, moderation was discovered, which allowed the lesser people to think that they were made equal to the leaders; and that was the single source of salvation for the state. "But there were the two Gracchi." And beyond them you can list as many as you like: since they are elected ten at a time, you will find in any period a number of dangerous tribunes, some frivolous ones, not responsible citizens. Perhaps there are quite a few. But the ruling order of society is not subject to hatred, and the plebeians on their own account create no dangerous struggles. [**25**] For that reason, either the kings should not have been expelled or the plebeians should have been given real, not nominal, freedom. It was in fact given in such a way that they were induced by many excellent customs to yield to the authority of the first citizens. In my own case, my beloved and admirable brother, I had troubles with the power of the tribunes but no quarrel with the tribunate itself. The plebeians were not stirred up to hatred of my actions: the slaves were unchained and stirred up, and fear of the army was added as well. My struggle at that time was not with that blight[27] but with the overwhelming crisis of the commonwealth; and if I had not given

[26] Tiberius Gracchus had Octavius, the tribune who vetoed his law, removed from office, a procedure of very questionable legality.

[27] *Pestis*, one of C.'s regular epithets for Clodius.

way, then the country would not have received a long-term benefit from my good deeds. The outcome demonstrated this: who was there, not only of the free population but even of the slaves worthy of freedom, to whom my safety was not dear? [26] If the outcome of my actions on behalf of the safety of the commonwealth had not been gratifying to all, and if the inflamed hatred of the raging mob had driven me out, and if the force of the tribunate had stirred the people against me, as was the case with Gracchus against Laenas and Saturninus against Metellus, then, Quintus, I would have endured it, and it is not so much the philosophers at Athens (who ought to have done so) who would have consoled me as the great men who were driven from that city and preferred to do without an ungrateful country than to remain in a wicked one.[28] As to your disapproval in this matter alone of Pompey's conduct, you seem to me not to recognize adequately that he had to pay attention not only to what was best, but to what was necessary. He recognized that that power could not be withheld from this state: how could a people that had so strenuously sought it before they had known what it was do without it once they knew it? A wise citizen should not dangerously have left some demagogue a cause that was in itself not dangerous and was so popular as to be irresistible. – You know, brother, that in a discussion of this sort, in order to be able to move to another topic, it is usual to say, "Quite so" or "True enough."

QUINTUS: Well, I for one do not agree; but I would like you to go on to the rest.

MARCUS: You at least are firm and stick to your old opinion.

ATTICUS: And I certainly don't disagree with Quintus. But we should hear the remainder.

[27] MARCUS: Next then: all the magistrates are given the right to take the auspices and give judgment. Judgments are given with the proviso that there is the right of appeal to the people; the auspices, so that delay can obstruct many useless but appealing initiatives. It is frequently the case that the immortal gods have, through the auspices, suppressed unjust impulses of the people.

As to the composition of the senate from those who have held office, it is certainly a popular measure to have no one reach the highest position without the approval of the people, eliminating cooptation by the censors. But this flaw is moderated by the fact that in our law the auth-

[28] Compare *On the Commonwealth* 1.6–9.

ority of the senate is strengthened: [28] what follows is "let its decrees be duly ratified."[29] For it works out that if the senate is in charge of public deliberation, and if the remaining orders are willing to have the commonwealth guided by the deliberation of the leading order, then it is possible through the blending of rights, since the people have power and the senate has authority, that that moderate and harmonious order of the state be maintained, especially if the following law is obeyed; for what follows is: "Let the senatorial order be free from fault; let it be a model to others."

QUINTUS: That is a fine law, brother, but to say that the order should be free from fault has very wide application and requires a censor to interpret it.

[29] ATTICUS: And although the senate is completely with you and retains the most grateful memory of your consulate, I must say (with apologies to you) that it could wear out not only the censors but all the judges as well.

MARCUS: Enough of that, Atticus! What I say does not refer to this senate or to men of the present, but to those of the future who may wish to obey these laws.[30] Since the law orders them to lack all faults, no one with faults will even enter the order. That is hard to accomplish without the proper education and training, and perhaps we will say something about that if time and occasion permit.

[30] ATTICUS: There will certainly be occasion, since you control the order of the laws; and the length of the day is generous with time. And for my part, if you should skip it I will ask you about the topic of education and training.

MARCUS: Please do, Atticus, about that or anything else that I skip.

"Let it be a model to others." If we can hold to that, we hold on to everything. Just as the entire state is likely to be infected by the desires and the faults of the leaders, so it is improved and corrected by their discipline. Lucius Lucullus was a great man and a friend to all of us. There is a story that when he was criticized for the grandeur of his villa at Tusculum, he replied with great amiability that he had two neighbors: on one side a Roman knight, on the other a freedman; and that

[29] In law, the senate had *auctoritas* ("authority, influence"; see "Text and Translation") rather than real power: its decisions were *senatus consulta*, "opinions of the senate," rather than laws. C.'s ideal laws give the senate more legal standing than in fact it had in Rome.

[30] Compare the use of the future tense in Laelius' description of natural law at *On the Commonwealth* 3.33.

since they had grand villas, he ought to be allowed what was permitted to men of lower standing. But Lucullus, don't you see that you are yourself the source of their desire, that if you did not behave this way they would not be permitted to either? [31] Who would endure such men when he saw their villas stuffed with statues and paintings, some of them public, some of them even sacred works of religion; who would not restrain their desires – if those who have the obligation to do so were not themselves in the thrall of the same desire? That the leaders have faults is not so bad – although it is of course a bad thing in itself – as the fact that a great many imitators of those leaders arise. If you review the course of past history, you can see that the state has been of the same character as its greatest men; and whatever moral alteration takes place in the leaders soon follows among the people. [32] That is quite a lot closer to the truth than Plato's opinion. He says that when musicians change their tunes the condition of states also changes; but I think that the character of states changes when there are changes in the life and habits of the nobles. Immoral leaders are all the more damaging to the commonwealth because they not only harbor their own vices but they instill them into the state; the fact that they are corrupted is not the only damage they cause, but the fact that they corrupt others: they are more harmful as examples than for their failings. This law is applied to the whole order, but it can be narrowed: there are relatively few men, bolstered by honor and glory, who can corrupt or correct the morals of the state. But that is enough on this subject for now, which I have dealt with more thoroughly in my previous book.[31] So we should turn to the rest.

[33] The next law concerns ballots, which I order to be known to the optimates but free to the people.

ATTICUS: I paid very close attention indeed, but I did not really understand what the law or those words meant.

MARCUS: I will tell you, Titus, and will consider a difficult and much-studied subject, whether the ballots in the election of magistrates, judicial verdicts, and approval of laws or other issues are better kept secret or should be open.

QUINTUS: Is even that open to question? I fear that I will disagree with you again.

MARCUS: No you won't, Quintus. I hold to the opinion that I know

[31] In particular, compare the fragments of *On the Commonwealth* Books 4 and 5.

you have always held, that there is nothing better than voting aloud. But we have to consider whether that is practicable or not.

[34] QUINTUS: But I hope you won't mind my saying, brother, that such an attitude both deceives people who are inexperienced and very frequently damages the commonwealth – when something is said to be true and right but not practicable, that is that the people cannot be resisted. The first line of resistance is firm action, and then it is better to be overcome by force for a good cause than to give way to a bad one. Who does not realize that the entire authority of the optimates was stolen by the ballot law? When the people were free they never wanted it, but they demanded it when they were beaten down by the oppressive power of leading citizens. And in fact, there are records of harsher verdicts against very powerful men given by voice than by ballot. For that reason the powerful should have been deprived of their excessive desire for balloting in bad causes rather than giving the people a hiding place in which the written ballot could conceal a flawed vote while the respectable citizens were ignorant of each person's sentiments. Therefore no respectable citizen has ever been found to propose or support such a measure.

[35] There are four ballot laws on the books.[32] The first one concerns the election of magistrates; that is the Gabinian law, carried by a low person of no background. Two years later followed the Cassian law on trials before the people, carried by Lucius Cassius, a noble, but – with apologies to his family – a man at odds with the respectable citizens and snatching at every wisp of popular support. The third law, on votes approving and disapproving legislation, belongs to Carbo, a seditious and wicked citizen; not even his reversion to respectability could gain him the protection of respectable citizens. [36] There was only one area left for voice votes, namely treason trials, which even Cassius had specifically exempted from his law. Gaius Coelius provided written ballots for this kind of trial too, and he regretted to the end of his days that in order to do in Gaius Popillius he had done harm to the commonwealth. Our own grandfather for his entire life resisted with great courage the attempt of Marcus Gratidius (whose sister, our grandmother, was his wife) to carry a ballot law in this town. Gratidius, as they say, stirred up a tempest in a teapot – something his son Marius later did in the Aegean Sea.[33] When this was reported to Marcus Scaurus the

[32] The four laws were passed in 139, 137, 131 or 130, and 107 BCE respectively.

[33] Marius Gratidianus; see biographical notes.

consul,[34] he said: "If only, Marcus Cicero, you had chosen to use your spirit and courage in the Roman commonwealth rather than in your small town!" [37] For that reason, although we are not now reviewing the laws of the Roman people but are either going back to ones that have been rejected or writing new ones, I think that you must speak not about what is practicable under the present political circumstances, but what is really best. Your beloved Scipio shoulders the blame for the Cassian law, which is reported to have been passed because of his support; but if you carry a ballot law, you will vouch for it yourself. I do not support it, nor does our friend Atticus, to judge from his expression.

ATTICUS: No populist measure has ever pleased me: I hold that the best commonwealth is that which Cicero here as consul established, one that is in the control of the best citizens.

[38] MARCUS: I can see that you don't need a written ballot to reject my law. But for my own part – even if Scipio said enough on his own behalf in my previous book[35] – I indulge the people in this liberty in such a way that the respectable citizens both have and use their authority. This is the wording of my ballot law: "let them be known to the optimates, free to the plebs." This law has the function of voiding all those laws which were passed later, which conceal the ballot in every way – that no one should look at it, ask for it, or question the voters. The law of Marius made the voting passages narrow.[36] [39] Most such laws are against bribery, and I have no objection to that; but if these laws still could not stop bribery, then let the people have its ballot as a badge of liberty – so long as it is shown willingly to the best and most respectable citizens. The liberty should consist in this, that the people are given the power of honorably pleasing the respectable citizens. A moment ago, Quintus, you observed that fewer people are condemned by the ballot than by voice vote; that is because the people are satisfied to have the right to vote, and so long as they have that, for the rest they follow people they respect or support. If I set aside votes that are corrupted by wholesale handouts, surely you see that – if bribery is not involved – the real issue in voting is what the most respectable citizens think? Therefore my law gives the appearance of liberty while keeping the authority of the respectable and eliminating an occasion for dispute.

34 The opening of the sentence is corrupt, and some words may be missing.

35 Cf. *On the Commonwealth* 4.8.

36 In 119. The intention was to limit physical access to voters and thus the opportunity for distributing bribes. Voters filed through a passage (literally, a bridge) to record their votes.

[40] The next law concerns those who have the right to conduct business before the people or in the senate. Then comes an important and in my opinion excellent law: "Let those things which are brought before the people or the senate be moderate" – that is decent and calm. The person conducting business directs and shapes not only the minds and wishes of his hearers, but almost their expressions as well. If . . . not difficult in the senate; a senator is someone who does not take his ideas from the speaker but who desires to be recognized for himself.[37] Senators are ordered to do three things: to be present (because the business of the senate gains solemnity from the number of senators present); to speak in his place, that is when asked his opinion; and to speak in measure, that is not endlessly. Brevity in giving one's opinion deserves great praise, not only in a senator but in a public speaker; there is never need for a long speech unless either the senate is misbehaving – which often happens through bribery – and no magistrate is helping out, when it is useful for the day to be wasted, or the topic is so important that it needs the full resources of an orator either to urge or to explain the case. Our friend Cato is a master in both these circumstances.[38] [41] The addition of "let him understand the concerns of the people" is because a senator must know the commonwealth. That is a topic of wide application: military and financial resources, the allies of the commonwealth, its friends and tributaries, the laws, agreements, and treaties governing each one. He must also know procedural matters and ancestral precedents. You see the type of knowledge, study, and memory without which no senator can be truly prepared.

[42] Then come dealings with the people, in which the first and most important provision is "let there be no violence." There is nothing more destructive for states, nothing more contrary to right and law, nothing less civil and humane, than the use of violence in public affairs in a duly constituted commonwealth. The law ordains obedience to someone interposing a veto, and there is nothing more valuable than that: it is better for a good thing to be blocked than to give way to a bad one.

As to my injunction that "it is the fault of the person in charge," that is entirely based on the opinion of Crassus, a very wise man. The senate accepted his view when it decreed, on the motion of Gaius Claudius the

37 Part of the sentence is lost, and part is corrupt, although the general sense is clear.

38 The younger Cato. C. in his correspondence expressed his annoyance at Cato's behavior for speaking "as if he were in Plato's *Republic* rather than among the dregs of Romulus" (*Letters to Atticus* 2.1.8).

consul concerning the sedition of Gnaeus Carbo,[39] that no sedition could take place against the will of the person in charge of the assembly: he has the opportunity to dissolve the meeting as soon as there is a veto and the beginning of disturbance. Someone who persists[40] when there is no possibility of formal action is looking for violence; and through this law he loses his means of avoiding punishment.

What follows is: "Let the citizen who intervenes in evil affairs be regarded as a savior of the community." [43] If he is praised by such an outstanding statement of the law, who would not eagerly come to the aid of the commonwealth?[41]

The next laws are part of our own public customs and laws: "Let them observe the auspices; let them obey the public augur." A good augur must remember that he ought to be at hand at the greatest public crises, that he is the assistant and aide to Jupiter the Best and Greatest just as those whom he has ordered to be present at the auspices are to him, that he has specific portions of the sky assigned to him, from which he can often bring aid to the commonwealth. Then come provisions about the promulgation of laws, about bills that deal with one thing at a time, about listening to private citizens or magistrates.

[44] Then come two magnificent laws that are taken from the Twelve Tables; one eliminates laws concerning single individuals, the other forbids action on the status of a citizen except in the greatest assembly.[42] And since at that time seditious tribunes of the people had not yet been created and not even imagined, it is remarkable that our ancestors had so much foresight. They did not want laws to be carried against private men – that is the meaning of *privilegia* – because there is nothing more unjust than that, since it is the essence of law to be a decision or order applying to all. They did not want votes on individuals except in the centuriate assembly: the distribution of the people by wealth, rank, and age brings greater wisdom to the ballot than when they are summoned broadly by tribes. [45] That makes all the more true the statement in my case of Lucius Cotta, a man of great talent and wisdom, that there had been no action at all about me: aside from the fact that that assembly took place with armed slaves, no validity could attach either to the

[39] In 92 BCE. [40] Conjectural; the text is corrupt.

[41] Compare *On the Commonwealth* 2.46 on Lucius Junius Brutus.

[42] Twelve Tables, fr. IX, 2 Crawford. The phrase *maximo comitiatu*, which C. interprets as meaning the Comitia Centuriata, probably meant "the fullest possible gathering." C.'s views on *privilegia* are probably tendentious, affected by the law under which he was exiled in 58.

vote of the tribal assembly on a citizen's status or to any vote concerning a single individual. And for that reason he said that I had no need of a law, since no legal action had been taken against me. But both you and other great men had a different opinion, namely to demonstrate what all Italy thought about someone about whom slaves and robbers claimed to have given an opinion.

[46] What follows concerns taking and giving bribes, and since laws must be given authority not so much by their words as by judicial decisions, the clause is added "let the penalty be equal to the crime," so that each person should be affected in the area of his fault: violence should be sanctioned by loss of civic status, greed by a fine, desire for office by disgrace.

The final laws are not in effect here but are necessary for the commonwealth. We have no method of protecting the laws themselves, and so the laws are what our clerks want them to be: we get them from scribes, and we have no authenticated public record in the public archives. The Greeks were more careful about this: they created "guards of the laws" who watched over not only the texts (that was customary among our ancestors too) but also men's actions, and brought them in line with the laws. [47] This responsibility should be given to the censors, as we want them to exist in the commonwealth at all times.[43] Before them too those who are completing their terms of office should state and explain their actions in office, and the censors should give an opinion about them. This takes place in Greece with publicly assigned prosecutors; but they cannot be taken seriously unless they are volunteers. For that reason it is better for accounts and explanations to be given before the censors, but the right of prosecution before a court should be preserved intact.

I have now said enough about the magistrates unless you want something more.

ATTICUS: Even if we say nothing, doesn't the subject itself remind you of what needs to be discussed next?

MARCUS: I suppose that you mean about the courts, Pomponius; that is certainly related to the subject of magistrates.

[48] ATTICUS: Don't you think that something needs to be said about the law of the Roman people, according to your initial plan?

[43] See above, n. 8. C.'s extension of the role of the censorship is one of the more important changes he makes to Roman practice, in accord with his discussion in *On the Commonwealth* Book 4.

MARCUS: What is it that you look for just now?

ATTICUS: Me? The subject that I think it most disgraceful for people involved in public life not to know. Just a moment ago you said that people get their laws from the scribes, and similarly I notice that most people holding office, because of their ignorance of the law, are just as knowledgeable as their assistants want them to be. For that reason, if you thought it necessary to speak about the alienation of sacred rites when you were expounding the laws of religion, so too, now that you have set up the magistracies in accordance with law, you must explain the law concerning official powers.

[49] MARCUS: If I can, I will do it briefly. Your father's friend Marcus Iunius wrote extensively to your father about this, and he did so, in my judgment, with learning and care. Our obligation is to think and speak about the law of nature independently, but to say about the law of the Roman people what has been handed down.

ATTICUS: That is my belief too, and what you just described is exactly what I am waiting for.

*

Fragments of *On the Laws*

1. We should count ourselves lucky, because death will bring us to a condition that is either better than that in life or at least no worse. If the soul is active without the body, then its life is divine; and if it has no sensation, then it is nothing bad. (Lactantius, *Inst.* 3.19.2)[44]

2. Since the sun has descended a little from midday, and this spot is not yet sufficiently shaded by these young trees, do you think we should go down to the Liris and pursue the remainder of the conversation under the shade of those alders? (Macrobius, *Saturnalia* 5.4.8; from Book 5)

[44] Placed by Vahlen in the gap after 2.53.

Biographical Notes

These notes include all persons named (omitting some mythological figures) in *On the Commonwealth* and *On the Laws*; consuls mentioned purely for dating purposes are not included. Note that the Latin (Ciceronian) spelling of Greek names is generally employed. These descriptions are very bare and concentrate on material relevant to the Ciceronian texts; further information on most of those named may be found in the *Oxford Classical Dictionary* (3rd ed., 1996).

ACCIUS, LUCIUS (170–*c*.84). Poet and tragedian and a scholar of grammar and literary history.

ACILIUS, LUCIUS (second century). Jurist and commentator on the Twelve Tables.

AELIUS PAETUS CATUS, SEXTUS (third–second century). Consul in 198, censor in 194; a renowned legal scholar who edited and commented on the Twelve Tables.

AELIUS STILO PRAECONINUS, LUCIUS (*c*.155–*c*.75). Grammarian and etymologist with Stoic leanings; also known as a speechwriter for others and as one of Cicero's teachers.

AELIUS TUBERO, QUINTUS (second century). The son of Scipio Aemilianus' sister Aemilia and a participant in *On the Commonwealth*. He was a considerable scholar and philosopher, but although he held the tribunate (at an uncertain date before 129), his Stoic austerity led to his failure to be elected praetor.

AEMILIUS PAULLUS, LUCIUS (d. 160). The natural father of Scipio Aemilianus; he defeated King Perseus of Macedonia at the battle of Pydna as consul for the third time in 168. The only booty he kept for himself was Perseus' library, which his sons used.

AEMILIUS SCAURUS, MARCUS (163–*c.*90). Consul in 115, censor in 109. One of the most influential conservative political figures of his time. Cicero much admired him; Sallust thought him corrupt and dishonest.

AESCHINES (fourth century). Athenian orator and statesman; his opponent Demosthenes in the speech *On the Crown* described with vitriol and much imagination his early career as a bad actor.

AFRICANUS: see CORNELIUS

AHALA: see SERVILIUS

ALEXANDER THE GREAT (356–323). King of Macedon; conqueror of the east.

AMPIUS BALBUS, TITUS (first century). Tribune and supporter of Cicero in 63, praetor in 59; supporter of Pompey in the Civil War. He was defended in court by Cicero and Pompey sometime in the late 50s.

AMULIUS. Mythical king of Alba Longa; Cicero's account omits the traditional story that he ousted his brother Numitor, the rightful king, and was himself killed by Numitor's grandchildren, Romulus and Remus.

ANAXAGORAS of CLAZOMENAE (*c.*500–428). Lived in Athens and taught natural philosophy for twenty years until prosecuted for impiety in 437/6; he was closely associated with Pericles.

ANCUS: see MARCIUS

ANTIOCHUS of ASCALON (late second century to 68/7). Head of the Academy, which he turned away from skepticism to what he called the "Old Academy," emphasizing the similarity among Stoic, Peripatetic, and Platonic ethical beliefs. Cicero heard him lecture in Athens in 79/8, and he had close connections with many Romans of high rank.

APPULEIUS SATURNINUS, LUCIUS (d. 100). Tribune in 103 and 100, he continued the radical policies of the Gracchi and supported Marius; the latter as consul took action against him, and despite a promise of safety, he was stoned to death while imprisoned in the Senate House.

ARATUS of SOLI in CILICIA (third century). A scholar and poet, whose *Phaenomena* versified the astronomy of Eudoxus and was phenomenally popular; it was translated into Latin by Cicero.

ARCESILAUS (316/5–242/1). Head of the Academy from *c.*268, he was the first of Plato's successors to turn the Academy to skepticism.

ARCHIMEDES (*c.*287–212). Engineer, inventor, mathematician; many of his works still survive, although his astronomical works are lost. He was killed in the siege of Syracuse.

ARCHYTAS of TARENTUM (fifth–fourth century). A Pythagorean philosopher and mathematician as well as a general, he had Plato rescued from the clutches of Dionysius II of Syracuse in 361.

ARISTO of CHIOS (third century). Stoic and pupil of Zeno; he espoused far more rigid ethical views than what subsequently became orthodox Stoicism.

ARISTODEMUS (fourth century). Originally from Metapontum in S. Italy but awarded Athenian citizenship; a renowned actor, he served as an ambassador for Athens in negotiations with Philip of Macedon.

ARISTOPHANES (fifth–fourth century). Athenian comic poet.

ARISTOTLE (384–322). A student of Plato and then founder of the Peripatetic school. The vast range of his writings includes scientific and logical works as well as ethics and politics (along with much else), but Cicero would have known few of the works now extant, using instead a number of more popular works in dialogue form (now lost), notably *On Justice* and *The Statesman* and his exhortation to the study of philosophy, *Protrepticus*.

ASELLIO: see SEMPRONIUS

ATILIUS CALATINUS, AULUS (third century). Consul in 258 and 254, dictator in 249, censor in 247; he was one of the military heroes of the First Punic War.

ATTICUS: see POMPONIUS

AURELIUS COTTA, LUCIUS (first century). Consul in 65 and censor in 64, he supported Cicero against Catiline in 63 and during his exile in 58–57.

BRUTUS: see IUNIUS

CAECILIUS METELLUS, LUCIUS (d. 221). Consul in 251 and 247; he defeated the Carthaginians at Panormus in the First Punic War. He was pontifex maximus from 247 until his death.

CAECILIUS METELLUS MACEDONICUS, QUINTUS (d. 115). Consul in 143, censor in 131; he was a political opponent of Scipio Aemilianus but (aside from what is said at *On the Commonwealth* 1.31) also hostile to Tiberius Gracchus.

CAECILIUS METELLUS NUMIDICUS, QUINTUS (second–first

century). Consul in 109, censor in 102. He went into exile in 100 rather than swear an oath to support the agrarian law of Appuleius Saturninus; he was recalled not long after.

CAECILIUS STATIUS (d. 168). Roman comic dramatist, greatly admired in antiquity; only fragments of his plays (of which some forty are known) survive.

CALATINUS: see ATILIUS

CALPURNIUS PISO FRUGI, LUCIUS (second century). An active soldier and statesman (tribune in 149, consul in 135, censor in 120); he wrote a history of Rome (*Annals*) from the beginning down to at least 146, in which he marked the beginning of Roman moral decline in 154.

CAMILLUS: see FURIUS

CARBO: see PAPIRIUS

CARNEADES (214–129). A skeptic and the head of the Academy; he was (with Diogenes the Stoic and Critolaus the Peripatetic) a member of the so-called philosophers' embassy from Athens to Rome in 155. His balanced speeches on justice and injustice on that occasion were shocking and notorious, and provide the basis for the debate on justice in Book 3 of *On the Commonwealth*.

CASSIUS, SPURIUS (sixth–fifth centuries). As consul in 486 he was accused of attempting a coup and was tried and executed in the following year. Both the nature of his attempt and the form of his trial are unclear.

CASSIUS LONGINUS RAVILLA, LUCIUS (second century). As tribune in 137 he carried a law (supported by Scipio Aemilianus) to extend the use of the written ballot from elections to trials before the people. He went on to become consul in 127 and censor in 125.

CATO: see PORCIUS

CATUS: see AELIUS

CHARONDAS (seventh or sixth century). Born in Catane (Catania) in Sicily; many of the cities of Sicily and southern Italy identified him as the author of their laws. The prologue to his laws quoted by Cicero in *On the Laws* (also preserved in the sixth-century Byzantine anthology of John of Stobi) is not authentic.

CHRYSIPPUS (*c.*280–206). The third head of the Stoa (from 232), after Zeno and Cleanthes; his copious writings (including a *Republic* and a work, *On Law*, used by Cicero) set out Stoic theory in a systematic form.

CICERO: see TULLIUS

CLAUDIUS MARCELLUS, GAIUS (d. 45 or earlier). Praetor in 80; he is mentioned as one of Cicero's fellow augurs at *On the Laws* 2.32.

CLAUDIUS MARCELLUS, MARCUS (d. 208). Consul five times and one of the great military figures of the middle Republic, he besieged and captured Syracuse in 212 during the Second Punic War.

CLAUDIUS MARCELLUS, MARCUS (d. 148). Consul in 166 and twice later and pontifex 177–148; grandson of the great Marcellus. He drowned in a storm while on an embassy to Masinissa.

CLAUDIUS PULCHER, APPIUS (d. *c.*131). Consul in 143, censor in 136, and a long-time political opponent of Scipio Aemilianus; he was a supporter of his son-in-law Tiberius Gracchus.

CLAUDIUS PULCHER, APPIUS (d. 48). Brother of Clodius and the only praetor to oppose Cicero's recall in 57, but later on good terms with him. He was consul in 54 and a member of the augural college. He dedicated his book on augural law to Cicero.

CLAUDIUS PULCHER, GAIUS (second century). Consul in 177, censor in 169; accused of treason by the tribune Rutilius.

CLAUDIUS PULCHER, GAIUS (second–first century). An opponent of Saturninus and consul in 92; also famous for exhibiting elephants in the games he gave as aedile in 99.

CLEON (fifth century). Demagogic Athenian politician during the Peloponnesian War, much ridiculed by Aristophanes.

CLEOPHON (fifth century). Like Cleon, a demagogue and politician in Athens.

CLINIAS (fourth century, if real). The Cretan participant in Plato's *Laws*.

CLISTHENES (sixth century). Athenian legislator whose reorganization of government in 508 was the basis of the democratic constitution.

CLITARCHUS (fourth/third centuries). Author of a history of Alexander the Great in twelve books more renowned for its style than for its historical accuracy or insight.

CLODIUS (early first century). Presumably the same as Q. Claudius Quadrigarius, author of a very rhetorical history of Rome from the Gallic sack of 387 to his own time.

CLODIUS PULCHER, PUBLIUS (*c.*92–52). Not named by Cicero in these works but very much present. A master of street politics and violence, he adopted the plebeian spelling of his family name and had himself adopted into a plebeian family in order to become tribune in 58, when he engineered the exile of Cicero. Their enmity arose from Cicero's evidence against him when he was tried for sacrilege in 61 for having violated the rites of the Bona Dea. He was murdered in a street fight on 18 January 52.

COELIUS ANTIPATER, LUCIUS (late second century). Author of a history of the Second Punic War in seven books.

COELIUS CALDUS, GAIUS (second–first century). Consul in 94; as tribune in 107 he passed a law extending the written ballot to trials for treason in order to convict Gaius Popilius, of whose treaty with the Tigurini he did not approve.

CORNELIUS SCIPIO, GNAEUS and PUBLIUS (third century). The father and uncle of the elder Africanus; they were killed fighting in Spain in the Second Punic War in 211.

CORNELIUS SCIPIO, PUBLIUS (second century). The son of the elder Africanus and the adoptive father of Scipio Aemilianus; his poor health kept him from entering public life.

CORNELIUS SCIPIO AFRICANUS, PUBLIUS (236–183). Consul in 205 and 194; he defeated Hannibal at Zama in 202 to end the Second Punic War.

CORNELIUS SCIPIO AFRICANUS AEMILIANUS, PUBLIUS (185/4–129). The natural son of Lucius Aemilius Paullus and adoptive son of Publius Cornelius Scipio; he was consul in 147 and 134 and destroyer in the following years of Carthage (in the Third Punic War) and Numantia in Spain; he was censor in 142. In real life he was both a consummate popular politician and a harsh and arrogant aristocrat, and tried to undo the popular measures of his cousin Tiberius Gracchus. In Cicero's writings he appears as a humane statesman of great intellectual abilities; he was certainly an acquaintaince of Polybius, Panaetius, and Terence. He is the protagonist of *On the Commonwealth*. His sudden death a few days after the dramatic date of the dialogue may have been natural, but Cicero thought he had been murdered.

CORNELIUS SCIPIO NASICA SERAPIO, PUBLIUS (second century). Grandson of the elder Africanus and thus a cousin of the Gracchi and (by his adoption) of Scipio Aemilianus; he was consul in 138 and pontifex maximus. As leader of the senate, he led the mob that killed Tiberius Sempronius Gracchus when Gracchus stood for reelection as tribune in 133. He was sent on an embassy to Asia by the senate immediately thereafter to get him out of Rome; he died before returning.

CORNELIUS SISENNA, LUCIUS (d. 67). A supporter of Sulla and later of Pompey, he was praetor in 78. He is best known as a historian of the Sullan period but also translated the salacious *Milesian Tales* of Aristides.

CORNELIUS SULLA, LUCIUS (138–78). From a decayed aristocratic family; he commanded troops in the Social War (90–89) and was consul in 88, when he marched on Rome to gain the command in the Mithradatic War which Marius was trying to obtain. After a rapid and inconclusive war (including a brutal siege of Athens), he invaded Italy in 84, defeated the supporters of Marius (or of the legitimate government) and had himself made dictator in 82, putting numerous enemies and wealthy people to death through proscriptions and establishing a reactionary senatorial government. He retired in 79 and died the next year.

CORUNCANIUS, TIBERIUS (d. *c.*243). Consul in 280; at some point thereafter he became the first plebeian pontifex maximus.

COTTA: see AURELIUS

CRASSUS: see LICINIUS

CURIATIUS, GAIUS (second century). As tribune in 138 he had the consuls Scipio Nasica and Iunius Brutus imprisoned.

CURIUS DENTATUS, MANIUS (fourth–third century). Consul in 290 (and three times thereafter) and censor in 272; a military leader renowned for his rectitude and frugality.

CYPSELUS (seventh century). Tyrant of Corinth in Greece for some thirty years beginning about 650.

CYRUS THE GREAT (sixth century). Founder of the Persian Empire and king 559–529. Xenophon's *Cyropaedia* (*The Education of Cyrus*), an edifying and fictional version of his life, was said to be the favorite book of Scipio Aemilianus.

DEMARATUS (sixth century, if real). A Corinthian noble who went into exile in Etruria because of the tyranny of Cypselus; the father of Lucius Tarquinius Priscus.

DEMETRIUS of PHALERUM (*c.*350 to after 283). Peripatetic philosopher and pupil of Theophrastus; he ruled Athens (317–307) on behalf of Cassander, the king of Macedonia. After the restoration of Athenian democracy by Demetrius Poliorcetes in 307 he went into exile, ending up in Alexandria, where he was an adviser to Ptolemy I on cultural matters. Cicero admired both his writings and his combination of philosophy with an active public life.

DICAEARCHUS (fourth century). A Peripatetic philosopher and pupil of Aristotle; Cicero made copious use of his many writings on government and cultural history.

DIOGENES of BABYLON (*c*.240–*c*.152). Pupil of Chrysippus and head of the Stoic school in Athens; he took part in the philosophers' embassy of 155 from Athens to Rome with Carneades and Critolaus.

DIONYSIUS II (fourth century). Tyrant of Syracuse 367–344 (with interruptions). Plato attempted without success to turn him into a philosopher king; he died in exile in Corinth.

DRACO (seventh century, if real). The alleged author of the first written Athenian law code, renowned for its severity. The extant homicide law from the late fifth century is ascribed to him.

DUILIUS, GAIUS (third century). Consul in 260, censor in 258; he defeated the Carthaginian fleet at Mylae in 260 and was the first person to be awarded a triumph for a naval victory.

EGERIA (eighth–seventh century, if real). A water nymph, associated with a spring near the Porta Capena in Rome; King Numa's significant other.

EMPEDOCLES of AGRIGENTUM (fifth century). Pre-Socratic philosopher, author of the poems *On Nature* and *Purifications*. Among his more important ideas are his belief in the four elements and in the transmigration of souls; he is said to have tested the latter by jumping into Mount Aetna.

ENNIUS, QUINTUS (239–169). The most versatile and original poet of early Rome, best known for his many tragedies and his epic *Annals*, on Roman history. Cicero admired him greatly and quotes him frequently.

EPICURUS (341–271). The founder of the philosophical school that bears his name. He was a materialist who believed that pleasure (defined in fairly austere terms) was the goal of life and friendship one of its greatest attributes; he rejected all strong emotions and (unless unavoidable) participation in public life. Cicero attacks his beliefs frequently and violently; they were made accessible and perhaps popular in Rome in the 50s through the brilliant poem *On Nature* (*De rerum natura*) of Lucretius.

ER the PAMPHYLIAN (imaginary). The soldier whose apparent death and subsequent resurrection are the occasion for the eschatological vision attributed to him (the Myth of Er) at the end of Plato's *Repub-*

lic, which is the model for Scipio's dream at the end of *On the Commonwealth*.

EUDOXUS of CNIDUS (*c*.390–*c*.340). Mathematician and astronomer; responsible for the theory of concentric celestial spheres. His astronomy was versified by Aratus.

FABIUS MAXIMUS VERRUCOSUS, QUINTUS (d. 203). One of the heroes of the Second Punic War (consul five times, dictator in 217); he was given the soubriquet *Cunctator* (Delayer) because of his tactics.

FABIUS PICTOR, QUINTUS (third century). An aristocrat and senator, he was the first Roman to write history, an account of Rome from the origins to his own time, in Greek. A Latin version was probably available in Cicero's time.

FABRICIUS LUSCINUS, GAIUS (third century). Consul in 282 and 278, censor in 275; he played a major role in the war against Pyrrhus and was renowned for his virtue.

FANNIUS, GAIUS (late second century). Two cousins almost impossible to distinguish. One of them was consul in 122, a son-in-law of Laelius, and a participant in the dialogue of *On the Commonwealth*; the other (probably) was a historian.

FIGULUS: see MARCIUS

FLAMINIUS, GAIUS (third century). Killed in 217 at the Battle of Lake Trasimene during his second consulate. As tribune in 232, he carried a law for distribution of land in northern Italy to Roman settlers; he was seen in the conservative later tradition as a precursor of the Gracchi.

FLAVIUS, GNAEUS (fourth century). The son of a freedman, he began as a scribe and became aedile in 304; he made public for the first time both the official calendar and the forms of legal procedure (*legis actiones*).

FURIUS CAMILLUS, MARCUS (fifth–fourth century). Military tribune with consular power in 401 and many times thereafter, dictator in 396 and after. The conqueror of Veii, he was then exiled for misappropriating booty; recalled and made dictator, he saved Rome from the Gauls in 387 and organized the rebuilding of the city.

FURIUS PHILUS, LUCIUS (second century). As consul in 136, he presided over an inquiry into Hostilius Mancinus' treaty with the Numantines. A close friend of Scipio Aemilianus, he is a participant in *On the Commonwealth*, in which he reluctantly delivers in Book 3 a version of Carneades' speech attacking justice.

GABINIUS, AULUS (second century). As tribune in 139 he carried a law requiring the use of written ballots in elections.

GALBA: see SULPICIUS

GALUS: see SULPICIUS

GELLIUS, GNAEUS (second century). A historian of early Rome whose *Annals* comprised at least thirty-three books.

GELLIUS POPLICOLA, LUCIUS (first century). From the anecdote reported by Cicero, he was no philosopher; he was, however, consul in 72 and censor in 70 and supported Cicero vigorously against Catiline in 63.

GRACCHUS: see SEMPRONIUS

GRATIDIUS, MARCUS (second century). He proposed a ballot law at Arpinum, which was opposed by his brother-in-law, Cicero's grandfather. He was killed in Cilicia in 102, where he was serving as a prefect in the war against the pirates.

HERACLIDES of PONTUS (fourth century). A pupil of Plato who wrote a wide range of philosophical works, some of them on political and legal theory, including dialogues which Cicero knew and used.

HERODOTUS (fifth century). Originally from Halicarnassus and a settler of the Greek colony of Thurii in southern Italy in 443; his Histories of the Persian Wars are the first work of Greek historiography, and he was (and is) regarded as the Father of History.

HOMER (tenth–ninth century, according to Cicero). The author of the *Iliad* and *Odyssey* (as well as other poems), according to ancient tradition; the date given by Cicero is somewhat earlier than modern scholars accept for the epics.

HORATIUS BARBATUS, MARCUS (fifth century). Consul in 449 with Lucius Valerius Potitus; they restored the Republic after the fall of the decemvirate.

HORATIUS COCLES (sixth–fifth century, if real). He foiled the attempt of the Etruscan king Lars Porsenna to take Rome and restore the expelled Tarquinius Superbus by single-handedly defending the bridge over the Tiber as it was destroyed beneath him.

HOSTILIUS, TULLUS (seventh century). The third king of Rome (672/1–640/39 Polybian), known primarily for his military accomplishments.

HOSTILIUS MANCINUS, GAIUS (second century). As consul in 137, he lost a battle to the Numantines and negotiated a treaty which the senate then repudiated, with his support, after an investigation by Furius Philus. He was surrendered to the Numantines in recompense; when they found the arrangement unsatisfactory and returned him to the senders, he was (after some debate) readmitted to citizenship and continued his career.

HYPERBOLUS (d. 411). Athenian politician and demagogue.

IULIUS, PROCULUS (eighth century, if real). Encountered Romulus on the Quirinal Hill after the latter's disappearance and learned that Romulus had become the god Quirinus.

IULIUS IULLUS, GAIUS (fifth century). Consul in 482 and one of the first board of decemvirs in 451; he allowed Lucius Sestius to appeal to the people.

IUNIUS BRUTUS, LUCIUS (sixth–fifth century). He led the overthrow of the monarchy and was one of the first pair of consuls, together with Tarquinius Collatinus.

IUNIUS BRUTUS CALLAICUS, DECIMUS (second century). Consul in 138, when he was imprisoned by the tribune Curiatius.

IUNIUS CONGUS GRACCHANUS, MARCUS (*c.*143–*c.*55). A friend of Gaius Gracchus in his youth (whence his cognomen); a historian and antiquarian, who dedicated his book on magistrates' powers to Atticus' father. He seems to have offered a more democratic interpretation of the Roman constitution than other writers.

LAELIUS, GAIUS (d. *c.*128). A close friend of Scipio Aemilianus and his legate in Africa; also Scipio's principal interlocutor in *On the Commonwealth*. As consul in 140 he proposed and withdrew an agrarian law; in 132 he was on the commission to punish the adherents of Tiberius Gracchus.

LAENAS: see POPILIUS

LARCIUS, TITUS (sixth–fifth century). The first dictator, in 498 (or 501), and also consul in one or both of those years; one of the military heroes of the first years of the Republic.

LICINIUS CRASSUS, LUCIUS (140–91). Consul in 95, censor in 92; Cicero, part of whose political education was supervised by him, thought him the greatest orator he had known and made him the principal speaker of *On the Orator*. He died suddenly in September 91, shortly after the dramatic date of the dialogue and just before the outbreak of the Social War.

LICINIUS CRASSUS MUCIANUS, PUBLIUS (d. 130). Consul in 131, pontifex maximus, a member of Tiberius Gracchus' agrarian commission, and father-in-law of Gaius Gracchus. He died in battle in Asia in 130 and was succeeded as pontifex maximus by his natural brother, Publius Mucius Scaevola.

LICINIUS LUCULLUS, LUCIUS (d. 56). A Sullan supporter; as consul in 74 and for some years thereafter, he fought against Mithradates until succeeded by Pompey. He retired to his luxurious villas in 59 to admire his fishponds, earning Cicero's scorn.

LICINIUS MACER, GAIUS (d. 66). After his praetorship in 68 and governorship (of an unknown province), he was tried and convicted for extortion in 66 in a court presided over by Cicero, dying shortly thereafter. As a historian of early Rome, in his *Annals* he took an antiaristocratic position; in life, he was similarly anti-Sullan.

LIVIUS ANDRONICUS (third century). A Greek captive from Tarentum; in Rome he wrote the first epic poem in Latin, a version of the *Odyssey* written in the archaic Saturnian meter; he also wrote both tragedies and comedies as well as a hymn to Juno in 207.

LIVIUS DRUSUS, MARCUS (d. 91). As tribune of the plebs in 91, he proposed a varied program of laws (including land distribution, citizenship for the Italians, and reorganization of the courts) that were intended to bolster senatorial rule but which satisfied no one. After his murder his legislation was annulled, and the disgruntled Italians seceded, beginning the Social War.

LUCILIUS, GAIUS (d. 102/1). A Roman knight and author of thirty books of verse satires including attacks on (or descriptions of) some of the major political figures of his time. He served at the siege of Numantia under the command of Scipio Aemilianus.

LUCULLUS: see LICINIUS

LUCRETIA (sixth century). Virtuous wife of Tarquinius Collatinus; her rape by Tarquinius Superbus' son Sextus and subsequent suicide were the proximate cause of the overthrow of the monarchy.

LUCRETIUS TRICIPITINUS, SPURIUS (sixth century). Father of Lucretia.

LUCUMO (eighth century, if real). According to Cicero, an ally of Romulus after whom the Roman tribe *Luceres* was named; his identity was a traditional antiquarian puzzle. Lucumo is also the original (Etruscan, not Greek as Cicero suggests) name of Lucius Tarquinius Priscus.

LYCURGUS (ninth century, if real). The mythical (or divine) figure who established Sparta's constitution and bizarre way of life in the early ninth century. He was also said by some to have founded the Olympic games a century later, leading to chronological problems (if he was not divine).

MACER: see LICINIUS

MAELIUS, SPURIUS (fifth century). Said to have distributed free grain in Rome to relieve a famine and to have aimed at tyranny; he was put to death by the master of the horse Servilius Ahala in 439.

MANCINUS: see HOSTILIUS

MANILIUS, MANIUS (second century). As consul in 149 he began the siege of Carthage in the Third Punic War and was Scipio's commander. One of the founders of Roman jurisprudence (and a participant in *On the Commonwealth*), he may have edited a collection of Numa's laws.

MANLIUS TORQUATUS, AULUS (second century). Probably an error for Titus Manlius Torquatus, consul in 165 and pontifex; renowned for his knowledge of civil and pontifical law.

MANLIUS CAPITOLINUS, MARCUS (d. 384). Consul in 392; while guarding the Capitol against the Gauls in 387 he was alerted by the sacred geese and repelled an attack. He was executed for plotting revolution in 384.

MARCELLUS: see CLAUDIUS

MARCIUS, ANCUS (seventh century). Fourth king of Rome (639/8–616/5 Polybian) and founder of Ostia.

MARCIUS FIGULUS, GAIUS (first century). Probably the consul of 64; nothing else is known about his fancy tomb.

MARCIUS PHILIPPUS, LUCIUS (second–first century). As consul in 91 (and an augur) he strenuously opposed the reforms of Livius Drusus; he switched sides judiciously during the civil wars, and as the oldest living senator supported the Sullan settlement against the revolt of Lepidus in 78.

MARIUS, GAIUS (*c.*157–86). Like Cicero, he was from Arpinum; although he did not reach the consulate until the age of fifty in 107, he proceeded to be elected consul each year from 104 to 100 to fight the Gauls. In old age in 88 he tried to claim the command against Mithradates, leading to civil war; he died soon after his capture of Rome in 86.

MARIUS GRATIDIANUS, MARCUS (d. 82). Nephew of Gaius Marius (both by birth and adoption) and the son of Marcus Gratidius, thus related to Cicero. Praetor in 85 and 84 as a Marian, he was brutally tortured to death by Catiline on Sulla's return in 82.

MASINISSA (*c*.240–149). King of Numidia; he wisely chose to support Rome at the right moment in the Second Punic War and was rewarded with an enlarged kingdom after the defeat of Carthage. He remained loyal to Rome until his death, shortly after the (fictional) visit to him by Scipio Aemilianus in 149 reported in *On the Commonwealth*.

MAXIMUS: see FABIUS

MEGILLUS (fictional). The Spartan participant in Plato's *Laws*.

METELLUS: see CAECILIUS

MILTIADES (*c*.550–489). Athenian general and victor at Marathon in 490. Fined for the failure of his expedition to conquer Paros, he died of a wound received on the expedition.

MINOS (mythical). King of Crete and (according to Plato) author of the Cretan law code; posthumously one of the judges in the underworld.

MUCIUS SCAEVOLA, PUBLIUS (d. *c*.115). Consul in 133 and supporter of Tiberius Gracchus. He succeeded his brother Publius Licinius Crassus Mucianus as pontifex maximus in 133; he was a renowned jurist and is said to have compiled from pontifical records the text known as the Great Annals (*Annales Maximi*). His son was Quintus Scaevola the Pontifex.

MUCIUS SCAEVOLA, QUINTUS (d. *c*.88). Known as the Augur to distinguish him from his cousin the Pontifex. The son-in-law of Laelius and a junior participant in *On the Commonwealth*, he was consul in 117, a distinguished jurist, and father-in-law of Lucius Licinius Crassus; he appears as an elder statesman in Book 1 of *On the Orator*.

MUCIUS SCAEVOLA, QUINTUS (d. 82). Known as the Pontifex to distinguish him from his cousin the Augur. The son of Publius Mucius Scaevola and like him (and his uncle and his grandfather) pontifex maximus. Consul in 95 and the author of a large treatise on civil law, he instructed Cicero in law in the mid 80s until his murder in 82 by the younger Marius.

MUCIUS SCAEVOLA, QUINTUS (first century). The grandson of Scaevola Augur, he was a friend of Cicero and his brother; aside from his verse in praise of Cicero's *Marius*, he is known to have written risqué poetry.

MUMMIUS, SPURIUS (second century). The brother of Lucius Mummius the destroyer of Carthage in 146, Spurius never reached the consulate, but he accompanied Scipio Aemilianus (and Panaetius) on an embassy to the east in 140–139. He is one of the participants in *On the Commonwealth*.

NAEVIUS, GNAEUS (third century). Roman dramatist and epic poet; his poem (*Bellum Poenicum*) on the First Punic War was the first Latin epic on Roman history. Few fragments of his poetry survive.

NASICA: see CORNELIUS

NAVIUS, ATTUS (sixth century, if real). A famous augur, known primarily for the encounter with Tarquinius Priscus: when he foretold that what Priscus was thinking would come true, he successfully accomplished it by splitting a whetstone with a razor.

NUMA: see POMPILIUS

OPIMIUS, LUCIUS (second century). Consul in 121, he played a large role in the death of Gaius Gracchus; his exile in 109, however, resulted not from that but from his having been bribed by the Numidian king Jugurtha.

PACUVIUS, MARCUS (220–*c.*130). Tragic poet and nephew of Ennius. Only fragments of his plays survive.

PANAETIUS of RHODES (*c.*180–*c.*110). Stoic philosopher and head of the Stoa from 129; his views about ethics and predestination were less rigid than those of the early Stoa. Not coincidentally, he was very much at home with Rome and the Roman aristocracy and accompanied Scipio Aemilianus on his eastern embassy in 140–139.

PAPIRIUS CARBO, GAIUS (d. 119). As tribune in 131, he carried a law requiring written ballots in votes on the approval or rejection of laws. Suspected of culpability in the death of Scipio Aemilianus, he later gave up his Gracchan sympathies and defended Opimius when he was accused of the murder of Gaius Gracchus. He committed suicide when convicted (of treason or extortion) in 119.

PAPIRIUS CARBO, GNAEUS (d. 82). Tribune in 92, supporter of Marius, and Marian consul in 85 and 84; he fled to Africa in 82 and was killed by Pompey in Sicily.

PAULLUS: see AEMILIUS

PERICLES (*c.*490–429). Athenian general, orator, and statesman, leader of the Athenian democracy from the mid fifth century until his death from the plague in 429.

PERSIUS, GAIUS (second century). Mentioned by Lucilius as too learned to be an ideal audience for his satires; known only from Cicero's references to this passage of Lucilius.

PHALARIS (mid sixth century). Tyrant of Agrigentum in Sicily, famous for the hollow bronze bull in which he tortured people by roasting. He was stoned to death by his grateful subjects; the bull, which had been taken to Carthage as a trophy, was returned to Agrigentum by Scipio Aemilianus after the sack of Carthage.

PHIDIAS (fifth century). Athenian sculptor, most famous for his statues of Athena in the Parthenon and of Zeus at Olympia.

PHILIP II (d. 336). King of Macedon 359–336 and father of Alexander the Great; he conquered Greece and was about to attack the Persian Empire when he was assassinated.

PHILIPPUS: see MARCIUS

PHILOLAUS (fifth century). Pythagorean, some of whose cosmological and metaphysical writings survive. Plato is said to have bought (or plagiarized) his books.

PHILUS: see FURIUS

PISISTRATUS (d. 527). Tyrant in Athens 561–527 (with interruptions).

PISO: see CALPURNIUS

PITTACUS of MYTILENE (seventh–sixth century). Lawgiver; one of the Seven Sages.

PLATO (429–347). Pupil of Socrates, founder of the Academy, teacher of Aristotle and many others. Cicero admired his dialogues and translated some of them; his *Republic* and *Laws* are the literary models for *On the Commonwealth* and *On the Laws*, although Cicero repeatedly attacks his political ideas as unrealistic and inhumane.

PLAUTUS (*c*.250–184). The manuscripts of his comedies (of which twenty survive complete) give his name as Titus Maccius Plautus, but it is very uncertain. He was credited in antiquity with having written at least 130 plays.

POLEMO (fourth–third century). Platonist; head of the Academy *c*.314–*c*.276.

POLYBIUS (*c*.200 to after 118). From Mantinea in Arcadia; he came to Rome as a hostage in 168 and stayed there to become a friend of Scipio Aemilianus, conversations with whom he records in his *Histories*, which narrate in Greek the history of Rome from the Second Punic War to his own time. His discussion of constitutional theory (extant) and of early Roman history (very fragmentary) in Book 6 is one of the sources and models for Books 1 and 2 of *On the Commonwealth*.

POMPEIUS, QUINTUS (second century). As consul in 140 he was defeated by the Numantines and made a disadvantageous treaty, which he disavowed as soon as it was safe; the senate approved his behavior, which Cicero contrasts with the more honorable actions of Hostilius Mancinus two years later. He was an active opponent of Tiberius Gracchus and became censor in 131.

POMPEIUS MAGNUS, GNAEUS (106–48). The dominant figure in Rome from the 70s to the Civil War in 49. As consul for the first time in 70 with Marcus Licinius Crassus, he undid many of Sulla's reactionary constitutional changes; as a general in the 60s he defeated the pirates and Mithradates, widely extending Roman rule in the east. His compact with Julius Caesar and Crassus in 60 ("the First Triumvirate") gave him a dominant role in Rome; he was consul for the second time in 55 and (during a period of extraordinary discord) sole consul in 52. In the Civil War he was defeated by Caesar at Pharsalus and murdered when he fled to Egypt.

POMPILIUS, NUMA (eighth–seventh century, if real). Second king of Rome (712/1–673/2 Polybian).

POMPONIUS ATTICUS, TITUS (109–32). A lifelong friend of Cicero and his brother (who was married to Atticus' sister), one of the interlocutors of *On the Laws* and the recipient of hundreds of extant letters from Cicero (*Letters to Atticus*, in sixteen books). A man of great wealth and wide financial interests and an Epicurean, he never entered public life; he remained a member of the equestrian order and lived for many years in Athens (hence his cognomen). Cicero relied on his support (financial and moral) and judgment on many occasions; he was astute enough to survive the proscriptions of the Second Triumvirate and lived to see his daughter married to Augustus' close friend and general Agrippa. A biography of him by his friend Cornelius Nepos survives.

POPILIUS LAENAS, GAIUS (second century). Accused of treason by the tribune Gaius Coelius Caldus in 107 for the terms he made as legate with the Gallic Tigurini after his commander was killed; he went into exile.

POPILIUS LAENAS, PUBLIUS (second century). As consul in 132 he opposed the plans of Tiberius Gracchus and was exiled through the efforts of Gaius Gracchus in 123 (and recalled two years later); the father of Gaius Popilius Laenas.

PORCIUS CATO, MARCUS (234–149). Consul in 196, censor in 184, and renowned for the stern morality of his character and opinions.

He was the greatest orator of his age and a man of considerable literary accomplishment: his treatise on agriculture survives, as do fragments of his history of Rome (*Origines*) and his speeches. Cicero often takes him as the model of civic virtue, particularly because he was, like Cicero, the first in his family to hold the consulate. The picture of him in Cicero's dialogue *Cato the Elder: On Old Age* presents a kinder, gentler Cato.

PORCIUS CATO, MARCUS (95–46). As rigid a moralist as his great-grandfather the censor and a doctrinaire Stoic as well; both an opponent of the First Triumvirate and singularly unlovable in his own right, he was praetor in 54 but failed to be elected consul. After he committed suicide after the Battle of Thapsus in the Civil War, he became (retroactively) the embodiment of principled republicanism.

POSTUMIUS TUBERTUS, PUBLIUS (sixth–fifth century). Possibly real but legendary hero of the early republic (consul in 505 and 503) who fought against the Sabines.

PROCULUS: see IULIUS

PUBLICOLA: see VALERIUS

PYRRHUS (*c*.319–272). King of Epirus from 297 to 272, he invaded Italy at the request of Tarentum and defeated the Romans twice (280–279) in battles so costly that "Pyrrhic victories" became proverbial. He was defeated at Beneventum in 275 and killed in street fighting in Argos three years later.

PYTHAGORAS (sixth–fifth century). Born in Samos but migrated to Croton in southern Italy, where he had a large political and philosophical influence. A vast range of numerological, theological, and philosophical beliefs are attributed to him; it is difficult, if not impossible, to disentangle his genuine ideas.

QUINCTIUS CINCINNATUS, LUCIUS (fifth century). Appointed dictator for the second time in 439 in connection with the alleged coup attempt of Spurius Maelius. In his first dictatorship in 458, he was summoned from his farm to stave off military disaster and became an emblem of the farmer-soldier.

QUINTUS: see TULLIUS

QUIRINUS: see ROMULUS

REMUS (eighth century, if real). The twin brother of Romulus, who (in some versions) killed him in a dispute over the foundation of Rome.

ROMULUS (eighth century, if real). The founder and first king of

Rome. After a long reign he mysteriously disappeared in a storm (or eclipse of the sun) and became the god Quirinus.

RUTILIUS RUFUS, PUBLIUS (late second to early first century). A student of Panaetius and protégé of Scipio Aemilianus, he became consul in 105. Tried and convicted (unjustly) for extortion in the 90s, he went into exile at Smyrna, in the province he was said to have mistreated. Cicero's description of his trial compares him to Socrates. Rutilius is also a participant in *On the Commonwealth*, and Cicero says that Rutilius told him about the conversation which *On the Commonwealth* claims to report.

SARDANAPALUS (seventh century?). King of Nineveh or Assyria, probably a distortion of Assurbanipal (668–625). One of the most frequently mentioned (with Semiramis) Asian monarchs, whose connection with historical fact is tenuous at best. The epitaph of which Cicero twice quotes the last two lines was widely known and was probably written in the fifth or fourth century.

SCAEVOLA: see MUCIUS

SCAURUS: see AEMILIUS

SCIPIO: see CORNELIUS

SEMPRONIUS ASELLIO (second–first century). A military tribune at Numantia under Scipio Aemilianus, he later wrote a history of his own time in at least fourteen books.

SEMPRONIUS GRACCHUS, GAIUS (d. 121). Tiberius Gracchus' younger brother and a member of his agrarian commission. As tribune himself in 123–122, he extended his brother's work of reform and was killed in a riot in 121.

SEMPRONIUS GRACCHUS, TIBERIUS (d. 154). Consul in 177, censor in 169, and a successful general; the father of the tribunes Tiberius and Gaius Gracchus.

SEMPRONIUS GRACCHUS, TIBERIUS (d. 133). Quaestor at Numantia under Hostilius Mancinus (and the negotiator of the repudiated treaty), he became tribune in 133. His program to distribute state land to the poor (and thus increase the number eligible for military service) met with violent opposition: he had his fellow tribune Octavius deposed and appropriated the bequest of Attalus III of Pergamum to pay for land distribution. While trying to be elected tribune for a second year he was killed by a mob led by the pontifex maximus, Scipio Nasica Serapio.

SERVILIUS AHALA, GAIUS (fifth century). As master of the horse in

439 he killed Spurius Maelius and as a result was forced into exile by popular hatred.

SESTIUS, LUCIUS (fifth century). During the first year of the Decemvirate, a body was found in his bedroom; he was tried for murder (and for burying a body within the city) before the popular assembly.

SIMONIDES (b. *c.*556). Greek lyric and elegiac poet, allegedly born in the same year that Stesichorus died.

SISENNA: see CORNELIUS

SOCRATES (469–399). Plato's teacher and the principal character in Plato's dialogues. An Athenian who resisted the tyranny of the Thirty at the end of the Peloponnesian War – some of whom were his friends and associates – he was accused of impiety and of corrupting the young in 399 and executed; Plato's *Apology, Crito*, and *Phaedo* represent his speech and his days in prison awaiting execution. As Socrates wrote nothing, his actual beliefs are uncertain, although most people believe that the early dialogues of Plato are close to his true manner of ethical disputation, in which his interlocutors are forced to question their own beliefs. All the major philosophical schools of the subsequent generations (except the Epicureans) claimed to be his followers.

SOLON (early sixth century). As archon of Athens in 594/3 he reorganized the constitution on the basis of property classes and abolished debt servitude. He was generally considered to have been the creator of Athenian democracy.

SPEUSIPPUS (fourth century). Plato's nephew and successor as head of the Academy from 347 to 339.

STESICHORUS (d. *c.*556). Greek lyric poet; he allegedly died in the year Simonides was born.

SULPICIUS GALBA, SERVIUS (second century). Consul in 144, previously acquitted in 149 for his massacre of Lusitanians who had surrendered to him. An augur and a famous orator, he was among those who heard Carneades in 155.

SULPICIUS GALUS, GAIUS (second century). Consul in 166 and a skilled astronomer who explained a lunar eclipse to the troops in Macedonia in 168.

TARQUINIUS, SEXTUS (sixth–fifth century, if real). The evil son of the tyrannical Tarquinius Superbus; his rape of Lucretia led to the overthrow of the monarchy.

TARQUINIUS COLLATINUS, LUCIUS (sixth century, if real). The husband of Lucretia and one of the first pair of consuls (with Lucius Junius Brutus); he was subsequently forced to abdicate because of his relationship to Tarquinius Superbus.

TARQUINIUS PRISCUS, LUCIUS (seventh–sixth century, if real). The son of Demaratus and an immigrant to Rome; he changed his name from Lucumo on being chosen fifth king of Rome (reigned 615/4–577/6 Polybian).

TARQUINIUS SUPERBUS, LUCIUS (sixth century, if real). The son (grandson in some versions) of Tarquinius Priscus; he and his wife Tullia murdered her father Servius Tullius and usurped the throne of Rome, whose seventh and last king he became (532/1–508/7). He was expelled because of his tyrannical behavior and the rape of Lucretia by his son Sextus.

TATIUS, TITUS (eighth century, if real). Sabine king; for a time he was co-ruler of Rome with Romulus.

THALES of MILETUS (seventh–sixth century). One of the Seven Sages and the first known natural philosopher. He is credited with being the first to explain eclipses (28 May 585) and the first creator of a celestial globe.

THEMISTOCLES (*c.*528–462). Athenian general and statesman, responsible for the naval victory over Persia at Salamis in 480. He was subsequently ostracized and condemned for dealings with Persia; he died as Persian governor of Magnesia.

THEOPHRASTUS (*c.*371–*c.*287). Aristotle's pupil and successor (in 322) as head of the Peripatetic School. His many works on political philosophy are almost completely lost, although they influenced Cicero greatly; what survives are two botanical works and his descriptions of personality types, the *Characters*.

THEOPOMPUS (eighth century). King of Sparta; responsible for the creation of the ephors as a limitation on monarchic power.

THEOPOMPUS (fourth century). A pupil of the rhetorician Isocrates, he wrote a Greek history in continuation of Thucydides and a history of the reign of Philip II of Macedon.

THESEUS (mythical). The semi-divine king of Athens and creator of a unified Attica.

TIMAEUS of LOCRI (fifth century). Pythagorean philosopher and the chief speaker of Plato's *Timaeus*.

TIMAEUS of TAUROMENIUM (*c.*356–260). Author of a massive history in Greek of Sicily and Italy, the first major work on the subject; his work was admired for its learning and its careful chronology.

TIMOTHEUS (*c*.450–*c*.360). Lyric poet from Miletus, whose innovations included an increase in the number of strings on the lyre. A substantial fragment of his *Persians* survives on papyrus.

TITIUS, SEXTUS (second–first century). Tribune in 99 and a follower of Saturninus; his agrarian law was blocked by bad omens and vetoed by other tribunes. He was later convicted of treason for keeping a bust of Saturninus in his house.

TORQUATUS: see MANLIUS

TUBERO: see AELIUS

TUBERTUS: see POSTUMIUS

TULLIUS, SERVIUS (sixth century, if real). The sixth king of Rome (577/6–532/1 Polybian), best known as the organizer of the division of the people into property classes and creator of the centuriate assembly.

TULLIUS CICERO, MARCUS (second century). Cicero's grandfather, a leading citizen of Arpinum.

TULLIUS CICERO, MARCUS (106–43). The author; also the principal speaker of *On the Laws*.

TULLIUS CICERO, QUINTUS (*c*.103–43). Cicero's younger brother, praetor in 62; a participant in *On the Laws* and the dedicatee of *On the Orator* and *On the Commonwealth*. At the dramatic date of *On the Laws* he was in fact a legate with Caesar in Gaul, where he wrote four tragedies in sixteen days while besieged in Alesia. He was proscribed and killed at the same time as his brother.

VALERIUS POTITUS, LUCIUS (fifth century). Consul in 449 with Marcus Horatius Barbatus; one of the restorers of the Republic after the Decemvirate.

VALERIUS PUBLICOLA, PUBLIUS (sixth–fifth century). A consul in the first year of the Republic and frequently thereafter; according to Cicero, one of the models of responsible constitutionalism.

VENNONIUS (second century). An otherwise unknown historian.

VERGINIUS, DECIMUS (fifth century). Roman soldier who murdered his daughter Verginia rather than abandon her to the lust of one of the wicked decemvirs (normally Appius Claudius, but not named by Cicero), leading to the overthrow of the Decemvirate. His name is elsewhere given as Lucius or Aulus.

XENOCRATES (396–314). Pupil of Plato and third head of the Academy.

XENOPHON (*c*.428/7–*c*.354). Athenian soldier and student of Socrates, author not only of the edifying *Education of Cyrus* but of a Greek history continuing Thucydides, an account of his adventures on the expedition of the younger Cyrus (*Anabasis*), and memoirs of Socrates (*Memorabilia*) as well as smaller works.

XERXES (d. 465). King of Persia. The immense expedition he led against Greece in 480 succeeded in burning Athens but was decisively defeated at Salamis and Plataea.

ZALEUCUS (seventh century). Lawgiver at Locri in southern Italy; said to have been the first author of written laws.

ZENO of CITIUM (334–262). Founder of the Stoic school (so named for its meeting place in the Painted Stoa in Athens) who outlined the basic doctrines later elaborated by Chrysippus. He wrote an influential *Republic* modifying Plato's *Republic*; it is known only through a few fragments but was very influential for Stoic political theory.

Index of Fragments

The following list includes all fragments printed either in the text of or the notes to *On the Commonwealth* and *On the Laws*, listed by source. The location of the fragments in Ziegler's editions is noted in square brackets between the source reference and the page in this edition; unless otherwise noted, references are to *On the Commonwealth*.

General Index

This index does not include characters in the dialogues (except for discussion in the Introduction) and some persons and places mentioned only once. Roman citizens are normally listed only under their family names (e.g. Aemilius, not Paullus); full cross-references will be found in the biographical notes, which include all named individuals.

Cambridge Texts in the History of Political Thought

Titles published in the series thus far

Aristotle *The Politics* and *The Constitution of Athens* (edited by Stephen Everson)
0 521 48400 6 paperback
Arnold *Culture and Anarchy and Other Writings* (edited by Stefan Collini)
0 521 37796 x paperback
Astell *Political Writings* (edited by Patricia Springborg)
0 521 42845 9 paperback
Augustine *The City of God against the Pagans* (edited by R. W. Dyson)
0 521 46843 4 paperback
Austin *The Province of Jurisprudence Determined* (edited by Wilfrid E. Rumble)
0 521 44756 9 paperback
Bacon *The History of the Reign of King Henry VII* (edited by Brian Vickers)
0 521 58663 1 paperback
Bakunin *Statism and Anarchy* (edited by Marshall Shatz)
0 521 36973 8 paperback
Baxter *Holy Commonwealth* (edited by William Lamont)
0 521 40580 7 paperback
Bayle *Political Writings* (edited by Sally L. Jenkinson)
0 521 47677 1 paperback
Beccaria *On Crimes and Punishments and Other Writings* (edited by Richard Bellamy)
0 521 47982 7 paperback
Bentham *A Fragment on Government* (introduction by Ross Harrison)
0 521 35929 5 paperback
Bernstein *The Preconditions of Socialism* (edited by Henry Tudor)
0 521 39808 8 paperback
Bodin *On Sovereignty* (edited by Julian H. Franklin)
0 521 34992 3 paperback
Bolingbroke *Political Writings* (edited by David Armitage)
0 521 58697 6 paperback
Bossuet *Politics Drawn from the Very Words of Holy Scripture* (edited by Patrick Riley)
0 521 36807 3 paperback
The British Idealists (edited by David Boucher)
0 521 45951 6 paperback
Burke *Pre-Revolutionary Writings* (edited by Ian Harris)
0 521 36800 6 paperback
Christine De Pizan *The Book of the Body Politic* (edited by Kate Langdon Forhan)
0 521 42259 0 paperback

Cicero *On Duties* (edited by M. T. Griffin and E. M. Atkins)
0 521 34835 8 paperback
Cicero *On the Commonwealth* and *On the Laws* (edited by James E. G. Zetzel)
0 521 45959 1 paperback
Comte *Early Political Writings* (edited by H. S. Jones)
0 521 46923 6 paperback
Conciliarism and Papalism (edited by J. H. Burns and Thomas M. Izbicki)
0 521 47674 7 paperback
Constant *Political Writings* (edited by Biancamaria Fontana)
0 521 31632 4 paperback
Dante *Monarchy* (edited by Prue Shaw)
0 521 56781 5 paperback
Diderot *Political Writings* (edited by John Hope Mason and Robert Wokler)
0 521 36911 8 paperback
The Dutch Revolt (edited by Martin van Gelderen)
0 521 39809 6 paperback
Early Greek Political Thought from Homer to the Sophists (edited by Michael Gagarin and Paul Woodruff)
0 521 43768 7 paperback
The Early Political Writings of the German Romantics (edited by Frederick C. Beiser)
0 521 44951 0 paperback
The English Levellers (edited by Andrew Sharp)
0 521 62511 4 paperback
Erasmus *The Education of a Christian Prince* (edited by Lisa Jardine)
0 521 58811 1 paperback
Fenelon *Telemachus* (edited by Patrick Riley)
0 521 45662 2 paperback
Ferguson *An Essay on the History of Civil Society* (edited by Fania Oz-Salzberger)
0 521 44736 4 paperback
Filmer *Patriarcha and Other Writings* (edited by Johann P. Sommerville)
0 521 39903 3 paperback
Fletcher *Political Works* (edited by John Robertson)
0 521 43994 9 paperback
Sir John Fortescue *On the Laws and Governance of England* (edited by Shelley Lockwood)
0 521 58996 7 paperback
Fourier *The Theory of the Four Movements* (edited by Gareth Stedman Jones and Ian Patterson)
0 521 35693 8 paperback
Gramsci *Pre-Prison Writings* (edited by Richard Bellamy)
0 521 42307 4 paperback

Guicciardini *Dialogue on the Government of Florence* (edited by Alison Brown)
0 521 45623 1 paperback
Harrington *A Commonwealth of Oceana* and *A System of Politics* (edited by J. G. A. Pocock)
0 521 42329 5 paperback
Hegel *Elements of the Philosophy of Right* (edited by Allen W. Wood and H. B. Nisbet)
0 521 34888 9 paperback
Hegel *Political Writings* (edited by Laurence Dickey and H. B. Nisbet)
0 521 45979 3 paperback
Hobbes *On the Citizen* (edited by Michael Silverthorne and Richard Tuck)
0 521 43780 6 paperback
Hobbes *Leviathan* (edited by Richard Tuck)
0 521 56797 1 paperback
Hobhouse *Liberalism and Other Writings* (edited by James Meadowcroft)
0 521 43726 1 paperback
Hooker *Of the Laws of Ecclesiastical Polity* (edited by A. S. McGrade)
0 521 37908 3 paperback
Hume *Political Essays* (edited by Knud Haakonssen)
0 521 46639 3 paperback
King James VI and I *Political Writings* (edited by Johann P. Sommerville)
0 521 44729 1 paperback
Jefferson *Political Writings* (edited by Joyce Appleby and Terence Ball)
0 521 64841 6 paperback
John of Salisbury *Policraticus* (edited by Cary Nederman)
0 521 36701 8 paperback
Kant *Political Writings* (edited by H. S. Reiss and H. B. Nisbet)
0 521 39837 1 paperback
Knox *On Rebellion* (edited by Roger A. Mason)
0 521 39988 2 paperback
Kropotkin *The Conquest of Bread and Other Writings* (edited by Marshall Shatz)
0 521 45990 7 paperback
Lawson *Politica sacra et civilis* (edited by Conal Condren)
0 521 39248 9 paperback
Leibniz *Political Writings* (edited by Patrick Riley)
0 521 36899 x paperback
The Levellers (edited by Andrew Sharp)
0 521 62511 4 paperback
Locke *Political Essays* (edited by Mark Goldie)
0 521 47861 8 paperback
Locke *Two Treatises of Government* (edited by Peter Laslett)
0 521 35730 6 paperback

Loyseau *A Treatise of Orders and Plain Dignities* (edited by Howell A. Lloyd)
0 521 45624 x paperback
Luther and Calvin on Secular Authority (edited by Harro Höpfl)
0 521 34986 9 paperback
Machiavelli *The Prince* (edited by Quentin Skinner and Russell Price)
0 521 34993 1 paperback
de Maistre *Considerations on France* (edited by Isaiah Berlin and Richard Lebrun)
0 521 46628 8 paperback
Malthus *An Essay on the Principle of Population* (edited by Donald Winch)
0 521 42972 2 paperback
Marsiglio of Padua *Defensor minor* and *De translatione Imperii* (edited by Cary Nederman)
0 521 40846 6 paperback
Marx *Early Political Writings* (edited by Joseph O'Malley)
0 521 34994 x paperback
Marx *Later Political Writings* (edited by Terrell Carver)
0 521 36739 5 paperback
James Mill *Political Writings* (edited by Terence Ball)
0 521 38748 5 paperback
J. S. Mill *On Liberty*, with *The Subjection of Women* and *Chapters on Socialism* (edited by Stefan Collini)
0 521 37917 2 paperback
Milton *Political Writings* (edited by Martin Dzelzainis)
0 521 34866 8 paperback
Montesquieu *The Spirit of the Laws* (edited by Anne M. Cohler, Basia Carolyn Miller and Harold Samuel Stone)
0 521 36974 6 paperback
More *Utopia* (edited by George M. Logan and Robert M. Adams)
0 521 40318 9 paperback
Morris *News from Nowhere* (edited by Krishan Kumar)
0 521 42233 7 paperback
Nicholas of Cusa *The Catholic Concordance* (edited by Paul E. Sigmund)
0 521 56773 4 paperback
Nietzsche *On the Genealogy of Morality* (edited by Keith Ansell-Pearson)
0 521 40610 2 paperback
Paine *Political Writings* (edited by Bruce Kuklick)
0 521 66799 2 paperback
Plato *The Republic* (edited by G. R. F. Ferrari and Tom Griffith)
0 521 48443 x
Plato *Statesman* (edited by Julia Annas and Robin Waterfield)
0 521 44778 x paperback

Price *Political Writings* (edited by D. O. Thomas)
o 521 40969 1 paperback
Priestley *Political Writings* (edited by Peter Miller)
o 521 42561 1 paperback
Proudhon *What is Property?* (edited by Donald R. Kelley and Bonnie G. Smith)
o 521 40556 4 paperback
Pufendorf *On the Duty of Man and Citizen according to Natural Law* (edited by James Tully)
o 521 35980 5 paperback
The Radical Reformation (edited by Michael G. Baylor)
o 521 37948 2 paperback
Rousseau *The Discourses and Other Early Political Writings* (edited by Victor Gourevitch)
o 521 42445 3 paperback
Rousseau *The Social Contract and Other Later Political Writings* (edited by Victor Gourevitch)
o 521 42446 1 paperback
Seneca *Moral and Political Essays* (edited by John Cooper and John Procope)
o 521 34818 8 paperback
Sidney *Court Maxims* (edited by Hans W. Blom, Eco Haitsma Mulier and Ronald Janse)
o 521 46736 5 paperback
Sorel *Reflections on Violence* (edited by Jeremy Jennings)
o 521 55910 3 paperback
Spencer *The Man versus the State* and *The Proper Sphere of Government* (edited by John Offer)
o 521 43740 7 paperback
Stirner *The Ego and Its Own* (edited by David Leopold)
o 521 45647 9 paperback
Thoreau *Political Writings* (edited by Nancy Rosenblum)
o 521 47675 5 paperback
Utopias of the British Enlightenment (edited by Gregory Claeys)
o 521 45590 1 paperback
Vitoria *Political Writings* (edited by Anthony Pagden and Jeremy Lawrance)
o 521 36714 x paperback
Voltaire *Political Writings* (edited by David Wiliams)
o 521 43727 x paperback
Weber *Political Writings* (edited by Peter Lassman and Ronald Speirs)
o 521 39719 7 paperback
William of Ockham *A Short Discourse on Tyrannical Government* (edited by A. S. McGrade and John Kilcullen)
o 521 35803 5 paperback

William of Ockham *A Letter to the Friars Minor and Other Writings* (edited by A. S. McGrade and John Kilcullen)
0 521 35804 3 paperback
Wollstonecraft *A Vindication of the Rights of Men* and *A Vindication of the Rights of Woman* (edited by Sylvana Tomaselli)
0 521 43633 8 paperback